PRAISE FOR *GLITTER UP THE DARK*

"Fortunately, there are progressive art objects. … art objects. But every now and then, we get revolutionary … that change how we talk, read, and think. Sasha Geffen's *Glitter Up the Dark* changed the way I hear music and the convenient way I understand gender and performance in and outside of music. One will not hear or reproduce traditional understandings of gender ever again after experiencing this boldly brilliant book."
—**KIESE LAYMON,** author of *Heavy*

"Sasha Geffen follows the glamour and the glitter across a musical universe of queer and trans performances. Not looking simply at particular stars nor following a musical movement like punk from its roots to its demise, *Glitter Up the Dark* travels the multiple lanes of a trans-musical express. With riffs on the trans voice; careful attention to histories of performance, reception, and fashion; and theories of queer time and space, this book sparkles and glows. Read it, listen to it, love it."
—**JACK HALBERSTAM,** author of *Gaga Feminism*

"With simply brilliant writing and joyfully queer insights, Sasha Geffen dives deep into rock's gendersmashing history, reminding us of the ecstatic potential when art and transgression collide."
—**MICHELLE TEA,** author of *Against Memoir* and creator of the Drag Queen Story Hour

"How does music make gender audible in all of its rich, expressive, shifting forms, far beyond binary definitions? How have artists as ubiquitous as the Beatles and as cult-yet-crucial as Poly Styrene and Wendy Carlos helped us hear and understand the truths of bodies who, as the author writes, demand to choose their own shapes? This scintillating and deeply considered account of pop's queer and trans history answers these questions with inspiring stories of rebellion and community, bratty punks and androgynous poets, studio inventors and prophets of the dance floor. An absolutely necessary account of what has always been at the heart of popular music: transformation."
—**ANN POWERS,** author of *Good Booty*

AMERICAN MUSIC SERIES

Jessica Hopper and Charles Hughes, Editors
Peter Blackstock and David Menconi, Founding Editors

ALSO IN THE SERIES

Hanif Abdurraqib, *Go Ahead in the Rain: Notes to A Tribe Called Quest*

Chris Stamey, *A Spy in the House of Loud: New York Songs and Stories*

Holly Gleason, *Woman Walk the Line: How the Women in Country Music Changed Our Lives*

Adam Sobsey, *Chrissie Hynde: A Musical Biography*

Lloyd Sachs, *T Bone Burnett: A Life in Pursuit*

Danny Alexander, *Real Love, No Drama: The Music of Mary J. Blige*

Alina Simone, *Madonnaland and Other Detours into Fame and Fandom*

Kristin Hersh, *Don't Suck, Don't Die: Giving Up Vic Chesnutt*

Chris Morris, *Los Lobos: Dream in Blue*

Eddie Huffman, *John Prine: In Spite of Himself*

John T. Davis, *The Flatlanders: Now It's Now Again*

David Cantwell, *Merle Haggard: The Running Kind*

David Menconi, *Ryan Adams: Losering, a Story of Whiskeytown*

Don McLeese, *Dwight Yoakam: A Thousand Miles from Nowhere*

GLITTER UP THE DARK

HOW POP MUSIC BROKE THE BINARY

SASHA GEFFEN

UNIVERSITY OF TEXAS PRESS AUSTIN

Printed in the United States of America
First edition, 2020

Requests for permission to reproduce material
from this work should be sent to:
Permissions
University of Texas Press
P.O. Box 7819
Austin, TX 78713-7819
utpress.utexas.edu/rp-form

♾ The paper used in this book meets the minimum requirements
of ANSI/NISO Z39.48-1992 (R1997) (Permanence of Paper).

Library of Congress Cataloging-in-Publication Data

Names: Geffen, Sasha, author.
Title: Glitter up the dark : how pop music broke the binary / Sasha Geffen.
Other titles: American music series (Austin, Tex.)
Description: First edition. | Austin : University of Texas
Press, 2020. | Series: American music series | Includes index.
Identifiers: LCCN 2019039555
ISBN 978-1-4773-1878-2 (paperback)
ISBN 978-1-4773-2083-9 (ebook)
ISBN 978-1-4773-2084-6 (ebook other)
Subjects: LCSH: Gender identity in music. | Sex roles in music.
| Popular music—History and criticism.
Classification: LCC ML3470 .G44 2020 | DDC 781.64086/7—dc23
LC record available at https://lccn.loc.gov/2019039555

doi:10.7560/318782

For my siblings

CONTENTS

GLITTER UP THE DARK

INTRODUCTION
An Alternate Ribbon of Time

The gender binary cannot really be broken because the gender binary has never been whole. It has always limped along in pieces, easily cracked by a brief foray into the historical record. The Christian colonialist construction of men as inseminating subjects and women as reproductive objects does not extend into ancient history, nor does it govern every facet of the present. Masculinity and femininity, so much as they refer to certain strategies for moving through the world, have never neatly corresponded to the two types of bodies defined in the opening passages of the Bible. Even human bodies don't hold true to the popular myth of strictly dimorphic sex, as anyone in the intersex community can tell you.

So the subtitle of this book is misleading, or rather it only holds true when viewed through a limited lens. There have always been more than two genders, and music and gender nonconformity have gone hand in hand since long before pop music emerged as a product—since before the concept of "product" existed. But the patriarchal order, in order to survive, needs to brand threatening ideas as artificial, superimposed, harmful, and new, so as to distract from the underlying truth: that patriarchy itself is artificial, superimposed, harmful, and not nearly as ancient or universal as it pretends to be. Hardly the natural order of the human being, patriarchy relies on the illusion of its own inevitability to survive.

The notion that only two genders exist, and that each gender prescribes specific behaviors, movements, and relations, has always been undercut by a thriving spectrum of deviant expressions that white capitalist patriarchy seeks to erase. When European settlers devastated the Americas, they "looked to the existing sexual and gender variance of Indigenous people as a means of marking them as racially inferior and uncivilized: a justification for a forever unjustified genocidal conquest," wrote Michael Paramo.[1] During the era of American slavery, white men and women similarly clung to the gender binary to distinguish themselves from the racialized people they were brutalizing, stamping out expressions of gender that didn't fit into the white Christian patriarchal mold as part of a long campaign of hellish state-sanctioned violence.[2]

The gender binary, which seeks to clearly label who can get pregnant and who can't, who should have power and who shouldn't, has served white supremacy for as long as white supremacy has existed. But cross-dressing, homosexuality, and fluidity of form sparkle throughout history. It's just that the powers that be still need the binary to persist to keep cis white men in charge and cast aside everyone else, and so they rigorously shutter the light that leaks in from just outside their cage.

Music shelters gender rebellion from those who seek to abolish it. In music, drag is not an aberration but a form of play. Women can sing with masculine bravado and men can adopt transcendent femininity: poses that were often dangerous to display offstage and outside the recording studio for people of all genders. Drag queens such as Julian Eltinge sang in vaudeville revues to broad acclaim while homosexuality was still illegal in the United States during the first decades of the twentieth century. Queer, trans, and gender nonconforming artists similarly populate the history of blues, R&B, jazz, and rock and roll. There's no pop music without artists who reveled in lashing out against the gendered expectations levied upon them from on high.

The blues as a cultural product begins with Gertrude "Ma" Rainey, the southern singer who in 1923 signed a record deal with Paramount and soon became famous throughout the United

States for her powerful, androgynous voice. Her friend and collaborator Bessie Smith, who had auditioned for Rainey's band in 1911, similarly became a star after signing to Columbia Records. Both women were black and queer, and both sang about lesbian love via barely coded lyrics. Rainey's song "Sissy Blues" also playfully celebrated feminine gay men: "My man's got a sissy / His name is Miss Kate / He shook that thing like jelly on a plate," she sings. In prewar America, major record labels were willing to sell gay records so long as they came from black women, whose voices and presences already deviated from mainstream norms.

"The blues songs recorded by Gertrude Rainey and Bessie Smith offer us a privileged glimpse of the prevailing perceptions of love and sexuality in postslavery black communities in the United States," wrote Angela Davis in 1998. "Both women were role models for untold thousands of their sisters to whom they delivered messages that defied the male dominance encouraged by mainstream culture. The blues women openly challenged the gender politics implicit in traditional cultural representations of marriage and heterosexual love relationships. Refusing, in the blues tradition of raw realism, to romanticize romantic relationships, they instead exposed the stereotypes and explored the contradictions of those relationships."[3]

Rainey and Smith, along with fellow blueswoman Lucille Bogan, set the stage for pop music's tendency to incubate androgyny, queerness, and other taboos in plain view of the powers that would seek to snuff them out. They were joined by Gladys Bentley, the stone butch blues singer who performed in a top hat and tails throughout the Harlem Renaissance in New York and whose deep, gritty voice foreshadowed the guttural howls of rock stars.

In 1938, the gospel guitarist Sister Rosetta Tharpe laid her music to tape for the first time at age twenty-three. Throughout the following decades, she would develop a style of playing electric guitar that would influence generations of rock musicians to come. Tharpe, too, was queer, and she adapted a phallic symbol of masculinity—the electric guitar—to her own gender-breaking whirlwind of a stage presence. "In that day it was still unusual to see a woman guitarist, in gospel or in any musical field," wrote Gayle Wald in a 2007 biography of Tharpe. "Not merely to play, but to wield the instrument with authority and ease, was to subvert convention and expectation."[4] Tharpe was doing the windmill on her guitar while Pete Townshend of the Who, the white man with whom the gesture is most commonly associated, was still learning to walk.[5]

Reach further back in time and you'll find a long and varied history of third, fourth, and other alternate genders—people who slip between the poles of the Western binary, often in keeping with musical and ceremonial traditions. Among indigenous Americans, Two-Spirited individuals manifest both male and female qualities. In India, third-gender Hijras who recently won the right to their own legal gender marker appear in ancient sacred Hindu texts, such as the Ramayana and the Mahabharata. In Bolivia, the China Supay—a devil character historically embodied by transfeminine performers—plays a key role in the Carnaval de Oruro festival. Contemporary electronic musician Elysia Crampton dedicated her 2018 self-titled album to Ofelia Espinoza, "one of the mariposas, or butterflies, who forever altered the costume of the china supay in the 1960s and 1970s, the Aymara femme devil performed by queer and trans bodies in the street festivities, which, though now formally Christianized, can be traced back to before the conquest," she said in a 2018 interview.[6] These identities only mirror the contemporary model of "trans" when viewed through a colonial lens. Within their original contexts, they do not mark a journey from one gender to another, but are natural and frictionless ways of being in their own right.

Many disruptive gender identities have deep ties to music. In Italy, for hundreds of years, a third gender was biologically created for an expressly musical purpose. From the sixteenth century until the early twentieth century, castrati sang in a third voice, neither male nor female. Castrated before puberty so that their voices would never drop, these singers paired the unthickened vocal cords of the soprano with the deep lung capacity of the baritone, resulting in a distinctively androgynous vocal quality. "Although the pitch may have been similar to that of a female, the timbre of the voice was different," wrote J. S. Jenkins.[7] In 1799, a French music critic "described the castrato sound as being 'as clear and penetrating as that of choirboys but a great deal louder with something dry and sour about it yet brilliant, light, full of impact.'"[8] For centuries, these voices were popular in opera and in Catholic choirs, though the practice of creating castrati was outlawed in the nineteenth century as industrialization and its attendant social values swept Europe.

The figure of the castrato and the invention of music recording technology briefly overlapped: only one castrato was ever known to make solo recordings. The last surviving Sistine castrato, Alessandro Moreschi, recorded a handful of songs on wax cylinders in 1902 and 1904. The recordings are remarkable. Moreschi's voice, reportedly past its prime at the time, has a coarse, rippled quality to it. He hits soprano notes with a guttural grain. The texture of his voice, combined with the ghostly quality of the recording, lends a spectral aura to the music. Moreschi does not sound like a combination of male and female vocal traits, but like a supersession of the gender binary altogether.

The availability of musical playback devices surged at the same time that the last of the castrati died. Recorded music, played at first within the inner sanctum of the home, severed the voice from the gendered body. The gramophone had no perceptible gender, and while commercially sold music often reinscribed conventional gender roles, it also frequently dismantled them. In his 1993 book *The Queen's Throat*, Wayne Koestenbaum theorizes a connection between the proliferation of recorded music and the articulation of homosexuality, with its associated androgyny, as a social category. "The category of 'homosexuality' is only as old as recorded sound," he notes. "Both inventions arose in the late nineteenth century, and concerned the home. Both are discourses of home's shattering: what bodies do when they disobey, what bodies do when they are private."[9]

In the first half of the twentieth century, black American musicians gave rise to new and dangerous genres, including jazz, rhythm and blues, and rock and roll. The history of American music is the history of black music, and since the gender binary is inextricably tied to whiteness, pop music's story necessarily begins slightly outside its parameters. It begins with queer black women like Sister Rosetta Tharpe and Billie Holiday; Ma Rainey, Lucille Bogan, and Bessie Smith, who wove references to lesbian sex into their lyrics; and Big Mama Thornton, who wore suits and ties while singing rhythm and blues. It begins with queer black men like Esquerita and Little Richard, early American rock performers who wore their hair fabulously high and swung their silky falsettos up to meet it. These artists formed the musical base that would give rise to the exceptional popularity of postwar white thieves such as Elvis Presley and the Beatles, who gave white record executives the opportunity to re-create old colonial dynamics by taking well-established cultural forms created by black people, feeding them through the throats of less talented white performers, and pretending that they were brand new.

Both Big Mama Thornton and Little Richard "cut their teeth as singers in the late 1940s in traveling troupes, where queer acts were part of the foundation of the early rhythm and blues music played to black southern audiences," wrote Tyina Steptoe.[10] These artists, some of the most influential in early rock history, made gay music from the start. Though they ultimately had to "dilute the queer content of their performances" while making mass-produced records, the vocal strategies they employed in their most brazen performances stayed with them: Richard's irreverent "woos" and Thornton's guttural croaks both broke out of the boundaries surrounding their assigned gender, and both vocal gestures made it to the recording studio. These musician's racialized and gendered voices, audibly othered and yet free in their otherness, influenced generations of singers to come.

Sanitized white covers of songs first performed by black musicians tended to sell better than the originals in mid-century America, and in the 1950s the recording industry capitalized extensively on this phenomenon by creating Elvis, whose cover of Thornton's "Hound Dog" became his best-selling single. If we take Elvis to be the first pop product, the first instance of musical monoculture whose open sexuality scandalized older generations of listeners and gave the nascent white teenager a foothold for its new identity, then the pop star, as a mythic figure, has always been somewhat androgynous. Elvis threaded together the vocal quirks of both male and female singers while bridging the black genre of R&B with the white country world. He was a prism of disparate influences and varied gender expressions; his broad success depended on his ability to be anything to almost anyone.

Elvis's breakthrough caused a stir among the old guard of music critics, who dismissed his performance style as too sexual and therefore too feminine. White men in postwar America were not supposed to exhibit so base an emotion as lust. In 1956, *New York Times* critic Jack Gould panned Elvis using the same language that many male writers still use to criticize female singers, effectively characterizing him as a male bimbo. "Mr. Presley has no discernible singing ability. His specialty is rhythm songs which he renders in an undistinguished whine; his phrasing, if it can be called that, consists of the stereotyped variations that go with a beginner's aria in a bathtub," Gould wrote. "His one specialty is an accented movement of the body that heretofore has been primarily identified with the repertoire of the blonde bombshells of the burlesque runway. The gyration never had anything to do with the world of popular music and still doesn't."[11]

It's difficult, in the twenty-first century, to conceive of Elvis as an androgyne, an effeminate threat to the gendered order. His iconography, sexual as it might be, looks purely masculine in retrospect. He sold so astonishingly well that American culture could not squeeze him out of its vision of maleness; unable to cast Elvis aside as a deviant distraction, mainstream America instead ate him up. If it can't get rid of them, patriarchy tends to devour its threats. Given enough time and financial motivation, normative masculinity will absorb even its boldest disruptions.

Why has music so often served as an accomplice to transcendent expressions of gender? Why did the query "Is he musical?" become code, in the twentieth century, for "Is he gay?" Why is music so inherently queer?

In the nineteenth century, the first glimmering of the modern gay rights movement cropped up among writers who theorized the existence of the Uranian or Urning—a third-gender person assigned male at birth who housed a feminine spirit. English author Edward Carpenter suggested that music was the form of expression most closely allied with the Uranian—that is, that music might be the gayest art possible. "As to music, this is certainly the art which in its subtlety and tenderness—and perhaps in a certain inclination to *indulge* in emotion—lies nearest to the Urning nature," he wrote.[12]

Music's ambiguity also enables the covert expression of queer desire and identity. "Historically, music has been defined as mystery and miasma, as implicitness rather than explicitness, and so we have hid inside music," wrote Koestenbaum. "In music we can come out without coming out, we can reveal without saying a word."[13] Because music is a language of subliminal expression, because it hides in paradox and contradiction, it has historically served as a safehouse for manifestations of nonnormative gender and sexuality. As Ann Powers writes in the introduction to *Good Booty*, "Popular music's very form, its ebb and flow of excitement so closely resembling the libido, drew people to it as a way to speak what, according to propriety, couldn't be spoken."[14] Music offers a more detailed, nuanced form of expression than even spoken language, and far more nuanced than the sex and gender binaries imposed from on high. And yet the powers that be do not always recognize music as subversion. Music is a space where singers can say what they mean without saying it, where melody and rhythm offer plausible deniability for even the most plainly sung truths. "BD women, you sure can't understand / They got a head like a sweet angel and they walk just like a natural man," Lucille Bogan sang on her 1935 recording of "BD Woman's Blues" (referring to "bull dyke women"). She openly celebrated her butch and transmasculine siblings decades before the fight for LGBTQ rights had entered the mainstream.

Listening to music is inherently a sensual exchange. Music enters the ear, causes pleasure, and inspires identification in the listener, who is not merely a passive participant in the encounter. The listener joins the singer in the song's ambiguous and ephemeral space, and is changed by the act of attentive, emotional listening. "The listener's inner body is illuminated, opened up: a singer doesn't expose her own throat, she exposes the listener's interior," wrote Koestenbaum. "Her voice enters me, makes me a 'me,' an interior, by virtue of the fact that I have been entered. The singer, through osmosis, passes through the self's porous membrane, and discredits the fiction that bodies are separate, boundaried packages."[15]

Anyone who has loved music has felt what Koestenbaum describes. The singer's voice enters the listener and becomes the listener's voice. The fan hears a beloved song and believes she is singing the words of the song, that they were written for her to sing. The division between artist and fan dissolves in the moment of impassioned listening, and with it goes the division between genders. In music, people are not separate; they cannot be divided up into two discrete categories.

At the 2018 Pop Conference at Seattle's Museum of Pop, the scholar E. Glasberg, while moderating a keynote panel called

"The Butch Throat," wondered what the contemporary analog to the castrato voice might be.[16] Whose voice soars above society's gendered poles? This book aims to offer some answers to this complex question, to shed some light on why music has become a unique cultural incubator for the expression of gender transgressions. It is not intended as a comprehensive catalog of androgyny in music; if it were, it would be much longer. Instead, it is meant as an investigation of the different strategies musicians have used to break out of the limited range of motion and expression mandated by gender essentialism. Many different types of artists populate this book. There are cis men and women who have used music as a temporary escape from their otherwise stable and socially ordained gender identity. There are trans men and women musicians who transitioned while in the process of making a pivotal work, perhaps seeing an opening in the music they were making at the time. And there are artists who defy labeling, who revel in music's ambiguity as it reflects their own. This book does not mean to equivocate among these identities—nonbinary trans people face different challenges and follow different trajectories than do trans women and men—but to illuminate their common strategies as they pertain to music's unique potential for defection from the status quo.

Over the past half century, music has accelerated the discussions of trans identity and gender fluidity that now command so much attention on a national scale. The second decade of the twenty-first century has seen growing mainstream support for trans people, though this wave of affirmation has also prompted considerable backlash, in turn. In 2014, *Time* magazine announced the "transgender tipping point" in popular culture via a cover story on actress Laverne Cox.[17] The article called attention to the fact that trans people exist, have existed for a long time, and are not going away, even as its enthusiasm for a bold new world may have been preemptive: the forty-fifth American presidential administration is currently working overtime to delete trans people from reality and make our lives as difficult as possible. But trans people, as history shows, are not so easy to erase.

In Colorado, where I live, it's now possible to get a driver's license with the gender marked "X" instead of "M" or "F." The *AP Stylebook* includes an entry on the singular "they" and advises calling trans people by their true names, not their dead ones. In interviews, mainstream pop stars such as Miley Cyrus and Sam Smith openly speak about their in-between gender identities, a feeling of neitherness that can be readily heard in the way they sing—in the creases of Cyrus's husky alto, in the way Smith's gossamer tenor lifts away from the diaphragm. In 2017, the pop songwriter Teddy Geiger, who has penned hits such as "Stitches" for Canadian singer Shawn Mendes, came out as a trans woman to the open excitement and joy of her famous collaborators. And in 2018, a giant projection of the late star Prince sang the lines, "I'm not a woman / I'm not a man / I am something that you'll never understand" during the halftime show of the fifty-second Super Bowl, echoing his real-life performance at the same show in 2007. Gender transgression crept its way into even that most ostentatious display of normative American manhood.

Something has changed in America. Among more and more people, gender is understood not as an inevitable, unchanging characteristic acquired at birth, but as a language, a technology, a system of communication with a full range of expression. Trans and gender nonconforming people have always survived with or without the acknowledgment of the dominant culture, and the dangers posed by the straight world persist, but at the very least it has become easier for us to find each other, to call out into the dark and hear a chorus of voices calling back in return.

In a song called "Don't Let Them In," the queer performer Perfume Genius sings against a delicate trill of piano, "In an alternate ribbon of time / My dances were sacred / My lisp was evidence / I spoke for both spirits." His voice carries the same ambiguity I hear throughout pop music's history: a sense of belonging to neither gender, floating beyond the impetus to box oneself in. This alternate ribbon of time is not a parallel universe. It winds through recent and ancient history, as musician after musician has opened space to dance outside the roles they were prescribed at birth. Listen and you'll hear it: a catch of breath, a euphoric wail, a skidding away from one way of being to another and back again.

Do not believe those bootlickers of the patriarchy who flailingly insist upon the androgyne's novelty, and don't listen to anyone who construes trans people as fictions. Trans people are as ancient as music. We have always been here, singing from the shadows, glittering up the dark.

1

SCREAMING THE BEATLES

The First Boy Band Breaks the Gender Mold

The first sound to hit is the scream. It crashes in before the first chord, whips around and through the band, suspends them as they play, and chases them long after they've dropped their instruments and sauntered off the stage. The scream announces and outlives the songs, which are incidental. The girls are not screaming in response to the music. The band is playing in response to the scream.

Before American viewers heard the Beatles on the *Ed Sullivan Show* in February 1964, they heard how the Beatles were adored. "The city never has witnessed the excitement stirred by these youngsters from Liverpool who call themselves the Beatles," Sullivan said by way of introduction.[1] He had welcomed Elvis Presley onto his show eight years prior; he knew the look of a frenzy, and he could tell that this one was different from the last. What he saw then, though no one quite knew it yet, was a new genus of fandom: new in intensity, but also in the quality of its symbiosis. Without Beatles girls, there's no Beatles. Each group forged its identity in relation to the other.

The religious ecstasy aroused in these women and girls can be heard not just as an accessory to the music of the Beatles, but as part of the music. It is impossible to think of the Beatles without thinking of the scream. In May 1964, the band aired a television special called *Around the Beatles* in which, to avoid technical difficulties, they lip-synced and mimed along to prerecorded tracks. The only live sound produced during the performance came from the dozens of girls who were there to scream their devotion.

On *Ed Sullivan*, the sound dwarfs them. The four men bop along, singing rudimentary melodies in accented voices, barely hitting their notes. They're not much to look at, except for the hair (scandalous: too long) and the delight that animates their faces when they watch the girls watching them. Paul, singing lead on "All My Loving," drinks it up. Ringo beams intermittently from behind the kit. Even George, the shy one, sneaks a look at the crowd during his first solo. That's where the show happens: not in the jangly rock-and-roll chords they scrape out, not in the flat, breathless harmonies or the childish dance moves, but in the faces of the Beatles as they look up into the stands where the real spectacle is taking place.

In 1964, the teenager was still a relatively new phenomenon, a fresh consumer class with money to burn and passion to invest. *Life* magazine published a profile of the teen in June 1954, noting that "young people 16 to 20 are the beneficiaries of the very economic collapse that brought chaos almost a generation ago. The Depression tumbled the nation's birth rate to an all-time low in 1933, and today's teenage group is proportionately a smaller part of the total population than in more than 70 years. Since there are fewer of them, each—in the most prosperous time in US history—gets a bigger piece of the nation's economic pie than any previous generation ever got."[2]

Contemporary reports often don't address race in the rise of the teenager, positioning white people as the neutral default actors of American society, but this prosperity and its cultural reverberations tended to be concentrated among white people during an era of legally enforced racial segregation in the United

States. The mostly white Baby Boomers claimed the freedoms of the teenager for themselves; a state of prolonged innocence between childhood and adulthood did not fully extend to black teens and other youth of color, who tend to be treated as adults long before their white peers. The teenager was—and in many cases still is—a white construction.

The financial solvency afforded to young white people in the '50s codified the teen as a figure with enough money to secure cultural agency but enough youth to use that agency recklessly. By the '60s, the postwar baby boom had led to a surplus of white teenagers who were still able to enjoy the previous decade's economic prosperity. Naturally, the music industry sought to capitalize on this thriving market, and the Beatles supplied the perfect opportunity. "There were more teenagers than there had been for Elvis or Sinatra, with more money in their pockets, filled with a powerful sense that society was changing," wrote Dorian Lynskey in 2013. "To love the Beatles in 1963 was to embrace modernity."[3]

The Beatles invigorated the role of the fan because they were the first cultural product to engage holistically with the figure of the teenage girl. They emerged onto ground broken by Elvis and then outpaced their predecessor creatively and commercially. Elvis supplied an avatar for the forbidden promise of sex, but his appeal rested in how easy he was to objectify, his obviousness. Cartoonishly handsome, he was a body onto which the teenage girl could project unspoken and illicit desire. He inspired adoration, but it could not compare to the ferocious awe frothed up among Beatles girls. There is no Elvis equivalent to the term "Beatlemaniac."

"To younger teenagers, the Beatles' cheerful, faintly androgynous sexuality was more approachable than Elvis's alpha-male heat," wrote Lynskey. The Beatles offered something more complex than an empty sexual template. They presented an opportunity for identification. A girl could invest her desire in the band, but she could also discover herself there.

The gaze cast on the Beatles was a queer one from the start. Before American women looked at the Beatles, they had been seen by Brian Epstein, the closeted gay record clerk who discovered and ferociously advocated for the band when record executives failed to give them a second glance. Watching them play a lunch hour show at a grimy club in Liverpool, Epstein picked up on the magnetic potential of the four young men. In Vivek Tiwary's graphic novel *The Fifth Beatle: The Brian Epstein Story*, artist Andrew Robinson closes the frame around the future manager's stunned face as he beholds the Beatles for the first time, as if he could sense his life pivoting around that one rapturous moment.[4] Reflecting on the show in his own words, Epstein himself was more measured. "There was some indefinable charm there," he wrote in his 1964 memoir *A Cellarful of Noise*. "They were extremely amusing and in a rough 'take it or leave [it] way' very attractive."[5] Upon becoming their manager, Epstein was tasked with convincing the world to see the Beatles the way he saw them: via a gaze that desired its objects without othering them. Heterosexual desire spans a chasm, coveting difference. Queer desire pulls together like elements, finding attraction in affinity.

That teen girls could even feel the kind of active, demanding sexual desire evinced by their screams was still a novel concept in the early '60s, which carried vestiges of the prior decade's postwar conservatism. "In a highly sexualized society (one sociologist found that the number of explicitly sexual references in the mass media had doubled between 1950 and 1960), teen and preteen girls were expected to be not only 'good' and 'pure' but to be the enforcers of purity within their teen society—drawing the line for overeager boys and ostracizing girls who failed in this responsibility," wrote Barbara Ehrenreich in a 1986 essay. "To abandon control—to scream, faint, dash about in mobs—was, in form if not in conscious intent, to protest the sexual repressiveness, the rigid double standard of female teen culture. It was the first and most dramatic uprising of women's sexual revolution."[6]

Befuddled by the Beatlemaniacs' exuberance, interviewers and critics (who were more often than not men) pinned the scream to a desire, of all things, to *mother* the band. "It has been said that you appeal to the maternal instinct in these girls," began an interviewer in 1964. John cut him off: "That's a dirty lie."[7] Joking or not, he was right. The dynamic at hand did not correspond to a mother/son model. Beatles girls wanted the way men were expected to want: unabashedly and directly, as active agents in the exchange of desire. There was nothing coy about their hunger.

Early reports of Beatles fandom in England noted that the band's teen girl following was driven to violence by their passion. While the lads recorded a session for the BBC in 1963, "the fans went mad and tried to tear the door of the Beatles taxi off its hinges." Outside a different show in Manchester, the fans succeeded in their destruction: "The audience refused to go until the boys came back for an encore. When the boys finally left the show, the taxi had its mirrors and aerial pulled off, and a window smashed."[8]

In the 1964 film *A Hard Day's Night*, girls chase the band by the dozens, screaming all the way—an inversion of the skirt-chasing gags that appeared throughout Marx Brothers comedies in the first half of the twentieth century. Beatlemania slotted the Beatles into a feminine position, the object of ravenous desire, and so enabled their female fans to assume a place of relative masculinity. By curating the band's aesthetic, Epstein primed teenage girls to see the Beatles the way a gay man might see them.

Before showing off his boys (his "artistes," as he called all the musicians he managed), Epstein dandied them up. He had them shed their heterosexual working-class signifiers, swapping out leather and denim for fitted mohair suits and ties. Without their straight-boy clothes, the band became effete. The suits paradoxically feminized them, rendering them soft enough for a female gaze to penetrate.

Because of their Liverpool accents and rambunctious demeanors, the Beatles appeared to bristle against their elegant costumes, which only made them look all the more irresistibly rebellious. Then there were the mop tops, styled by Astrid Kirchherr, the German photographer who would take the band's first group photos at a fairground in Hamburg. Not a girlish cut, exactly, the mop top connoted an unkempt masculinity. It spilled over the boys' ears and down the backs of their necks, crossing over the hard lines of their shirt collars. The Beatles didn't look like women; they looked as though they lacked the discipline to look like men, which landed them in uncharted territory between established gender forms.

The mop tops are the stars of *A Hard Day's Night,* a rock musical where the only thing that happens is that the Beatles make trouble. They gallivant through cityscapes and frolic through a field, escaping their handlers and showing up late to absolutely everything. They embrace their childishness and especially relish how it annoys the parental figures responsible for them. John plays with a toy submarine in a bathtub while he's supposed to be getting ready for a press conference. George trash-talks a teenage influencer (a proto-Instagram star) to her TV executive boss. At one point, Ringo links up with a schoolboy who's playing hooky with three of his friends. The four young boys hold a mirror to the Beatles, who act like they're in the fifth grade throughout the film. The hair supplies a symbol for this irreverence. It makes them look like four men in their twenties who refused to grow up and enter the straight world, which is represented in the movie by a series of stodgy authority figures—cops, managers, and TV producers, all men, all smart-suited, clean-shaven, and neatly barbered. The invocation of a scrappy eternal boyhood appealed to teen girls, who were themselves not quite adults, but it also had an effect on rebellious boys. As Roger Ebert put it in his 1996 review of the film, "[*A Hard Day's Night*] was so influential in its androgynous imagery that untold thousands of young men walked into the theater with short haircuts, and their hair started growing during the movie and didn't get cut again until the 1970s."[9]

The long hair posed a threat to traditional American masculinity. In a 1979 piece on the legacy of the Beatles, rock critic Greil Marcus noted parenthetically, "One acquaintance argued with great vehemence that it was physically impossible for male hair—at least, *normal* male hair—to grow to Beatle length" [emphasis in original].[10] In mid-1960s America, gender norms were so deeply inscribed that even a few extra inches of hair appeared not just as a social lapse but as a biological anomaly. The shirt collar represented the barrier between normative and deviant masculinities; by letting their hair cross it, the Beatles broke a long-held agreement of what it meant to look like a man. "There they were in America, all getting housetrained for adulthood with their indisputable principle of life: short hair equals men, long hair equals women," said Paul in 1966. "Well, we got rid of that small convention for them."[11] The band's betrayal of hard masculinity opened them up to a new breed of fan devotion. They didn't inspire awe in teen girls by casting femininity as the antithesis to their own manhood. They wove girlishness into their boyishness, inviting the girls who loved them to participate directly in their spectacle.

One reviewer, writing for the *Toronto Telegram* in 1964, posited that the Beatles' attractiveness originated not in the band itself but in the way girls looked at the band: "They don't rely on obvious sexuality, either in movement or song, but obviously there is a large element of sexuality in their appeal. Any sexuality is once removed: it occurs in the eye of the beholder rather than from any overt action by The Beatles."[12] This dynamic represented a sea change from Elvis, who oozed sexuality. Elvis was dominant; he inspired sexual longing because there was no choice but to see him as a sexual object. The Beatles, in their passivity, invoked a more active sexuality in their fans. Beatles girls took charge: they outscreamed the Beatles. "Tonight was, you know, marvelous. Ridiculous," John said after a concert at the Washington Coliseum in 1964. "Almost eight thousand people all shouting at once, and we were trying to shout louder than them with microphones, and we still couldn't beat 'em."[13]

It helped that there were four of them. A single musician, like Elvis, is a monolith: either he attracts a look or he repels it. The presence of four musicians adds dimension to the act of looking. Because they dressed in near-identical black suits in the early years of their career, because they all wore the same haircut, the Beatles invited the gaze to sink in deeply, past the uniform and into their faces, their affect, their quirks. If one Beatle deflected desire, another might invite it: they were different enough from each other to attract an equivalent variety of fans.

"We reckoned we could make it because there were four of us," said John. "None of us would have made it alone, because Paul wasn't quite strong enough, I didn't have girl-appeal, George was too quiet and Ringo was the drummer. But we thought that everyone would be able to dig at least one of us, and that's how it turned out."[14]

Their difference compelled girls to identify with one in opposition to the others. You loved John or you loved Paul, or you were strange and latched onto George, or you were receptive to pathos, in which case your eye followed Ringo. The best scene in *A Hard Day's Night* comes when the Beatles start playing "She Loves You" and four girls each shout out the name of their favorite player with equally tearful fervor. These powerful affinities revealed self-knowledge. Teen girls could excavate their own emergent personalities by shooting their gaze into the Beatles and seeing where it landed.

Onstage and on film, the Beatles modeled a novel form of homosociality. They didn't perform like the male vocal groups that preceded them in the 1950s. Their movements were not so formal, and not always outward facing. They performed for the audience but also for each other. Because they had no clear leader, they didn't move like their rock-and-roll ancestors either. When they appeared on TV, the camera cut from one member to another, allowing each of them a roughly equal portion of the viewer's gaze.

Through a certain lens, the way the Beatles move onstage brushes up against the edge of the homoerotic. On *Ed Sullivan*, the stage is set with only two microphones, one for Paul and one for John. If George wants to sing backup, he has to wander over to one of his bandmates, who steps aside to make room for him. Two singers share a mic, facing each other, the necks of their guitars thrust out in opposite directions. Musically, performatively, they play off each other, sharing unspoken jokes or knowing facial expressions. These subtle intragroup dynamics are more fascinating to watch than even the raunchiest Elvis performance. They speak to an inner world, a communion among boys only partially visible to the audience, who get an intoxicating glimpse. The scream didn't only express sexual desire for the band; it also functioned as a bid for entry into the world the Beatles shared with each other.

Contemporary pop groups model the same internal difference, and so it's tempting to label the Beatles as the world's first boy band, the wellspring that gave rise to commercial titans such as the Backstreet Boys and One Direction. But the Beatles didn't engender the form from scratch; they transposed it across racial, gendered, and geographic borders. They derived much of their sound from black American men, including Chuck Berry and Fats Domino, but they also absorbed plenty of musical innovations from black women. Their vocal delivery, their harmonies, and their in-group dynamics already had a model in the American girl group.

The Beatles' debut studio album, 1963's *Please Please Me*, boasts three covers of songs previously recorded by black American girl groups. "Chains," a Gerry Goffin/Carole King composition originally released by the Brooklyn trio the Cookies in 1962, speaks to a stifled, passive form of desire. "I'd like to love you, but darling, I'm imprisoned by these chains," George Harrison sings on the Beatles' cover. His voice melts into the voices of his bandmates, just as the Cookies' three voices braided tightly together. Their harmonies connoted feminine commiseration, a woman lamenting her impossible yearning to her sympathetic friends. Girl groups such as the Cookies modeled sisterhood; even when their songs were written in the first person, speaking to an unapproachable "you," they sounded as though they were speaking to each other, letting multiple women shoulder the weight of one girl's romantic suffering. The Beatles mimicked that form of delivery exactly. They didn't masculinize "Chains" by thrusting George out to the front of the mix. They sang, as the Cookies did, like sisters soothing each other.

"Boys," the only song on *Please Please Me* to feature Ringo on lead vocals, similarly mirrors its original girl group recording. As a 1960 Shirelles B-side, "Boys" saw lead singer Shirley Owens gush about the delights of loving men. "I'm talking 'bout boys!" she sings, and further back in the mix, the rest of the group agrees: "Yeah, yeah, boys!" The Beatles tweaked the lyrics slightly to make clear that they were the boys capable of providing girls with pleasure, but the song's vocal relationship remains intact, as does the enthusiasm for boys as a general concept. "I'm talkin' 'bout boys / What a bundle of joy," sings Ringo, and the band chimes behind him in agreement. As a Beatles recording, the song invites female listeners to occupy the position of desirer while the band plays the role of the boys eager to be desired. "Boys" endows girls with agency, opening a door into active female participation in sexual desire while simultaneously inhabiting a girl's headspace as she fantasizes about loving boys.

On the band's second album, *With the Beatles*, John Lennon sings lead on a cover of the Michigan group the Marvelettes' 1961 hit "Please Mister Postman." His northern accent sets his vocal delivery apart from Gladys Horton's—the Beatles had no qualms about sounding English, which helped them stand out on American radio—but he readily interpolates the grain of Horton's voice into his own. Where she fries her voice, he fries his. The rough edges of his singing now tend to be associated primarily with the Beatles, but the band derived the technique from black American singers—listen to *The Soul of Ike & Tina Turner*, released by the then-married musical duo from Saint Louis in 1961, and you'll hear in Tina Turner's delivery the seeds of what's now considered the Beatles voice. On "Please Mister Postman," John even preserves Horton's patois pronunciation of the line, "Deliver de letter / The sooner de better."

The Marvelettes' "Please Mister Postman" toyed with an urgent passivity. The song is about a woman waiting for the mail. There's no action in the narrative; nothing happens, and yet Horton sings as though she's determined to make something happen, if only she can sing hard enough about her waiting. She occupies a traditionally feminine role, biding time until the man she loves decides to show affection. The song isn't even addressed to her boyfriend. She sings to the postman, a neutral intermediary, but the quality of her voice suggests an impatience reserved for the man who's ignoring her from afar. She sounds like a woman bristling at the confines of femininity, sloughing sweetness and patience and identifying with anger and frustration instead. The Beatles may have changed the word "boyfriend" to "girlfriend," but the timbre of Horton's voice persists in their iteration of the song. They're boys emulating girls who have grown tired of gender scripts: boys trying to be girls who are sick of what it means to be a girl.

American femininity is necessarily bound up with whiteness; being black, singers such as the Marvelettes could never fully adhere to idealized womanhood in the eyes of a racist country. A racialized figure already carries the specter of gender subversion when gender ideals are coded white. Black American girl groups sang differently from white American women, just as

Chuck Berry and Fats Domino performed differently from their white peers. From the margins of a culture that systemically privileged whiteness, these artists cultivated invigorating new forms of music that marked them aurally as living somewhat outside the status quo. The Beatles latched onto that difference, integrating it into a sound that would distinguish them from other white men in turn.

Paul and John's fondness for girl groups seeped into their own songwriting. The original compositions on the first few Beatles albums integrated the vocal relationships modeled by the Shirelles, the Marvelettes, the Cookies, and the Ronettes. Each of John's effervescent "yeahs" on "It Won't Be Long" gets answered by his bandmates, who intensify the word and cause John to excite it even further: a snowballing of vocal energy into a torrent of "yeah." Like "Please Mister Postman," "It Won't Be Long" is a song about enthusiastic waiting. (In the 2007 jukebox musical film *Across the Universe*, the song gets sung by a girl who's waiting for her boyfriend to return from war—it neatly suits a female perspective.) "It won't be long / Till I belong to you," John sings. Though "till you belong to me" is a metrically identical line, he opts for surrender over possession. In the world of the song, he's both domestic and utterly passive, cooped up in the house pining for his love, and yet he sounds thrilled about it. So does the rest of the band, who serve as confidantes to his loneliness and champion the willing return of the woman who left.

Though girl groups provided much of the foundation to the Beatles' sound, queer male sexuality also left its mark on the band. John's "woo!" on "I Saw Her Standing There," the first track on the first Beatles album, comes straight from Little Richard's "Tutti Frutti"—a song originally written about topping ("tutti frutti / good booty" went the chorus before it was straightwashed). If the references to gay sex were scrubbed out by the time Little Richard laid the song to tape, the thrill of singing about such a topic lingered in the recording that became a

1955 hit. "Good booty" became "oh Rudy" and Richard casually mentions a handful of girls, but the bright falsetto "woo!" in the second chorus remains, an artifact of queer euphoria. John utters the same "woo!" in "I Saw Her Standing There," breaking from his chest voice to his head voice as if wanting to dance with a girl were as illicit as nonnormative sex. (It wasn't, but singing about sexuality in any form still carried its own taboo.) The "woo" gets its own line, mid-thought: "How could I dance with another? / Woo! / When I saw her standing there."

The song opens with the lines "Well she was just seventeen / You know what I mean / And the way she looked was way beyond compare," a sequence of thoughts that has not exactly aged well. In one light, the lyrics to "I Saw Her Standing There" objectify a vulnerable subset of the population, marking a minor as a sexual object. In another, they acknowledge and validate that same subset. The teenage girl exists in the world of the Beatles' music. She dances among them, inspiring their affection as much as they inspire hers. By speaking her age, the Beatles make her real—and acknowledge her agency. Rather than sing from the perspective of a boy chasing down a girl, the Beatles use "I Saw Her Standing There" to hint at romantic mutuality. The "she" of the song has a will of her own: "She wouldn't dance with another," John assures us. By rendering a seventeen-year-old girl as not just an object of desire but also a subject, the Beatles instigated a break from 1950s visions of femininity. The Beatles girl is not just a future wife, not a vision of domestic potential to be tapped by an opportunistic man. She has her own desires, and she has some measure of freedom to pursue them.

There's one shot in *A Hard Day's Night* that disappears almost as quickly as it comes on-screen. It's during the "She Loves You" sequence, when the camera darts from girl to girl, delighting in their delight. Many pull their hair or bury their face in their hands. One of them is so overcome by emotion that she turns away from the stage and collapses into a hug with her friend. This moment, more than any other in the film, clarifies what the Beatles did to people—specifically, what they did to girls. They drew forth devotion, but they also supplied a foundation on which girls could bond with each other. Their influence is felt here, in the intimacies of fandom, more than it's heard in any of the music they inspired. In many ways, they cleared room for the figure of the fan: a passionate participant in pop music with a fierce queer gaze, wanting the pop star while also wanting to be the pop star—wanting a form of impossible mutuality and forging bonds with others based on the strength of that desire.

The groundwork of the Beatles phenomenon had already been well established by the time the band flickered onto American TV screens. There's very little the Beatles did musically that hadn't been done better by black artists years before; their gender transgressions arose not from direct innovation but from the repackaging of black musical idioms into a group of pretty white English boys. The Beatles were thieves, but in their immense popularity, they shook loose brittle gender roles in a way that made white American record executives and their target markets sit up and take notice, broadcasting androgyny across the States on an unprecedented scale.

2

OH! YOU PRETTY THINGS

The Glitter Revolution

The year 1970 opened a strange new decade. Americans had walked on the moon one year earlier, sealing a major victory for the Space Race without purging the atmosphere of its Cold War anxiety. Midway through 1969, the gays, lesbians, trans women, and drag queens who frequented the Stonewall Inn in New York's Greenwich Village decided they'd had enough of police harassment and rioted for days in an act of cathartic rebellion that would come to be seen as the birth of the modern LGBTQ rights movement. These glimpses of futurity and progress were punctuated by cultural and literal deaths. In the summer of 1969, actress Sharon Tate was murdered in her Los Angeles home by members of the Manson Family cult. The Beatles broke up in 1970; that same year, Jimi Hendrix and Janis Joplin died within a month of each other, both at age 27. The utopianism of the flower children failed to manifest on a broad scale. Strident attempts by the hippie counterculture to love the world back to health had not, in fact, brought about the end of the Vietnam War, and now the movement's heroes were dying. A vacuum grew inside pop music and youth culture; to fill it, certain musicians looked back to the early days of rock and roll, subsuming its chunky rhythms, sexual vocalizations, and guitar prowess, with a twist.

Both glam rock and punk rock ultimately crystallized in New York, but their roots spread further out across the United

States. At the end of the '60s, a five-piece garage rock band from Phoenix, Arizona, packed up their gear, moved to Los Angeles, and changed their name from the straitlaced Spiders to the gender-confounding Alice Cooper. "Alice Cooper, as most avid music buffs in this locality are no doubt aware, is not a newly-arrived musical counterpart to Kate Smith or one of the Lennon Sisters," read a 1969 article in the *Arizona Republic*. "Nor is Alice Cooper even another Janis Joplin or Aretha Franklin."[1] Alice Cooper—both the name of the band and the stage name of its front man, Vince Furnier—was one of the incendiary acts that would bend American rock out of its introverted and gender-essentialist psychedelic phase into the norm-flaunting era of glam.

The name might have started as a gimmick, but Furnier and his band integrated it holistically into their act. As Alice Cooper's music grew blunter (their 1969 debut, *Pretties for You*, is more or less cloaked in psychedelic mannerisms, a pretense they would start to shed on 1970's *Easy Action* and would drop entirely by 1971's *Love It to Death*), so did their act. The band drew ire for a 1969 stunt in which Cooper threw a live chicken into the audience to its death. But among journalists, the way the band looked sparked as much confusion as its animal cruelty.

By 1970, Cooper had begun to desecrate gender boundaries so brazenly that even rock critics had to admit they were shocked. John Mendelsohn, writing for *Entertainment World*, noted Cooper's "garish drag-queen eye makeup" and said he looked "like a nightmare vision of unisex run amuck."[2] In *Creem*, Marvin H. Hohman Jr. drew an explicit line between Cooper's appearance and the specter of queer deviance: "Alice Cooper is the living embodiment of those dangerous freaks that the straights keep shouting about."[3] Albert Goldman, writing for *Life* in 1971, had a more visceral reaction. "The advance publicity for Alice Cooper almost turned my stomach," went the opening line of an article called "Rock in the Androgynous Zone."[4] Other contemporaneous headlines similarly jumped on Cooper's gender presentation.

"Alice Cooper: Are You a Boy, or Are You a Girl?" asked a 1971 issue of *Crawdaddy*.[5] "Alice Cooper of Freaky Rock Fame Is Just an All-American Boy-Girl" responded the *Milwaukee Journal* the same year.[6]

Alice Cooper lapped up the ambivalent attention. He liked pushing buttons—his stage antics included being wheeled around in a straitjacket and feeding a live snake—and he knew that, in America, gender was a big button to push. In interviews, he doubled down on his clashingly androgynous look by insisting, presciently, that it was the most natural thing in the world. When the *Milwaukee Journal* asked about the name, Cooper said simply, "It's such an American name. We're such an American band. We're the ultimate American band." He was fond of telling journalists that "biologically, everyone is male and female." In a 1969 interview for *Poppin*, he added, "People don't accept that they are both male and female, and people are afraid to break out of their sex thing because that's a big insecurity that's doing that. Consequently, people will make fun of us."[7]

This line of reasoning invited a curious paradox. Cooper knew that a man wearing copious eyeliner onstage would shock American audiences as much as a man shoveling live mice into the mouth of a boa constrictor. By insisting on the naturalness of his gender presentation, he drove that shock deeper. As other glam musicians would soon come to discover, playing off drag as if it were second nature (*Oh, this? I just threw it on*) was a surer way to highlight its disruptive potential than acting like a self-conscious rabble-rouser. The blasé attitude with which Cooper wore his own androgyny ended up hammering the point home. In the *Crawdaddy* feature, Ben Edmunds and Lenny Kaye noted that Cooper's "transvestite" inclinations were developed in response to "a growing frustration with an inability to get jobs or other meaningful employment"—in other words, a failure to complete the historical rites of masculinity. "The ultimate rebellion of our time is the simple refusal to be a man," Goldman wrote in *Life*, presumably after recovering from his nausea at seeing Cooper's made-up face.

In England, where gay sex acts had only just been decriminalized in 1967, a small crop of songwriters was quietly nursing its own refusal of traditional masculinity. Born Mark Feld, the singer and guitarist who named himself Marc Bolan navigated a similar musical transition to that of Cooper, shaking off the florid trappings of psychedelic rock to uncover a raw, primal, and glittering form of music underneath. Bolan's first four albums with the band Tyrannosaurus Rex indulged his love of high fantasy against a soft bucolic backdrop. Although those albums more or less fell within the parameters of what was considered acceptable hippie masculinity at the time, Bolan's vocal delivery pushed at the edges of his assigned gender. "Bolan sang in a high-pitched, somewhat nasal, heavily vibrato-laden tenor voice that was completely idiosyncratic and unmistakable," wrote Philip Auslander in his 2006 book *Performing Glam Rock*. "A highly mannered voice . . . seems theatrical, artificial, and perhaps unmasculine—one commentator described Bolan's voice at the time as possessing a 'soft but sinister androgynous vibrato.' In opting for a highly mannered vocal presentation, Tyrannosaurus Rex set themselves apart stylistically from psychedelic rock in ways that anticipated glam in its use of sexually ambiguous and artificial-seeming voices."[8]

Bolan carried that voice into T. Rex, the glitter-dusted incarnation of the same band who, with the help of producer Tony Visconti (who would go on to work with David Bowie for decades), would establish the sound of UK glam on the seminal 1971 album *Electric Warrior*. The shaggy-haired front man retained the sense of wonder he felt for unicorns, sea monsters, and wizards across the Tyrannosaurus Rex albums but refocused it into more quotidian, rock-and-roll concerns: sex, love, dancing, and cars. The music was simplified, too, retreating into the open chords and bass/snare drum shuffles of '50s rock music.

This retro template rooted T. Rex's music, giving the band room to dive into emotional nuances that their psychedelic records crowded out. The sublime "Cosmic Dancer" threads Bolan's high, nasal voice through a rock ballad as he subtly claims a kind of interstellar queerness. "I was dancing when I was twelve . . . / I was dancing when I was out . . . / I danced myself right out the womb," Bolan sings. "Is it strange to dance so soon?" The lines, anodyne at a glance, suggest a feeling of otherness compounded by his feminine delivery. The pubescent age of twelve, the double meaning of "out," and the repeated question—"Is it strange to dance?"—all point to a coded disclosure of Bolan's own bisexuality. His assertion that he danced himself out of the womb predates Lady Gaga's explicitly pro-queer anthem "Born This Way" by exactly forty years.

T. Rex's effeminate underpinnings were not lost on music critics at the time. In a 1972 review of *Electric Warrior* for the *Village Voice*, Robert Christgau sourly described Bolan's performance as "fey."[9] Ben Gerson's *Rolling Stone* review of the same album opened with a nearly identical quip about the singer's presentation: "So elegant, so fey." Gerson would go on to note Bolan's "effete vocal" and close the piece with a joke about his height: "With *Electric Warrior*, Marc Bolan establishes himself as the heaviest rocker under 5'4" in the world today."[10]

Around the release of *Electric Warrior*, T. Rex made an appearance on *Top of the Pops* that, according to Auslander, "fully launched" the glam rock phenomenon in the UK. Strumming a flying V guitar, Bolan appears in pink slacks, a silver blazer, and a gleaming green top. Most notably, each of his cheeks is adorned with a big glitter tear. While the glitter on his face can't precisely be called feminine—it wasn't a look worn regularly by women at the time—the very fact of his wearing makeup disqualified him from masculine standards too. It was as though Bolan were striking a pose between, or beyond, the two socially ordained genders. Not fully male and not fully female, he floated, a cosmic dancer, in his own space.

Another London native would soon cement the link between the cosmos and earthly queerness. Like Bolan, the singer born David Jones dabbled in a variety of genres, with limited success, before he launched himself out of the atmosphere. He was a saxophone player and a long-haired folkie before he became an alien, though a 1969 hit timed to the launch of the Apollo 11 moon mission established David Bowie's early interest in space. Though it capitalized on the spectacle of the successful moon landing, "Space Oddity" came loaded with a healthy distrust of a society that would happily shoot people into the sky. The song's speaker, Major Tom, is interviewed right before launch, not about his mission, but about his clothes. His journey's derailment makes it clear that the people back on earth care more about his celebrity than his well-being; once aloft, something goes wrong in his spaceship and he floats off into the unknown. Certainly not a celebration of the American space program, "Space Oddity" can be read more easily as a parable of human frailty. "Planet earth is blue and there's nothing I can do," Bowie sings at the chorus, his high tenor crackling.

Bowie's skepticism about the state of affairs down on earth soon metamorphosed into one of the most spectacular rejections of gender conventions in pop history. He carried androgyny into the mainstream on the strength of his weird charisma, but Bowie didn't invent his look or his sound; like most famous rock artists, he (allegedly) stole it. Bowie settled on a feminized alien aesthetic after seeing the Andy Warhol stage play *Pork*, which opened in London in the summer of 1971. Warhol, a gay artist famous for integrating the imagery of advertising into fine art, cultivated an artistic community of gay men, drag queens, and trans women in the '60s and '70s. One of the artists in his circle was Jayne County, front woman of the proto-punk band the Electric Chairs. She played the character Vulva Lips in *Pork* and met Bowie and his wife, Angie, backstage. "When we went to London to do *Pork*, we had heard about David Bowie who had long hair like Lauren Bacall and wore these baggy clothes and makeup—we were fascinated by him," County said. "But Angie [Bowie] was looking for a new image for him because he was getting stalled with that image. So they came to see us at *Pork* and hung out in the dressing room and became friends with the cast."[11]

County would later credit this encounter for Bowie's dramatic reinvention. "We influenced David to change his image," she said. "After us, David started getting dressed up. I'd gotten the shaved eyebrows thing from [fellow Warhol superstar] Jackie Curtis, and David started shaving his eyebrows, painting his nails, even wearing painted nails out at nightclubs, like we were doing. He changed his whole image and started getting more and more freaky."[12]

Bowie took much of his look from County and other trans women in the Warhol universe; County has also claimed that he stole a good amount of her music. "David loved my songs and so I sent him my demos. He loved them and wanted more so I sent him three sets of demos: 'Man Enough to Be a Woman,' 'Are You a Boy or Are You a Girl,' 'Queenage Baby' . . . He wanted to take me into the studio and produce an album, so I sent all my music and little bits and pieces started showing up on his albums," she said.

That Bowie became a star and not County speaks to the rigid maze gender-transgressive pop stars had to navigate in the 1970s. If Bowie had actually been trans, his face likely wouldn't be plastered across every form of pop culture debris from bumper stickers to emoji. His cis masculinity gave many listeners—and record executives—a sense of plausible deniability. Vaulting an actual transsexual to the status of celebrity would have been too disruptive, too risky, and so the industry settled on a man who could do the best impression of a trans person while staying tethered to relative normalcy. Bowie self-identified as gay at the start of his career, but he was married to a woman who gave birth to their son. His flamboyant performance was ultimately grounded in the reassuring symbol of the heterosexual nuclear family.

Though his image was hardly original, Bowie still managed to drive a new vision of androgyny into mainstream culture, a Trojan horse carrying the notion that it was possible to betray the regressive models of gender foisted upon young people at the time. Like Bolan, he used his music to occupy an ambiguous middle space outside prescriptive imaginings of binary gender. Over clunky rock chords, he shouted out to queers and androgynes on the 1971 song "Oh! You Pretty Things." "Don't you know you're driving your mamas and papas insane?" he sings, identifying his audience as young people beginning to disavow the rigid constraints of their parents' generation. "Gotta make way for the homo superior," he concludes at the end of the chorus, deliciously punning on "homo" while insinuating that the future belonged to the gays.

There were few names for such a figure as Bowie in the early '70s, so the singer invented his own: Ziggy Stardust, the protagonist of the 1972 album *The Rise and Fall of Ziggy Stardust and the Spiders from Mars*. Many young people in the UK caught their first glimpse of Bowie in his gender-smeared glory that year, when he and the Spiders from Mars debuted the album's first single, "Starman," on *Top of the Pops*.[13] While Bolan had already introduced the idea of glam to the program the year before, the lithe and luminous Bowie and his glitter-spangled smirk were something altogether new, more mischievous, and ultimately more dangerous.

Dressed in a Lurex jumpsuit with fire-engine-red hair, Bowie flirts unabashedly with the camera as he navigates the chorus's flamboyant octave leap—a nod to Judy Garland's "Somewhere over the Rainbow" from *The Wizard of Oz*, a recognizable symbol of in-group belonging in twentieth-century gay culture. He fixes his eyes on the camera, makes sure he's being seen, and then throws his arm around Mick Ronson, his long-haired guitarist, a move that in 1972 could only be seen as a flaming middle finger to the straight world. Such open displays of homosocial affection lacked precedent on network TV; judging by his defiant gaze into the camera, Bowie knew the gesture would be read as homoerotic.

Homosexuality had been ostensibly legal for just five years in England, though many queer men were still getting arrested for consensual sex acts. (LGBTQ activist Peter Tatchell noted in 2017 that "the partial decriminalization of homosexuality in 1967 was very partial indeed.")[14] That February, Bowie had casually told *Melody Maker* he was gay, and a few months later, in July, two thousand people marched through London in the UK's first-ever pride rally.[15] "Starman" gathered that momentum and projected it into suburban homes, landing an ecstatic gesture of queerness squarely in the domestic sphere. "I had to phone someone, so I picked on you," Bowie sings, pointing his finger directly into the camera and wagging it around. "If we can sparkle, he may land tonight / Don't tell your papa, he'll get us locked up in fright." As with "Oh! You Pretty Things," Bowie stakes out territory that belongs exclusively to young, glittering aliens—no parents allowed.

Ziggy Stardust—a bisexual, polyamorous, alien rock star who descended to earth to show kids a groovier way of life—broke apart the common script of queerness as perversion, aberration, or anomaly. If it was unearthly to be queer, then "Starman" proved that the queer kids came from a world brighter than Earth. Bowie cast his transgression not as a failure of masculinity but as a transcendence of masculinity, of joyous belonging to a celestial world beyond our own.

Back in the United States, another troupe of pop aliens was slowly ascending into the outer atmosphere. After a decade of recording as Patti LaBelle and the Bluebelles, the vocal trio of LaBelle, Nona Hendryx, and Sarah Dash rebranded, simply, as LaBelle and began plotting a course out of doo-wop and into glam rock by way of soul and funk. After renaming themselves, LaBelle began wearing silver jumpsuits with high, space-age collars and dazzling glitter makeup. Originally based in Philadelphia, the trio earned a devoted following in New York, attracting a "multiracial, multi-sexual, and multicultural crowd" (as Hendryx would put it) to their extravagant and life-affirming shows.[16]

In October 1974, LaBelle made history when they became the first black pop group to play the Metropolitan Opera House. If the Met's audience was normally full of relatively discreet homosexuals, LaBelle, who had just put out the hit album *Nightbirds* a month prior, drew out a more ecstatically visible breed of gay. Writing for the *New York Times*, critic John Rockwell described the scene in a tone of barely polite bewilderment. "If one wanted to be catty about it, one could suggest that Sunday's crowd was the Met's opera audience come out of the closet: there can rarely have been so many bearded gentlemen in dresses, razzledazzle sequins and arched eyebrows at a Met performance before," he wrote. "Met officials have announced themselves in the past as being highly selective as to the type of pop audience they would allow within the sacred portals. Nobody was available for comment this week as to future plans for pop, but after Labelle, one can only wonder if the next step won't be Wayne County on Halloween."[17]

He was referring to Jayne County with the name she used pre-transition; the snotty implication seemed to be that LaBelle's flamboyant performance was one step away from a trans woman in fullregalia on the sacrosanct stage of the Met. Dismissive as he may have been toward overt expressions of queer joy, Rockwell was right, in a sense: LaBelle knocked something loose in New York's concert scene. Gays, drag queens, and trans women felt free to dance in the aisles of the Met, no longer buttoning themselves up to pass in polite society. The group's music proved a fitting soundtrack for these pockets of queer celebration. "Lady Marmalade," LaBelle's enduring hit single, sang the praises of a sex worker in New Orleans, and the song became an anthem of sorts for those who found avenues of survival and joy outside the status quo.

In 1976, Martin Weston gave the LaBelle phenomenon a name in the pages of *Ebony*. "The former doo-wah ladies of the Apollo Theater in Harlem are in the forefront of outrageous unisexual futurism in rock music show biz," he wrote. "Such lyrics as *Somebody somewhere / has all the answers to the questions on our minds* appeal to a generation of young people—some of whom are black, some of whom are gay—for whom there are few spokesmen. The Labelle renaissance was a complete break from traditional mores in public entertainment, and it opened some taboo areas of human sexuality and racial oppression to free musical discussion and uninhibited stage display."[18]

From Judy Garland to Lady Gaga, the history of gay men seeing themselves reflected in exaggeratedly feminine cis women stretches for nearly a century. LaBelle tapped into this phenomenon, but they were also an artistic outlet for a woman who was herself queer. By 1975, Nona Hendryx, who by her account wrote the majority of LaBelle's material, was known for her "proud lesbianism." (These days, she identifies as bisexual.) In his review of *Nightbirds*' follow-up *Phoenix* for *Creem*, Wayne Robins wrote that Hendryx's queerness and the queerness of the group's fans had thrust LaBelle into "a socio-sexual vanguard."[19] Using the same tools as Bowie and Bolan—alien costumes and glitter makeup—LaBelle orchestrated sites of political rebellion and personal freedom at their concerts. They took glam's futurism and plugged it back into the here and now, creating space for fans at the margins to express themselves freely. Known for the performing poet and musician Gil Scott-Heron's black radical anthem "The Revolution Will Not Be Televised," LaBelle made it clear they intended themselves to be not just a pop spectacle but a vital political force too. The glitter and the melodies got attendees in the door; once they were inside, LaBelle's powerful stage presence and incendiary lyrics could open their eyes. "A lot of people don't want to see groups who sing about any sort of problems or 'revolutionary' material," noted Hendryx in 1975. "But if you dress up your message it's like people seeing a glittering sign."[20]

In a 1975 article complaining about the state of pop in New York City, *New York Times* critic Ken Emerson drew a direct line between LaBelle's gleaming queer appeal and the white male performers who would come to crowd them out in the glam rock canon. (LaBelle may well have made the best music of the glam era, but rock history plays favorites, and those favorites tend to be overwhelmingly white and male.) "Perhaps the first performers to attract simultaneously large numbers of white teenagers, blacks and gays, Labelle is not the only New York group whose allure is based in part on sexual ambiguity," he wrote. "On stage, Lou Reed seems to flirt with every persuasion but finally appears to be, like Warhol, beyond sex."[21]

If LaBelle sneaked messages of revolution to eager audiences by stunning them with sequins and three-part harmonies, Reed found that such a message could be dressed down too. After releasing *Ziggy Stardust* to critical acclaim, David Bowie started working with the former front man of the Velvet Underground, the experimental band that had caught Warhol's ear in the '60s. The Velvet Underground couched Reed's lazy vocal performance in simple drum beats, screeching violas, and shuffling electric guitars. His lyrics breached topics like drug abuse and BDSM; his delivery, alongside the band's low fidelity recordings, drove home the sense that such taboos were no big deal to a group of misfits in New York. Though he had a tortured relationship with his own sexuality at the time and ultimately ended up marrying multiple women, Reed was out as gay in the '70s; his origin story involves getting electroshock therapy for the "homosexual urges" he experienced as a teen. (Like many origin stories, his was probably exaggerated. After Reed's death in 2013, his sister denied that the therapy was intended to cure anything other than mental illness, but the lore was already fixed.)[22] Compared to Bowie and Bolan, Reed's was a more abject, self-loathing mode of queerness, not a voyage to the stars but a plummet down into the mud.

Along with Mick Ronson, Bowie and Reed recorded *Transformer*, Reed's second solo album, in London in August 1972. Though a more modest singer than Bowie and Bolan, Reed nevertheless contributed to glam's reimagining of the male voice. He sang in halting phrases, at times almost speaking, as though he were making passing commentary to a friend on the street. Often, he sounded bored, aloof, even numb. Bowie complemented Reed's singing style with earthy bass tones and spacious arrangements, creating a sound that was casual without being ignorable.

Reed wears heavy eye makeup on the cover of *Transformer*, an album whose title and content also suggests gender malleability. The enduring hit "Walk on the Wild Side" pays direct homage to the trans women and drag queens who ran alongside Reed in Warhol's orbit. Reed names Holly Woodlawn, Candy Darling, and Jackie Curtis as characters in the song, all Warhol superstars who acted in the artist's films and plays. In contrast with Bowie's ecstatic celebration of queer aliens, Reed sings of a more quotidian magic. "Plucked her eyebrows on the way / Shaved her legs and then he was a she," goes the first verse of "Walk on the Wild Side," describing Woodlawn's transformation upon arriving in New York for the first time. That Reed refers to her as "he" at all is in keeping with his general air of callousness, but he only deploys that pronoun once. Woodlawn is introduced as "she," implying that the beauty rituals of plucking her eyebrows and shaving her legs are not trickery, not an attempt to obfuscate a "true" former self, but spells of becoming. They allow passage from Miami to New York, from a life spent hiding to a life lived in the open.

On the song "Make Up," directly after "Wild Side" in the track list, Reed suggests an affinity with these women as well as an admiration. After describing a "slick little girl's" morning makeup routine, Reed sings, "Now, we're coming out / Out of our closets /

Out on the streets." The woman in the song, described as though she is Reed's lover, first appears as a feminized other: someone who, unlike Reed, applies makeup while he looks on. Halfway through the song, he flips the script. Reed is not only in awe of his partner; he's a lot like her, cooing over the shades of eyeshadow she chooses, maybe dipping into them himself. Together, they form a "we." Over triumphant and comical spats of tuba, the two of them come out.

The vision of queerness that *Transformer* offered—gentle, sly, and appreciative rather than rambunctious and outré—was quiet enough for Nick Tosches of *Rolling Stone* to dismiss the album as "artsyfartsy kind of homo stuff."[23] Even critics who were ostensibly on board with the sexual ambiguity glam offered seemed to find Reed's take on the genre lacking. "God knows rock & roll could use, along with a few other things, some good faggot energy, but, with some notable exceptions, the sexuality that Reed proffers on *Transformer* is timid and flaccid," Nick Tosches wrote. Even within a genre known for disavowing traditional masculinity, artists like Reed could catch bad press for being insufficiently masculine. Though more subtle and less resplendent than Bowie or LaBelle, Reed added dimension to the glam phenomenon, laying to tape his own distinct flavor of musical queerness.

By tapping into the structure and energy of early rock-and-roll songs, glam furthered rock's initial impulse to covertly express illicit sexualities within an oppressive culture. Not only could glam artists sing about sex; they could sing about sex with both genders while dolled up like extraterrestrial androgynes. Their music opened a gateway to a form of expression that was only possible on a massive scale with the mediation of the stage or the recording studio. "On that stage, I'm at liberty," Marc Bolan said in a 1970s BBC interview. "I'm in a realm of fantasy. I can do whatever I want to do and get away with it."[24] With its penchant for science fiction narratives, outrageous costumes, and abundant makeup for everyone, glam rock got away with what mainstream culture couldn't: an open, exuberant display of gender beyond a strict binary. Without codes and without masks, glam made it out onto the streets.

3

WHINING IS GENDER NEUTRAL

Punk's Adolescent Escapism

On the cover of the Stooges' 1970 album *Fun House*, Iggy Pop melts into a torrent of orange. His arms are thrust up behind him. He wears shiny black opera gloves to the elbow. His hair is long for a boy, and it looks like he hasn't washed it in weeks—it glints with built-up grease. He looks down at himself, his eyes closed and peaceful but his lip twisted up into a sneer. It's a submissive pose: his arms aren't tied but they're positioned like they could be, like he's bound on the floor ready for a beating. The gloves make him look feminine but also primed for deviant, scatological sex. Maybe he just doesn't want to get his hands dirty.

In the late 1960s, the proto-punk band the Stooges seized on femininity as part of a broad arsenal of shock tactics. Before they had played a single song together, the members of the band incubated a bratty punk attitude in their stifling midwestern hometown of Ann Arbor, Michigan. They were bored kids seeking escape in the taboo. As a teen, Stooges guitarist Ron Asheton coveted the aesthetics of the Beatles as readily as he adorned himself in Nazi imagery; both Chelsea boots and Iron Crosses got a rise out of his teachers and peers, but it was the long hair that ultimately got him expelled from high school. He and future Stooges bassist Dave Alexander went on a pilgrimage to England to marinate in the aura of the Beatles, the Rolling Stones, and the Kinks, icons of visceral rebellion that they clung to while enduring middle America. "When Dave and I got home we got kicked out of school because we had super-long hair," said Asheton in 1996.[1] Femininity, then, was more distressing to behold on a boy than fascist regalia.

The collective cultural memory of the '60s suggests the decade was a safe haven for male femininity. Long hair on both genders abounds in retellings of the era—the hippie is a soft and shaggy archetype. But most of the imagery now associated with the '60s didn't arrive until the end of the decade. The United States was slow to metabolize shifting gender norms; years after the Beatles were televised into American homes, men could still catch flak for wearing their hair past their collars. "People would chase you for ten blocks, screaming, 'Beatle!' They were out of their fucking minds—that was the reality of the sixties," said artist Ronnie Cutrone. "Nobody had long hair—you were a fucking freak, you were a fruit, you were not like the rest of the world."[2]

Trans punk singer Jayne County similarly remembered getting flak in high school for growing her hair out like the Beatles. "I walked all the way [to the record store] and back and every once in a while somebody would yell out their car, 'Sissy!' or they'd yell, 'Look, it's Ringo!' because I had a little Beatles haircut and everything," she said. "Way back in the dark ages, when I was in high school, people still didn't know what gay or queer was or anything like that."[3]

That the word "Beatle" could ever have been used as a homophobic slur—that it fit right next to "sissy" in the vocabulary of bigots—seems outrageous by contemporary standards. In retrospect, the Beatles' gender transgressions look as tame as their innocent melodicism. But the Stooges grew up in an environment that punished deviations from normative masculinity, and being bored numb by their surroundings, they sought as much punishment as possible.

A more or less straitlaced high school kid, Jim Osterberg absorbed his future bandmates' rebelliousness as he started remaking himself as Iggy Pop. He grew his hair after watching Ron and Dave grow theirs. Like the drag queens and trans women in Andy Warhol's circle in New York, Iggy took an ambiguously gendered and obviously artificial stage name. He had a "Jr." tacked onto the end of his birth name, the same name as his father, so "Jim Osterberg" obviously had to go. He didn't want to be anyone's sequel.

Piecing together his persona and his songs, Iggy made himself into a collage of disparate cultural and musical influences. In 1966, he dropped out of high school and voyaged to Chicago to learn the blues from the prolific drummer Sam Lay. He ended up staying with Bob Koester, who ran the Jazz Record Mart in the city's River North neighborhood, in between playing gigs. Playing with Chicago bluesmen made Iggy realize that he wasn't interested in simply mimicking their sound, even if he was fascinated by it. "These guys were way over my head," he said. "What they were doing was so natural to them that it was ridiculous for me to make a studious copy of it, which is what most white blues bands did." Instead, he absorbed their idiosyncrasies into the newly chaotic form of rock he was developing. "I appropriated a lot of their vocal forms, and also their turns of phrase—either heard or misheard or twisted from blues songs," he said.[4]

Iggy had a keen ear for speech patterns. After moving back to Michigan, he hung around town and siphoned slang from local teenage girls. The Stooges' song "TV Eye" originated with a phrase dropped by Ron's sister Kathy Asheton. "'TV Eye' was my term. It was girl stuff. My girlfriends and I developed a code. It was a way for us to communicate with each other if we thought some guy was staring at us," she said in an interview for *Please Kill Me: The Uncensored Oral History of Punk*. "It meant 'Twat Vibe Eye.' Like, 'He's got a TV Eye on you.' Iggy overheard us and thought it was really funny. That's when he wrote the song 'TV Eye.'"[5]

Iggy begins "TV Eye" with a three-part scream: a long, guttural bellow, a shriek, and a tossed-off exhale. He sounds electric and vicious on the take that made it to *Fun House*. "She don't care / Yeah, I love her so / She got a TV Eye on me," he brags, relishing his position as a sexual object to be looked at, and also as an insider privy to the vocabulary of teen girls. Compositionally, the song's a rut. Like its predecessor "I Wanna Be Your Dog," from the Stooges' 1969 self-titled debut LP, "TV Eye" is anti-libidinal. It never erupts from simmering tension into orgasmic catharsis the way most pop songs do. There are no chord changes, and both the bassline and the guitar riff follow the vocal melody. The drums adopt a comically simple pattern: an upbeat and a downbeat repeated infinitely in quick succession. The song's magnetism comes from the way the band strains against the structure. Iggy and Ron sound like they're trying to out-sneer each other from behind the mic and the fretboard, respectively. After Ron sprays off into a chaotic solo, the band regroups into a one-chord chug, packing in the song until it clogs.

The irreverence, confrontationality, and messiness of "TV Eye" would form a cornerstone of the genre yet to be known as punk. So would Iggy's atypical position in the song's matrix of desire. As a front man, he was less willing to project power and confidence than he was to subject himself to humiliation. Much of the Stooges' shock value came from Iggy's abject stage presence. In photos from the late '60s and early '70s, he wears dog collars and crawls on all fours, staring wide-eyed at the camera as if begging the photographer to debase him. He's almost always shirtless, and he moves as if his partial nudity were just as shocking as a woman's would be. Titless, he struts like he's got his tits out for all to see.

Years before David Bowie made a spectacle out of face paint, spandex, and hair dye, Iggy pranced onstage in what he's called "a maternity dress" (Ron described it as an "old white nightshirt from the 1800s that went all the way down to his ankles"). He shaved his eyebrows, painted his face white, and wove aluminum foil into his hair. By the time the Stooges booked their first New York show, Iggy had pared down the look to something more convincingly androgynous. "This guy with blond bangs—who looked like Brian Jones—came out onstage and at first I thought he was a chick," said Alan Vega of the New York band Suicide, another proto-punk outfit with an ear for the macabre.[6] This anecdote, in which Iggy is simultaneously mistaken for a Rolling Stone and a woman, epitomizes the singer's complex and chimerical presence.

Iggy voraciously interpolated femininity into his outlandish stage costumes. In a series of photos from 1973, he's wearing one-legged sequined tights and knee-high leather boots; in an image shot by queer photographer Leee Black Childers the same year, he pairs an embroidered peasant blouse with tight jeans and what looks like toenail polish, though it could just as easily be blood pooled beneath the nail. Vega recalled seeing him perform in "dungarees with holes, with this red bikini underwear with his balls hanging out."[7] In many shots, Iggy's contorted to the point of defying physics, bent over backwards like he's about to snap in half. He looks possessed. His performance tested the limits of physicality. He would binge on hard drugs and vomit onstage, first discreetly behind an amplifier, later onto the front row of the crowd. He'd fall off the stage and keep singing while bleeding.

On the cover of the Stooges' 1973 album *Raw Power*, shot at London's King Cross Cinema in 1972, Iggy wears heavy eyeliner and a deep red lip, painted on in the green room before the show by guitarist James Williamson's then girlfriend. He has a Marilyn Monroe beauty spot on his left cheek, and the edge of his silver leather pants glints from his waist. What he's doing isn't exactly drag. He's not smiling, and his pose—both hands gripping the microphone as he leans precariously to the left of the photo's frame—suggests a defensive stance rather than an enticing, playful one. He pouts a little as he stares into the crowd, as if trying to make out how they're seeing him. The makeup invites confrontation. By mapping Marilyn's face onto his own, replicating her like Andy Warhol did in silkscreens from the early '60s, he corrupts the actress's image, turning her into a snarling, feral villain. A perfectly poised and deeply mythologized symbol of femininity becomes a carnival mask.

The makeup and clothing Iggy wore onstage had little to do with glamour. It accentuated his abjection, intensifying the band's violently masculine provocations. It wasn't that Iggy wanted to embody femininity's poses, mannerisms, and affectations. He exploited femininity's markers to call attention to the brittleness of American manhood, and to repel the eye that tried to gender him. It worked for his bandmates in high school, and it worked for him onstage.

The musical and aesthetic grotesqueries of the Stooges, like the blasé affectations of the Velvet Underground, proved foundational to punk. At its root, punk is a negative music. It doesn't offer an alternative vision to the world so much as it bites at the world as it stands, which is why it's most effective when it sounds like shit. Sing well and you reinforce artistic hegemony. Sing like an asshole and you prove that music's appeal is more elusive than its gatekeepers say.

In May 1970, Warhol superstar Jackie Curtis put on a stage play she had written called *Femme Fatale: The Three Faces of Gloria*. She had intended the play to star her friends Penny Arcade and John Christian, but John had become addicted to drugs. Paranoid, he would not leave his apartment for rehearsals. Jackie instead cast a newcomer to the scene: a twenty-three-year-old woman from New Jersey named Patti Smith.

Smith, who hung at the periphery of Warhol's crew with her then-boyfriend Robert Mapplethorpe, looked enough like a man to pull off the role. "She was really skinny and dressed weird. She had this look that was completely her own, which in retrospect was a precursor of the whole punk thing," recalled Penny Arcade. "She wore these espadrille-type wrestler's shoes, skinny black pants, and usually a white man's shirt, tucked in, with a Guido type of undershirt underneath. She didn't wear a bra, and she had a very gaunt face and very dark hair."[8]

Before she had written or recorded a single song, Patti Smith worked hard to piece together an image that felt like home. She found the spectrum of 1960s feminine expression lacking. "The boys had Bond and Brando. They beat off to Bardot. The girls had the pale range of Doris Day to Sandra Dee," she wrote in a 1993 essay. "All through childhood I resisted the role of a confused skirt tagging the hero. Instead, I was searching for someone crossing the gender boundaries, someone both to be and to be with. I never wanted to be Wendy—I was more like Peter Pan. This was confusing stuff."[9]

In a poem penned when she was still a teenager, Smith articulated some of the nuances of this confusing stuff: "Ever since I felt the need to choose I'd choose male," she wrote. "I felt boy rhythms when I was in knee pants. So I stayed in pants. I sobbed when I had to use the public ladies room. My undergarments made me blush. Every feminine gesture I affected from my mother humiliated me."[10]

As a teen, Smith found her obscure gender reflected back to her on the cover of a paperback. A photograph of Arthur Rimbaud, the nineteenth-century French poet who produced an influential body of work between the ages of seventeen and twenty-one, stared up at her. "His haughty gaze reached mine from the cover of *Illuminations*. He possessed an irreverent intelligence that ignited me, and I embraced him as compatriot, kin, and even secret love," she wrote in her 2010 memoir *Just Kids*.[11] The photo she describes is in all likelihood the one taken by Étienne Carjat when Rimbaud was seventeen. The poet's hair is mussed, spiking out at odd angles, and he peers past the viewer's left shoulder, not at the camera lens. Beardless and thin, he is young enough to carry an air of androgyny. Smith seized him. She shoplifted the book and carried Rimbaud around as a spiritual guide through her artistic career. "We are trapped in our own teenage skins. We long for a way out but lack the right moves, verbs, and curves," she wrote nearly thirty years later. "So we lift a hair, a gesture, a way of dress. Any means necessary to break out."[12]

Another complication threatened to cage Smith into a life she didn't want. When she was nineteen and studying to become a teacher in New Jersey, she got pregnant. She was not ready to become, as she put it, "just another unmarried mother in South Jersey, living on welfare with a nine year old kid."[13] She had the baby, put it up for adoption, and got the hell out of her hometown.

In 1967, Smith broke out of the feminine mold she hated by moving to New York, writing poetry, making art, and metabolizing the men with whom she felt a keen identification. She moved in with Mapplethorpe, the boundary-breaking photographer who turned out to be gay but who remained Smith's guiding light and platonic soulmate until his death from AIDS in 1989. Sick of the long folksinger tresses she had imported from New Jersey, she cut her hair like the Rolling Stones' guitarist Keith Richards, a man who had grown his hair past the limits of acceptable American masculinity.

"Patti kept saying to me, 'Do I look like Keith Richards?' You know, 'How does my hair look? Does it look like Keith Richards?' I said, 'Yeah, kind of,' because I didn't understand why anybody would wanna look like Keith Richards," recalled Penny Arcade.[14] But Smith coveted the ambiguity a Rolling Stone haircut lent her, the freeing limbo it opened. "Someone at Max's asked if I was androgynous," she wrote in *Just Kids*. "I asked what that meant. 'You know, like Mick Jagger.' I figured that must be cool. I thought the word meant both beautiful and ugly at the same time. Whatever it meant, with just a haircut, I miraculously turned androgynous overnight."[15]

In her work and her stage presence, Smith activated a space between genders. "I don't consider myself a female poet," she told Victor Bockris during her first-ever interview in 1972. "It's only lately that I've been able to consider myself as a female at all. But I don't consider myself a female artist. I don't think I hold any sex. I think I have both masculine and feminine rhythms in my work."[16] Smith wrote poems after the style of Rimbaud and read them in the style of Bob Dylan, sneering her way through the text. "In her performance, she was able to play at being this male presence, sort of alternatively female and male, or androgynous," said fellow poet Ed Friedman.[17] In a subculture where women aspired to hyperfemininity and many men reached out to join them, Smith's masculine affect stood out. Her masculinity was so concrete that the gay poet Allen Ginsberg once tried to cruise her at a Manhattan Automat, thinking she was an effeminate boy.

She carried those combined rhythms into her music. Though Smith didn't intend to become a bandleader, reading poetry while guitarist Lenny Kaye improvised planted a seed in her mind. She realized the spoken word and the sung one had a lot in common, and that rock instrumentation could supply a natural bolster for poetry.

Smith taught herself to sing by listening to Stooges records and mimicking Iggy Pop. "We'd put on 'Gimme Danger' and try to imitate the attitude of the vocals, trying to get it right in our throats. Patti would say, 'Yeah, this is how you learn to sing,'" said musician and model Bebe Buell.[18] It's a fantastic image: Patti Smith hunched by a turntable, taking Iggy's crimped, abject voice into her own throat, singing along as he decomposes from a forced croon into a ragged scream. The song ends, and she drags the needle back to the beginning to undergo the transformation all over again.

A little of Iggy creeps into "Gloria: In Excelsis Deo," the first track from Smith's 1975 debut album *Horses*. The song mixes "Gloria," a 1964 B-side by Van Morrison's garage rock band Them, into Smith's own poetry. Morrison mingles with Iggy and Bob Dylan in her voice. "My sins my own / They belong to me," she snarls, repeating the "me" at the low end of her range, folding gravel into the grain. She dares the listener to identify the "me," to place the "I" that is singing within a spectrum of gender. As Smith moves from the words of her poem "Oath" to Morrison's "Gloria," she assumes a masculine gaze, gleefully pursuing the eponymous woman. "I'll put my spell on her," she promises, and she does, and it works: Gloria walks up the stairs and knocks on the speaker's door. It's not exactly a lesbian encounter (Smith has said she tried sleeping with female friends and discovered in herself a strong preference for men), but more of a heterosexual one where Smith casts herself in the male role. If masculinity was the most readily available access point to the activity of looking, desiring, and pursuing another, then Smith would assume masculinity. She was to be the subject in the world of her art.

"'Gloria' gave me the opportunity to acknowledge and disclaim our musical and spiritual heritage," Smith wrote in her 1998 lyrics collection *Complete*. "It personifies for me, within its adolescent conceit, what I hold sacred as an artist. The right to create, without apology, from a stance beyond gender or social definition, but not beyond the responsibility to create something of worth."[19]

Smith framed her gender within the trappings of masculinity, but she consistently referred to her desire to supersede the available binary. Like Bowie, she would look to the stars for a third option beyond male or female. On "Birdland," she sings of Peter Reich looking for his father, Wilhelm Reich—the controversial psychoanalyst who believed sex gave off cosmic energy that could control the weather—in an alien spaceship. It's not that Wilhelm has been abducted; it's that he was always an alien, and, having died, has returned to his people. Peter may be an alien, too, if only the ship would come to take him home. "We are not human," Smith sings, pronouncing an identity beyond the mundane for the Reichs but also for herself. "From very early on in my childhood—four, five years old—I felt alien to the human race," she said in a 2005 interview. "I felt very comfortable with thinking I was from another planet, because I felt disconnected—I was very tall and skinny, and I didn't look like anybody else, I didn't even look like any member of my family."[20]

On the cover of *Horses*, shot by Mapplethorpe, Patti Smith leans against a bare white wall, her tie undone and her jacket flung over her right shoulder in tribute to Frank Sinatra. Her Keith Richards haircut casts a black halo. She looks at once serene and defiant, gazing into the camera but seeing only the man behind it. "When Robert took pictures, I could see his face," she said. "When I remember it, I never see a camera there. I always see his eyes squint, the way he looked at me, or the way he checked to make sure everything was right."[21] Looking at a queer man looking at her, Smith softened the supposed difference between them. Her husband, Fred "Sonic" Smith of the Detroit proto-punk band MC5, would later comment that Patti always looked like Mapplethorpe in his photos. Mapplethorpe strained against masculinity and Smith strained against femininity, and they met in the middle through a camera lens. "When I look at [the cover of *Horses*] now, I never see me. I see us," Smith wrote in *Just Kids*.[22] She looks at him looking at her; she sees herself in him as he sees himself in her. The gaze reverberates.

Smith's androgynous otherness manifested in her voice, which swung from deep, guttural grunts to piercing staccato shrieks. Across *Horses*, she sounds perpetually out of breath. She slants her voice into a knowing sneer, the vocal equivalent of Rimbaud's askew and haughty gaze. It's a voice between genders, high enough in pitch to register as a woman's voice but irreverent, arrogant, and blunt like a man's. The burgeoning genre that would come to be known as punk dispersed this voice. (The word "punk" meant "bottom" at the time, lending the genre's name an air of queer deviance from the start.) Both Iggy and Patti echoed in acts that would typify punk, such as the Ramones, the Buzzcocks, and the Clash, whose singers found a grunt to work as well as a wail. Punk's songs got shorter and its players grew more abject. The genre manifested androgyny by casting off gender along with a host of other societal norms. Gender conformity was still conformity, and both men and women performers defied standards of voice, dress, and appearance in their stage presence.

A whine is a childish vocal expression. Adjacent to a nag, it's often coded as feminine—there's no counterpart to "whiny bitch" that can be aimed squarely at a man—but it registers uniformly as abject, which suited it perfectly to punk. The genre's devotees appropriated childishness to cast off the confines of the rigid adult world. "[Punk] was about real freedom, personal freedom. It was also about doing anything that's gonna offend a grown-up," said music journalist Legs McNeil, who cofounded the influential *Punk* magazine in New York at age nineteen.[23]

One of the first bands to whittle punk rock down to its bare essentials, the Ramones were four boys from Queens who, as a gimmick, all adopted the same last name as if they were brothers. After aging out of a glam phase inspired by the raucous and flamboyant local band New York Dolls, they donned skinny jeans and tight T-shirts emblazoned with cartoon characters, like siblings wearing each other's hand-me-downs. They adopted diminutive versions of their given first names for their stage monikers: Johnny, Joey, Dee Dee, and Tommy. It was like each of them was vying to be the littlest brother in the group. If glam was all about being a glitter-streaked alien, then punk, as the Ramones envisioned it, was more about being an obnoxious kid.

On their early records, the Ramones sound like children let loose in a recording studio, grunting their way through the lyric sheet and barely able to play their instruments. (Dee Dee's count-off at the start of many of their songs rarely corresponds to the song's actual tempo.) Their lyrics veer from the absurd to the deranged to the bitterly ironic. They often identify girls as fellow punks: Judy, Sheena, and Suzy all have songs to their name where the band inducts them into the cult of their own making. A few songs use homosexuality as a punch line, including "We're a

Happy Family," in which Joey ends a stanza about a dysfunctional nuclear arrangement with the line "Daddy likes men."

The Ramones' references to deviant sexualities often took an aloof, cynical tone, as they were singing about the existence of gay people from a straight vantage. None of them identified as queer, but before they adopted their leather and denim uniforms, they flirted somewhat sardonically with the sheen of glam. "Joey was the one that really got into glitter," remarked Mickey Leigh, Joey Ramone's actual brother. "Dee Dee and those guys would ridicule me. I was still hanging out every day and Dee Dee would come by with his arm around this guy Michael, acting all fruity. They did it on purpose—to shock and separate themselves from everybody. I guess it made them feel cooler."[24]

By the time they released their debut self-titled album in 1976, the Ramones had shed their effeminate costumes, but a few traces of the time they spent playing gay crept into their music. Dee Dee, for one, may have been doing more than just playing. The song "53rd and 3rd" reportedly tells the true story of his brief stint in sex work, hustling a popular cruising spot among men looking for boys. "I remember driving by Fifty-third Street and Third Avenue and seeing Dee Dee Ramone standing out there," said Leigh. "He had a black leather motorcycle jacket on, the one he would later wear on the first album cover. He was just standing there, so I knew what he was doing, because I knew that was the gay-boy hustler spot. Still, I was kind of shocked to see somebody I knew standing there, like, Holy shit. That's Doug standing there. He's really doing it."[25] The song ends with the speaker murdering the first man to solicit him, which may have been an embellishment on Dee Dee's part to reassert his heterosexuality within the context of a devoutly straight band. He only ever spoke cryptically of the song. "'53rd & 3rd' speaks for itself," he's quoted as saying in *Please Kill Me*.[26] "Everything I write is autobiographical and very real. I can't write any other way."

Punk made its way across the Atlantic by way of Malcolm McLaren, an English Svengali who had tried and failed to manage the unruly New York Dolls. While that band was imploding, McLaren dreamed up another, linking together a group of young English musicians and encouraging them to call themselves the Sex Pistols. The UK's most infamous punk act was, in effect, a boy band: a group of pretty young things spliced together by an opportunistic older man. McLaren and his partner, designer Vivienne Westwood, cultivated the Pistols' look, drawing from both BDSM looks and New York punks such as Richard Hell of Television and the Voidoids, who's credited with being the first musician to use safety pins as a fashion statement.

If New York punk looked ragged, filthy, and overtly masculine, English punks were more open to carrying elements of glam rock into their getups. They paired schoolboy blazers with spiked hair and eyeliner. Fans of acts that formed in the Pistols' wake, such as the Buzzcocks, mixed gender signifiers readily; in photos of the Manchester band's audience from the late '70s, women wear loose ties and tattered button-ups alongside purses and nail polish. Their hair is cropped and unruly, mirroring the musicians onstage. Through self-infantilization and abjection, punk muddied the distinction between genders.

This blurring spread through the English punk singer's androgynous, sneering voice, which stood apart from the Ramones' half-conscious grunts. Pete Shelley of the Buzzcocks and Poly Styrene of X-Ray Spex, both English singers whose bands debuted their first records toward the end of the '70s, belted out notes in an elongated, nasal whine. Each singer made occasional pointed use of vibrato, an operatic flourish at odds with the seedy, barbed language of their lyrics. This particular punk voice bristled against both male and female vocal norms, aligning itself more closely with the child, whose prepubescent voice sounds the same regardless of assigned gender.

Born Marianne Joan Elliot, Poly Styrene was a former hippie and teenage runaway who had been trained to sing opera when she was young. Traces of her education linger even in her brash, unashamed punk belt. Her voice rings out from her gut on X-Ray Spex's 1978 debut album *Germfree Adolescents*. She begins the record with a bellow reminiscent of Iggy Pop's on "TV Eye": an indication of tremendous presence, and a statement of purpose to be as loud and obnoxious as possible. Styrene does not sing quietly or gently like a woman might be expected to sing. She is not here to soothe the ear or sedate it with traditional beauty. She yells every song on the record as if trying to give directions from across an aircraft hangar, and in doing so she cracks the casing around the so-called female voice. Unlike Patti Smith, she doesn't make much of a bid for masculinity; there's no growl to her voice, no deep, earthy foundation underpinning her words. Critic Nitsuh Abebe called it "a way of singing that's fierce, but fiercely feminine—that sounds like it's bursting free from expectations."[27] She sings like a girl primed to throttle the next person who tells her to be quiet, a girl fed up with the decibel range that's been imposed on her for her entire life.

If she sounded more feminine, Styrene did share with Smith the sense of channeling androgynous rhythms while performing—the feeling that in the sanctified circle of the stage, there was no need to select one of two genders to embody. "If somebody said I was a sex symbol, I'd shave me'ead tomorrer," she said in a 1977 interview. "In fact I don't even think of myself as a girl when I'm on stage. I think I'm sexless."[28]

Germfree Adolescents came out on November 10, 1978. That week, Donna Summer's "MacArthur Park" and Anne Murray's "You Needed Me" held the number one and two spots on the *Billboard* Hot 100, respectively. Both showcase a gentle and unobtrusive vision of femininity: a woman as a wellspring of affection and maybe melancholy, but never anger. Summer's hit took on a revitalizing disco strut, but "You Needed Me" is as languid as ballads come, a fossilized artifact of easy listening. Barbra Streisand and Olivia Newton-John also clung to the charts at the time, two slight-voiced singers whose sappy throwback singles couldn't be further from punk's scorch. Poly Styrene's inflamed singing style bristled at the docile sound of 1970s pop femininity, casting off the need to please and making an uproarious mess instead.

Because adult women are not supposed to scream outside of emergencies, Styrene's voice renders her childlike. She calls upon Peter Pan, Smith's symbol of genderlessness, on the 1979 single "Highly Inflammable." "You thought I was a woman / I thought you were a man / I was Tinkerbell / And you were Peter Pan," she sings over bulges of saxophone and metallic waves of synthesizer—a rare instance of electronic instrumentation in the band's catalog that reiterates the magic of her fairy tale imagery. Both Peter Pan and Tinkerbell stand for a refusal to enter the world of adults. One gloss of the song's lyrics shows her scolding a boy for his immaturity, but by casting herself as Tinkerbell, Styrene identifies with his instinct to sequester himself from adult responsibilities. Her delivery makes it seem as if she can shout away the obligation to grow up.

At the volume she maintains throughout *Germfree Adolescents*, Styrene's wry criticisms of ad-sodden, identity-obsessed culture ring clearer. She shouts, and in shouting she propels herself to the edge of the social categories boxing her in. Beyond the perimeter, she can see consumer society more lucidly as the sham that it is. On "Identity," another track introduced with a scream, she rallies against the supposedly natural process of gleaning identity from mass media: "Do you see yourself / On the TV screen? / Do you see yourself / In the magazine?" she seethes. On the chugging "I Am a Poseur," she declares tautologically, "My facade is just a fake." Styrene locates the television as the production site of the perfect, docile worker on "Genetic Engineering," while "Warrior in Woolworths" imagines a low-wage service worker scheming his way out of the system. Skeptical of everything she can see, especially the social expectations levied upon her, Styrene hollers loud enough to expose the cracks in capitalism's flimsy trappings. She knows there's no such thing as authentic self-expression in a consumer society, just different ways of negotiating with the false.

Men who made use of punk's vocal idioms also crossed social boundaries, though not due to their loudness, to which they already had a right. On '70s Buzzcocks recordings, Pete Shelley's reedy tenor hardly seems to resonate in his diaphragm or his rib-cage; it's all nose, making him sound smaller and more effeminate than a grown man. He looked the part too. In a 1978 live review, the *New Musical Express* noted that Shelley "had bleached blonde hair and, from a distance anyway, appeared like some effeminate elf complete with a high-pitched Northern accent."[29]

Unlike New York punks who reveled in abject masculinity, Shelley cultivated a romantic vision of androgyny. He laced indications of his own queerness into both his music and his presence. Unlike his former bandmate Howard Devoto, who quit the Buzzcocks just as they were gaining steam, Shelley didn't use gendered pronouns in his lyrics. "Devoto would sing 'he' or 'she.' But Pete, who sports a Campaign for Homosexual Equality button badge, has altered definite pronouns to 'you' or 'people,'" wrote Caroline Coon in a 1977 *Sounds* profile of the band. The CHE was founded in the UK in 1964 and fought to decriminalize gay sex; by visibly displaying his support for the organization, Shelley dropped a big hint as to his own inclinations, even if he wouldn't name them at the time. Coon noted that the singer was "low profile about his sexual preferences." "I don't want specialist treatment," he said. "There isn't any implied gender in our songs now because we think it's boring singing about one thing when it could apply to both sexes. Our songs are bisexual."[30]

Though Shelley refused to slap a label on himself, Buzzcocks fans, it seems, were able to read between the lines. A 1978 profile of the band in *NME* mentioned the fan letters he would get "seeking advice and counsel on topics running from homosexuality to joining the army."[31] In 1979, he finally offered some clarity, stating that he was "attracted to people rather than genders"—a pioneering pansexual.[32]

Many of the Buzzcocks' songs alluded generously to Shelley's queerness. "Noise Annoys," from 1978's *Love Bites*, calls out to "pretty girls / pretty boys," an echo of David Bowie's undivided "pretty things." In "Ever Fallen in Love (With Someone You Shouldn't've)," Shelley bemoans the pain of a deviant affection: "You disturb my natural emotions," he sings, relishing his s's in a flamboyant display, meaning either that love has ruptured his default aloofness or that a particular attraction has rerouted his supposedly natural heterosexuality. The latter interpretation has more textual support: "We won't be together much longer / Unless we realize that we are the same," he continues, as if begging the object of his interest to stop denying their mutual deviance and give in to their attraction.

Shelley's tormented lyrics on "Ever Fallen in Love" play against the song's outwardly triumphant arrangement. Steve Diggle's lead guitar rings out like a victory bell between lines throughout the verse, while the quick tempo and vocal melody of the chorus insinuates a love successfully pursued. The song's sheer exuberance and irresistible catchiness was enough for it to land, as a sanitized cover, on the *Shrek 2* soundtrack. On the surface, it's bright enough for children to pick up on its glee.

In the lyrics, the Buzzcocks stage a queer emotional conflict. The taboo relationship is at its root a joyful one: mutual, playful, and rewarding. But Shelley enters it knowing full well the danger of doing so. The "shouldn't've" weighs heavy on the rest of the lyrics, even though he pronounces it so quickly and sloppily it can easily be heard as a "should've," like he's trying to slur out the negative in the center of the contraction. The excitement of the speaker is matched only by his anxiety, and the two twirl together until they're nearly indistinguishable. Shelley gets away with the forbidden in the broad daylight of a punk song, where deviants can parade around without a second glance.

The punk whine appears in its purest form on the Buzzcocks' song "Why Can't I Touch It?" A nearly seven-minute B-side compiled on the 1979 collection *Singles Going Steady*, "Why Can't I Touch It?" speaks to a stifled love, an attraction just behind the boundary of consummation. Shelley can see, feel, taste, and hear this encounter, four senses out of five, but he stops short of being able to reach out and grab it. At the chorus, he wrings out the word "why" until he almost runs out of breath. The verse melody ends in an upturn, but the "why" spirals down to the bottom of the key. It's like Shelley has been climbing a ladder to see his beloved, only to be knocked back down into the alley the second he reaches the sill. The invisible membrane separating the two potential lovers could be any social norm, even bad luck, but the course of Shelley's vocal melody suggests another forbidden encounter. He rises up to the top of his range, flirting with audible markers of femininity, only to be flung rudely back down to earth.

The whine survived the rise of hardcore, lying dormant while a new generation of punks doubled down on their masculinity in an appeal to working-class signifiers. California band Black Flag and DC outfit Minor Threat mostly whisked away the petulant adolescent tics of their predecessors, replacing the Ramones' churlish gripes and the Buzzcocks' open complaining with ferocious political diatribes and urgent bids for agitation. Minnesota's Hüsker Dü, meanwhile, staged emotional torment against pummeling drumbeats on the 1984 punk opera *Zen Arcade*. They were more prone to melodicism than many of their hardcore peers, but they were also much queerer; singer and guitarist Bob Mould was officially outed as gay in the '90s, while drummer and vocalist Grant Hart identified as bisexual. Both musicians, however, downplayed their sexuality in their music and their lives.

"According to Hart, both men took lovers on tour and their orientation was an open secret in the indie community," wrote Michael Azerrad in *Our Band Could Be Your Life*. "But most people who knew cared very little. Part of the reason it was never a big deal was that the band never emphasized sexuality—theirs or anyone else's—in their music or their performance."[33] Hüsker Dü may be a canonically queer punk band, but they omitted the winking androgyny that Pete Shelley had relished in his own music.

The drug-soaked nihilism that had plagued early punk music started to ebb away, leaving concrete anger in its wake as America's social inequities came into focus under the sharp light of the Reagan administration. The songs grew shorter, the drums faster, and the guitar tones got even rougher around the edges. Punk's annoying teenage boy grew up into a righteously outraged man, and so his gender solidified. Hardcore's voicings integrated more gruffness into their timbre, shying away from punk's childish and gender-smearing roots. But the whine resurfaced among a crop of bands that found commercial success in the '90s. California trios Blink-182 and Green Day reinvigorated the vocal form as punk rock made its way to pop radio.

Before Green Day climbed the Top 40 with the sentimental acoustic ballad "Good Riddance (Time of Your Life)," from 1997's *Nimrod*, they stirred up a uniquely Californian flavor of obnoxious infantilism. "Dear mother, can you hear me whining?" front man Billie Joe Armstrong asks on Green Day's 1991 single "Welcome to Paradise." Though he sings in a blunt, unadventurous tenor, his words echo Pete Shelley's queries on the Buzzcocks' "Noise Annoys" as he addresses the mother figure directly, asking if his whine is even registering with its target. On the same album, *Kerplunk*, Armstrong throws on a fake southern accent over the twang of a banjo while begging to become "your dominated love slave," wryly poking holes in country music's cult of masculinity.

In 1994, in "Basket Case," Armstrong asked his listeners directly, "Do you have the time / To listen to me whine?" By naming the whine and positioning it as a justifiable mode of expression—"Welcome to Paradise" and "Basket Case" both describe concrete social distress—Green Day reintroduced punk as a queer-inflected genre to a mainstream audience. On "Basket Case," he visits a female therapist who diagnoses him with sexual frustration, and then he sees a male sex worker, who pegs the singer as a good old-fashioned "bore." Too horny to live and too boring to die, he retreats into his weed-enhanced ennui, surviving the only way he knows how: by complaining loudly into a microphone that's just a little too tall for him.

Armstrong doubled back to the impulse to wear eyeliner that had coursed across '70s punk bands in the UK. He and his bandmates dyed their hair and wore short-sleeve button-ups with skinny ties, like toddlers at church. Fellow Californians (and better classical whiners) Blink-182 joined Armstrong in the early-'90s display of boyishness, spinning yarns about their own immaturity in an exaggerated valley-boy yawp. The huge commercial success of these bands marked a second coming for punk and opened up a space for an even more flamboyant subgenre in the growing sector of alternative radio. After '90s pop punk came 2000s emo, a histrionic, self-pitying, and cathartic flavor of rock music that launched androgynes such as Gerard Way of New Jersey band My Chemical Romance to fame.

In the early aughts, alternative rock soared up the pop charts. Nu-metal bands like Linkin Park had hits alongside glossy pop powerhouses like Britney Spears and Backstreet Boys, while post-grunge—the mealy-mouthed descendant of influential '90s bands like Nirvana and Alice in Chains—clogged the radio with power ballads. If punk and grunge once professed to stand apart from the capitalist machine, they had both been thoroughly eaten by it. But there were still rough, abrasive punk bands making music with tiny DIY labels. One of them hailed from Gainesville, Florida, and called themselves Against Me!

Led by a singer and guitarist then known as Tom Gabel, Against Me! put out the 2001 *Crime* EP on the scrappy Indiana folk-punk label Plan-It-X Records. Their debut LP, *Reinventing Axl Rose*—a reference to the lead singer of Guns N' Roses, who in the '90s had become a kind of emblem of hair metal's shitty hypermasculinity—came out on the punk label No Idea, and it established the band as one of the most original voices in contemporary punk. Gabel sang about poverty, politics, and yearning, about the swamp hell of Florida, about the hypocrisy of American liberalism. The band's career picked up throughout the aughts, and in 2007 Against Me! released an album on the major label Sire Records. They lasted three years there, leaving after the 2010 album *White Crosses*. No one else knew it yet, but the pressure on Gabel to perform as a popular punk rock front man was growing intolerable.

In 2012, the lead singer of Against Me! formally came out as a transgender woman by way of a comprehensive profile in *Rolling Stone*, where she announced her real name: Laura Jane Grace.[34] She had known she was trans her entire life and frequently alluded to her real gender in song lyrics, but she repeatedly brushed away the yearning to transition, fearing it would get in the way of her work as a musician. As a young child, she saw Madonna on TV and felt drawn to her image as a female performer. Upon hitting puberty, she had prayed alternately to God and to the devil that she would wake up as a cis girl. She stole women's clothes and wore them in private. Once, she pilfered a roommate's birth control pills to see if taking them would have a physiological effect akin to estrogen.

When Against Me! grew successful and started touring frequently, Grace felt boxed in to masculinity. "I felt more and more like I was putting on an act—like I was being shoved into this role of 'angry white man in a punk band,'" she said. At twenty-five, she told herself she would never come out, that she would force herself to play a man for the rest of her life: "We were about to go on a long period of touring, and I was like, 'That's it. I'm getting rid of all this. I'm male, and that's it.'" By the time she was thirty-one, she had decided to cast off that guise and come out on one of the most public stages imaginable. She gave the *Rolling Stone* interview before she had even told her parents that she was trans—her dad found out when he picked up a copy of the magazine—and set to work recording *Transgender Dysphoria Blues*, the 2014 Against Me! album on which she could finally sing explicitly about her gender.

Grace's voice sounds the same on *Transgender Dysphoria Blues* as it did on the band's previous albums. She sings, as she's always sung, like a woman sick of hiding her anger, a woman availing herself of gruffness, sorrow, and rage. She wasn't the first female punk singer to make use of such a grain: pioneering trans punk singer Jayne County also commanded a fearsome, tragicomic snarl, while Wendy O. Williams, the cis front woman of the New York band the Plasmatics, sang from the very bottom of her diaphragm in a sandpaper contralto. But Grace was the first widely known punk singer to re-gender her voice retroactively.

Reinventing Axl Rose begins with a song about her grandmother's unwavering grief in the wake of her grandfather's death from alcoholism. At the chorus, Grace sings, "Just like James / I'll be drinking Irish tonight," but it's her grandmother Evelyn she identifies with throughout the verses. Her voice quavers as she sings, "It's been thirty-seven years since James died / On St. Patrick's Day in 1964 / She could not hold it against him." Her voice breaks on that last line, lending the song an intoxicating vulnerability. While she can easily envision her own early death ("if we're never together / if I'm never back again"), she can just as easily cast herself in the role of the woman left in mourning ("I swear to God that I'll love you forever"). Grace sounds strung between two futures, but by inhabiting Evelyn's emotions with so much delicate empathy, she seems to have already chosen who she is going to become.

Grace thought she had already outed herself back in 2007, five years before she would come out to the world officially. On "The Ocean," from the Against Me! album *New Wave*, she sings, "If I could have chosen, I would have been born a woman / My mother once told me she would have named me Laura / I would grow up to be strong and beautiful like her." It's all there, down to the name she would ultimately use. "There's no metaphor to the line," she said in 2016.[35] She assumed everyone around her would pick up on her overt confession of dysphoria, but couched in a song, it glanced off the world.

Music supplies the perfect alibi: you can sing the truth about yourself as many times as you like, but it'll stay in the realm of the imaginary. It's the perfect place to say something without saying it, to dance between genders without having to confront the material reality of transition. Inside a song, every singer is exactly who she says she is in the moment her voice passes through her throat. The voice makes reality, even if that reality evaporates, like a dream the second the tape stops rolling.

4

WRECKERS OF CIVILIZATION

Post-punk, Goth, and Industrial

Ian Curtis's voice darkened between 1978's *An Ideal for Living* and 1979's *Unknown Pleasures*. On the former, the Manchester band Joy Division's debut EP, he's in command of a tattered punk-rock bark, singing about Nazi leader Rudolf Hess with enough zeal to make the Stooges' Ron Asheton beam. By the time he got to singing "Disorder," the opening track of the post-punk band's most iconic album (the one whose cover you've seen on T-shirts), he had retreated inward, away from punk's irreverent shock tactics and into deep personal horror. He sounds like a different person.

Joy Division formed in the late '70s among the glut of Sex Pistols knockoffs that dominated the UK in the punk band's wake. At their very first gig, they opened for fellow Mancunians the Buzzcocks; according to critics at the time, it was a fairly lackluster set. "They played under the name Warsaw (having rejected Pete Shelley's suggestion of Stiff Kittens) and their morbidly dull music failed to penetrate even the most eagerly-trained ear," wrote critic Mick Middles.[1] As they drifted away from punk toward the next phase of musical British complaining, Joy Division gathered a darkness around themselves. The postindustrial landscape of Manchester seeped into their haunted songs. If the Buzzcocks sought relief from their surroundings through irreverent play, Joy Division decided to marinate in their personal hells instead.

In the few years that Joy Division made music together before Curtis's death in 1980, the singer lingered at the very bottom of his vocal range. He often sounds like he's straining to stay there, like he can't quite summon enough breath to round out his melodies. His lungs sound empty at the end of his lines on "Disorder"; he comes in a little sharp on the lowest notes of "Candidate" and again on the unusually long and increasingly desperate howls of "New Dawn Fades." He falters while singing "Atmosphere," sinking down into a strained baritone while his vowels split at the seams. Curtis's voice aligned with the band's guitar tone on the earliest Joy Division recordings. By the time they assembled their debut LP, he had identified firmly with the bass: low and somber, articulating few notes but singing them with enough gravitas to chill the sound of the whole arrangement.

If punk's whiny breaks into falsetto connoted frustration mixed with the occasional bout of ecstasy, then Curtis's six-feet-under moan suggested irreconcilable sadness. It also served to exaggerate his masculinity, making him sound far older than he ever became. He was twenty-three when he took his own life, and his features never wore out their boyishness. He looked fresh out of high school throughout Joy Division's tenure. It's uncanny to look at photos of the singer and imagine that deep, world-weary bellow coming out of him. He sings as if possessed. Something else must be producing that voice—a foghorn on a ghost ship, maybe. That he sang without playing an instrument, with no physical shield between himself and his audience, only exacerbated his hauntedness. Onstage, he seemed impossibly vulnerable, his face blank and his eyes wide open. In live videos of the band from their television appearance on the youth program *Something Else* in 1979, Curtis looks as if there's something behind his eyes animating him. That he danced like a marionette controlled by a tweaking puppeteer only reinforced the illusion of possession.

Curtis often sang seriously of his illnesses—he had epileptic seizures and bouts of severe depression—which set him apart from the punk front men squealing their way across his native England. Illness tends to be feminized: suffering itself is fair game for song lyrics, but chronic, unyielding depression with no clear instigating event falls outside the usual parameters of masculine expression. In punk, mental illness was often satirized if it came up at all. The Sex Pistols mentioned institutionalization, on "Problems," as a tangential threat to their chaotic personal freedom. The Ramones touched on depression in the upbeat, smirking "Gimme Gimme Shock Treatment." Sickness didn't happen to men, and if it did, it got rerouted into a joke so that men would not have to identify as sick people, but as temporary sufferers of a comic derailment.

The impulse to outsource illness to women was so strong that Curtis devised a female avatar to sing about his epilepsy. "She's Lost Control" positions the speaker as an onlooker to a woman's seizure. Over a beat that sounds like it's puffing smoke across Manchester's industrialized landscape, Curtis rattles off a chain of echoing syllables. The bass line is played high on the neck for most of the song, tracing a queasy, winding riff. The guitar, a low, distant grunt, ascends through the verse as the bass descends, staging a tense melodic confrontation. The environment closes in on the voice. This is a horror story: sickness grips the body of a nameless woman in a polluted, hostile city.

Curtis switches between speakers throughout "She's Lost Control." As the bystander, he repeats the song's title at the end of the first two lines; then, by the third, he's singing "*I've* lost control," directly quoting the woman having the seizure. The ambiguity between the "she" and the "I" deepens by the final verse. "She expressed herself in many different ways until / She lost control again / And walked upon the edge of no escape and laughed / I've lost control," Curtis sings. The "I" here can be attributed to the "she," laughing out the refrain, or it could represent a new thought, the sole instance of Curtis himself claiming to lose control. "Walked" and "laughed" have no pronoun; the "she" hangs back in the stanza. The action blurs, as if Curtis were steadily identifying more and more with the female stranger throughout the course of the song, until he finally admits that he, too, has lost control.

The city encroaches on Curtis again during "Interzone," in which he alternates between his nascent punk voice and the voice of the demon squatting inside him. Named for the decrepit, surrealist setting of William S. Burroughs's 1959 novel *Naked Lunch*, the song envisions Curtis scouring the city for "some friends of mine," only to conclude, "I guess they died some time ago." "Dead Souls," a track that would not see release until after Curtis's suicide, provides yet another haunting, this time by long-dead "conquistadors." "They keep calling me," Curtis repeats in his brassy chest voice, as if the ghosts were speaking not only to him but through him.

Curtis sang about illness obliquely, not in the mode of the straight-faced confessional but by way of fiction's distortions. In "She's Lost Control," he plays the helping person, not the sick one, even as he feels his affinity with the seizing woman loom. The more classical horror stories peppering Joy Division's catalog allow a similar defense against the literal admission of illness. Demons, spirits, and other intangible antagonists act as a reliable ciphers for intrusion into the organized self. Disease, puberty, and deviant desires are easier to imagine in stories where they do not originate inside the body. They come from somewhere else, disrupting the body's rhythmic march through time. Horror stories permit the unhappy ending. They are one of the few media where the body and its defections can share a single narrative.

Punk reveled in the forbidden, but post-punk grappled with the labor of carrying its weight. Tempos slowed and grew more brutal; voices dropped from a yelp to a grumble, as if suffering a testosterone-rich puberty. Curtis carried his low voice as though it were new and unfamiliar to him, like that of a pubescent child whose vocal cords thicken before he enjoys a growth spurt: a small, infantile body emitting a grown man's baritone. The discordance unsettles. This puberty play-acting rendered childhood not as an opportunity for reckless freedom but as a site of abject powerlessness. Curtis's boyishness accentuated his vulnerability. He wore his gender like it was too heavy for him, like he had not yet grown into it.

"Could these sensations make me feel the pleasures of a normal man?" he asks during the first verse of "Disorder"—a loaded question. Which sensations, what pleasures, and what does he mean by "normal man"? He's "waiting for a guide" to lead him forward, away from his own corrupt rendering of masculinity, maybe, and into a more acceptable mold. Curtis clatters off the words to "Disorder" too quickly for their meaning to sink into the ear, and even on the page, they're murky. The song is a blurry rumination on otherness, a garbled transmission from a man lurking on the periphery of recognizable human experience. Curtis knows something is not quite right about himself. The best he can do about it is groan his way through it, vocalizing discomfort as he bristles against an ill-fitting role.

Post-punk excised the obvious, slapdash comedy that had attended punk's antisocial bent. While punks sneered at preordained social roles, post-punk musicians made use of horror techniques to enact symbolic violence on those norms. Murder, self-harm, and sexual violence were all fair game within the genre, which sought to expose through lyrical narratives those social ills that seemed inseparable from the social order, even as the order tried its best to brush them under the rug. The Ramones made fun of the image of the heterosexual household in "We're a Happy Family," joking about the dysfunctions that hide within even the most normal-seeming homes. Post-punk bands, by contrast, staged horror stories in those same homes, identifying them as sites of terror and violence. Patriarchal propaganda asserts that marriage is a natural form and a social good, but many marriages simply serve as cover for domestic abuse. By singing about violence in the home, post-punk and industrial musicians peeled back the skin on patriarchal myths to reveal the festering terror underneath.

In 1977, the New York noise duo Suicide released their debut self-titled album, a harrowing journey through a cramped electronic soundscape. On the standout song "Frankie Teardrop," vocalist Alan Vega intensifies the punk yelp into a full-blown death howl. "Frankie Teardrop" tells of an underpaid, overworked factory laborer who comes home from work one day and, seeing no other option, murders his baby and his wife, then shoots himself. Vega sets up the song in a thin voice that rattles with fear and stress. Over keyboardist Martin Rev's ticking drum machine and oscillating bass drone, Vega offers a measure of empathy for the twenty-year-old Frankie: "He's just trying to survive / Let's hear it for Frankie / But Frankie can't make it / Cause things are just too hard." The vision of America where a man with a low-wage job can provide for his family collapses beneath the feet of the song's eponymous character. Frankie can't feed his family and he can't pay rent; living expenses have risen and wages have not met them. But he internalizes the failure and, seeing no story other than the one he's been fed throughout his American childhood, decides an early death is the only way out of his living nightmare.

Vega yelps when Frankie shoots his six-month-old baby. He shrieks when Frankie turns the gun on his wife, and screams when finally Frankie puts the gun to his own head and pulls the trigger. Having completed his three-point tour of domestic carnage, Frankie goes to hell, which is where Vega screams his most tailbone-rattling scream: a high-pitched expression of agony that echoes away into a squeal of feedback. In 1978, critic John Tobler called it "one of the most psychotic screams ever committed to vinyl."[2]

The scream carried far: in 1982, the all-American power dad Bruce Springsteen released the haunted folk album *Nebraska*. On the song "State Trooper," he sings from the perspective of a man pulled over by a cop on the New Jersey turnpike. "Maybe you got a kid, maybe you got a pretty wife / The only thing that I got's been bothering me my whole life," he sings over an urgent acoustic strum. Then, at the end of the song, he pleads for "somebody out there" to "deliver me from nowhere," and screams in a perfect imitation of Vega. By way of Springsteen, that acid shriek made its way onto a major label album. (Curiously, on the Nebraska song "Highway Patrolman," Springsteen sings about a brother named Frankie who "ain't no good.")

The shriek is the province of the horror movie victim. Killers don't shriek; behind masks or faces fixed with sociopathic grins, they hardly emote at all. Vega shrieks for Frankie's family and then he shrieks for Frankie himself, rendering the character as his own victim, or maybe the victim of the storyteller, who carries the pressures of industrial capitalism out to their ghoulish ends. "We're all Frankies / We're all lying in hell," Vega concludes, looping his audience into Frankie's shattering. The horror of the song originates not in Frankie's impulse to murder his family, but in the conditions that drive him there: a ten-hour shift that doesn't pay enough to feed two adults and an infant, a stubborn vision of men as providers in an economy that bars them from providing. Vega's shriek accentuates Frankie's failure to conform to myths of masculinity. He can't be a man, can't be a father, so he falls, feminized, into hell.

The house band for the avant-garde arts collective Coum Transmissions, UK quartet Throbbing Gristle similarly told horror stories about fissures in the nuclear family, though they took a more literal approach to the castration of the patriarch. In 1976, the outfit made its official live debut at a Coum exhibition at the London Institution of Contemporary Arts called *Prostitution*, whose abundant display of nudity and viscera made headlines when a conservative member of Parliament declared the group "the wreckers of civilisation."[3] Their debut album, 1977's *The Second Annual Report of Throbbing Gristle*, includes audio from that performance. On "Slug Bait," singer Genesis P-Orridge plays a miscreant who breaks into a married couple's house, castrates the husband, and forces him to eat his own balls in front of his pregnant wife. P-Orridge shrieks midway through the castration, repeating the word "knife" in the same register as Vega's piercing cries on

"Frankie Teardrop." The husband bleeds to death, and the speaker cuts open the woman's abdomen in order to consume her fetus. If the reproductive heterosexual family formed the irreducible base unit of "civilisation," as a right-wing politician might argue, then Throbbing Gristle, if you took their lyrics literally, did seem hell-bent on wrecking it.

Both Throbbing Gristle and Suicide positioned the shriek as the vocal expression of the depraved and irredeemable criminal who falls just short of what it means to be a man. "Slug Bait" and "Frankie Teardrop" feminize the sociopath as he attacks and degrades the nuclear family. If Frankie's murder-suicide can be read as a symbolic feminization, as he fails in his duty to be a productive masculine subject under capitalism and subsequently tumbles into hell, then the speaker P-Orridge voices in "Slug Bait" renders the same emasculation more viscerally: the balls come off. P-Orridge's shriek unites the cannibalistic speaker and the fresh eunuch, wrapping both into the horror of lost masculinity. The husband bleeds to death from his mutilated genitals while P-Orridge's voice leaps from a traditionally "male" range to a feminine falsetto.

In calling the label they founded Industrial Records, Throbbing Gristle were the first artists to apply the word "industrial" to their music, connecting the dystopian drudgery of factory work to the clattering, metallic sounds they produced with modified synthesizers. "The 'Industrial Music' that . . . Throbbing Gristle pioneered takes the mechanized factory sounds of everyday life—the acoustic evidence of the working-class's subjugation—and recontextualizes it as a form of political art," wrote Douglas Rushkoff in *Painful but Fabulous: The Lives and Art of Genesis P-Orridge*.[4] Much of the band's work sounds like machinery: metal clanks against metal while voices reverberate through sheets of reverb, making P-Orridge sound like a worker (or a sadistic overseer) shouting into a warehouse. The band made use of glitching electronics and uncanny vocal processing to construct a sickly environment where P-Orridge's voice could walk a knife's-edge between allure and repulsion, between fleeting power and permanent helplessness.

Though most Throbbing Gristle songs forewent traditional structures entirely, a few toyed with the scaffold of the pop song. The early single "United" traces an upbeat, catchy vocal melody over a harshly distorted drum machine that accentuates the gendered ambiguity of P-Orridge's reedy vocal tone. "Weeping" from 1978 pairs cloyingly sweet lines such as "I want to make you happy just a little" with references to depression and self-harm: "You didn't see me weeping on the floor / My arm is torn open like a wound." Beneath P-Orridge's plaintive voice, detuned strings moan and coast aimlessly across the sound field. Like so much of Throbbing Gristle's work, the song seizes on the listener's expectations of musical progression only to reroute and disappoint them. There's no release, no chorus to let out the tension, only anxiety and nausea coursing through an endless verse.

"We opened up a hole in reality. We smashed a hole through rock and roll," P-Orridge said in *The Ballad of Genesis and Lady Jaye*, a 2012 documentary about h/er work, marriage, and subsequent gender transition.[5] In 1995, P-Orridge married Jacqueline Breyer, a dominatrix who went by Lady Jaye when P-Orridge met her, as a client, in New York. "Lady Jaye dressed me in her clothes the first day we met," said P-Orridge. "The love we had was so strong we wished we could become one. Then we thought: why shouldn't we?"[6]

Together, P-Orridge and Breyer embarked on the Pandrogyne Project, a body modification endeavor in which they each worked to resemble each other and close the space between their respective physical forms. For P-Orridge, who identifies as third gender and uses the pronouns s/he and h/er (pronounced aloud like "she" and "her"), the project effectively comprised a transition from one gender to another. S/he wore h/er hair long and blond like h/er wife's; the couple got breast augmentations and rhinoplasties at the same time, waking up from anesthesia next to each other in the same recovery room. Though both participants in the project modified their appearances, P-Orridge was the one who more forcefully ruptured gender boundaries, adopting feminine features that complemented the unusual and ambiguously gendered name s/he had chosen for h/erself at age sixteen.

Released nearly twenty years before the Pandrogyne Project began, "United" foreshadows P-Orridge's unique transition. "You become me / And I become you / She is she / And she is you too," s/he sings. It's a love song of sorts, a song about a romantic union so complete it obliterates the division between bodies. Amid jagged industrial noise, it avails itself of pop music's recognizable signs of joy: a quick tempo, chirping synthesizers, an ascending vocal melody. But it's not a heterosexual couple casting off their individuality to become one. Both partners, it seems, use the pronoun "she."

P-Orridge and Breyer conceptualized the Pandrogyne Project as an alternative to traditional familial forms. "Instead of having children," P-Orridge asks in *The Ballad of Genesis and Lady Jaye*, "what if we made ourselves the new person instead?" Rather than braiding together their DNA via procreation, P-Orridge and Breyer decided to make each other into their own child in a show of defiance at what was expected of them as a couple. There was no need to vest their collective hopes in a third being. Together, through their art, they could make themselves anew.

"I deliberately chose to distort the DNA of my body as a rebellion against predestination," said P-Orridge.[7] The idea of glitching one's gender as a show of defiance against normativity had long preoccupied the artist. S/he learned the mutability of the body at an early age when s/he suffered a long childhood illness (h/er chosen last name derives from the breakfast food s/he says cured h/er). Unlike people who grow up healthy and correctly gendered, P-Orridge never harbored any illusions about the body's inviolability. For h/er, the body was constantly in motion and could be changed according to one's will. There was nothing sacrosanct about a given name, a given body, or a given gender; all were materials to be used in the lifelong artistic project of creating and re-creating the self.

Many transition narratives entertain the idea of a "true self" with a true gender lying in wait, eager to be expressed. By using h/er marriage as a catalyst for h/er transition, P-Orridge branched away from that limited archetype. H/er transition was an expression of the self, but no more than h/er art projects had been throughout h/er life. Always in motion, the body served as just another canvas for the articulation of spiritual ideas—in this case, a love so strong it broke down the boundaries around the individual and forged a new being, a single soul that called two different bodies its home.

"The person who invented this creature Neil Andrew Megson [P-Orridge's birth name] who surrendered to Genesis P-Orridge in 1965 as an art project, he just moved away and died and left a character and a caricature and this is, in a sense, the beginning of that character learning again to be a SELF," P-Orridge said in 2001. "That to me is a very sacred act. To give more credence to the universe and consciousness than to one's own inherited idea of Self. . . . So you can set yourself free, and once you are free you can keep exploring the intersections to determine, to decide how to live a life, to try to live a life as 'spirit,' to try to live a life as ideas, to try and finally to find a number of languages for what appears to be there."[8]

In a video from a 1981 Throbbing Gristle concert in London, Genesis P-Orridge speaks into a microphone while h/er bandmates mutilate h/er voice.[9] The pitch bubbles around the octave, echoing from a chirp down into a growl. As s/he begins to scream, it sounds as if there are multiple P-Orridges, each with a different vocal range, leaping through the air. An unruly crowd emanates from a single body. "I WANT! DISCIPLINE!" s/he repeats, gripping the microphone with both hands and prowling the stage like a caged leopard. S/he rocks h/erself on the floor like an abused child trying to self-soothe. S/he leans into the crowd and offers them the microphone, encouraging them to scream the word "discipline" through the storm of vocal effects. H/er voice undergoes two stages of laceration: one in h/er throat, where it's organically fried via the intensity of the scream, and one in the machine, where it's distended, multiplied, and made uncomfortably loud. At one point, synthesist Chris Carter tweaks the reverberation to the point that P-Orridge's voice comes out as a squeal of feedback. Toward the end of the song, P-Orridge leans over and kisses an audience member, a blond man with a buzzcut who writhes ecstatically at the fleeting contact. The boundary between performer and audience melts; the crowd both screams along with P-Orridge and even interacts with h/er sensually, charged by the energy of the performance.

The hole that Throbbing Gristle tore open in reality began with a corruption of pop music's typical exchanges. Instead of offering pleasure by way of melody, the band challenged and irritated the ear. Instead of treating the stage as a pedestal, positioning themselves as artists bestowing upon their audience the gift of their art, Throbbing Gristle debased themselves. Throughout the 1981 performance of "Discipline," P-Orridge begs to be punished. S/he revels in h/er own sense of powerlessness and invites the crowd to share in what power s/he does have: access to the microphone. These subversions opened up space for spontaneous, creative exchanges. By breaking apart popular music and stitching it back together incorrectly, Throbbing Gristle allowed new forms to emerge. Balances of power could be upended, the unspeakable could be spoken, and the scripts of everyday life could be at least temporarily rewritten. "Civilization," such as it was in twentieth-century England, hardly sufficed to contain the whole of human experience, and Throbbing Gristle were keen on surfacing what had been left out of the normative story. "I was looking for some kind of devotion and holiness, but in a contemporary way, I was trying to rediscover what it is in our culture that's been taken from us," P-Orridge said.[10]

That the holy could be pursued through what seemed on its surface to be demonic was not a new idea (Throbbing Gristle were big fans of occultist Aleister Crowley, who espoused similar ideas), but it did find new terrain in pop music. Through Throbbing Gristle (and later with the band Psychic TV), P-Orridge could burrow away from mundane expectations of personhood and arrive at a sense of the liberated spiritual self. "The state of 'wakefulness' is described as a magickal space that provides the practitioner with tools to reveal and describe and physically adjust the fundamentals of the Self," wrote P-Orridge's friend and collaborator Julie Wilson (making use of P-Orridge's spelling idiosyncrasies) in *Painful but Fabulous*. "P-Orridge describes this space of wakefulness as an infinitude ov perceptive spaces and points ov observation, where 'down,' 'up,' 'across,' 'distance' and other faded directional terms becoum redundant as do the notions of fixed identity and of male and femaleness."[11]

Music, here, is magic; gender, too. Both supply raw material for reordering the physical world, allowing the artist to roil the orderly, upset the ordinary, and make a new home for the chaotic and constantly changing inner self. For P-Orridge, reality was not to be imposed on the individual by authority, but generated within the individual and shared communally with others. "Genesis challenges us to co-author the collective story," wrote Douglas Rushkoff in *Painful but Fabulous*. "[S/he] insists that if we don't create reality ourselves, someone, somewhere will surely do it for us. And that person will not have our best interests at heart."[12]

On Throbbing Gristle's first run of recordings, taken years before h/er physical transition, P-Orridge's voice already sounds androgynous. It's thin and it quavers; it plays in the space between tenor and alto. Long before s/he manifested h/er femininity physically, s/he approached it vocally, singing h/er way to a space beyond the two socially acceptable genders, outside the rigid standards of behavior enforced from on high. Before it appeared to h/er in other forms of language, P-Orridge sang h/er reality, and invited others to join h/er there, in that space where the self can break out from the claustrophobic channels of the status quo.

Vampires, like punks, don't age. They skulk in perpetual youth, outside the world but also more powerful than its uninfected citizens, isolated and free. Given the glamour of the vampire, it was inevitable that the horror figure would cross over from film to music, where its supernatural androgyny felt right at home.

The term "gothic rock" was first applied to California band the Doors' twelve-minute detour into oedipal madness, "The End."[13] Presaging Alan Vega and Genesis P-Orridge's lyrical corruptions of the family, Jim Morrison sneered his way through a scene in which he kills his father and rapes his mother. Though the Doors evaded many of the hallmarks of what would come to be known as goth music, this one song and its concentrated, anti-familial negativity opened a wide, gloomy space for the brooding masses to come into.

If Joy Division grew somber, ethereal dramas from the dregs of punk, then English bands like the Cure, Siouxsie and the Banshees, and the Smiths took up the darker edge of glam rock in their own presentation. Regardless of gender, goth rockers tended to look the same: dark hair, dark clothes, dark eyeliner framing an open, mournful gaze poured directly into the camera lens. One of the most visually iconic goth front men, Robert Smith of the Cure started presenting himself androgynously in the early '80s, after the band had moved away from more or less straitlaced post-punk toward a more dizzying, reverb-swathed form of rock. He teased up his hair, applied copious eyeliner, and started wearing red lipstick.

Unlike the chameleonic Bowie, who eased up on the alien makeup in the '80s, Smith retains his femme getup to this day. It complements the Cure's music, which seeks out femininity not as a shock tactic but as an entry point into the subtler shades of desire and suffering that cascade throughout the band's discography. With a keen appreciation for reverb and a puckered whine, Smith softened post-punk into an emotional miasma where he could excavate the hurt that lingers in joy, and vice versa. He sings "Lovesong," an expression of eternal romantic devotion, in the same tone he employs on "Pictures of You," a pop confection that might as well be a dirge. "Plainsong," a sweeping ballad ostensibly about the literal end of the world, plays as though the speaker and his lover have arrived at an unshakable inner peace just as civilization collapses around them.

One Cure song in particular indulges the sensation of simultaneously wanting someone and wanting to become them: the upbeat, frantic "Why Can't I Be You?" Taken from 1987's adventurous hodge-podge *Kiss Me Kiss Me Kiss Me*, the single follows an uncharacteristically fun guitar riff and synthesized brass line. "You're so gorgeous / I'll do anything," declares Smith, who then at the chorus asks repeatedly, "Why can't I be you?" A songwriter less fond of ambiguity might have offered the line "Why can't I *have* you?" but Smith sees no reason to maintain the hard line between himself and the feminine object of his desire. Throughout the song, his voice breaks into falsetto, as if he's trying to shuck its masculine connotation and ascend to the vocal range of the person he desires. For him, the ultimate consummation of romantic affection isn't domination over the other. It isn't wanting and then getting; it's a joining, a blurring of the self that obliterates the categories of "lover" and "beloved" entirely, creating a new, third being beyond heterosexual gender arrangements. The suggestion that men could, in their desire, *become* women was so offensive to contemporary sensibilities that certain American listeners reportedly went so far as to label the song "satanic."[14]

The cover of *The Queen Is Dead*, the 1986 album by Manchester rock band the Smiths, depicts French actor Alain Delon in repose.

The title hovers in pink serif above him, and of course it's a bit of a joke. The LP's title track, which opens side A, bitterly criticizes the monarchy, but it's hard to ignore the word "queen" in pink, decorating the image of an effeminate man lying perhaps lifelessly on his back.

The Smiths' singer, Morrissey, designed the cover. While he has famously never come out as anything in particular (when pressed on the subject, he's tended to give a rough summary of pansexuality and declare himself a "humasexual," as in attracted to people in general), he saturated the Smiths' music with references to queer historical figures and stifled, forbidden love.[15] Much of his lyricism is cloaked in bitter irony, and his ventures into vocal androgyny are no different.

An early example of the now-ubiquitous practice of pitch-shifting appears on the single "Bigmouth Strikes Again," where Morrissey plays a verbally abusive jack-off who transmogrifies himself into the victim of the fraught exchange. "Sweetness, I was only joking when I said / By rights you should be bludgeoned in your bed / And now I know how Joan of Arc felt," he sings. When he repeats that last unbelievable line with increasing dramatic fervor—"*now I know how Joan of Arc felt!*"—a second voice joins him, identical in flamboyance but higher in pitch. The Smiths credited this backing voice as "Ann Coates," a play on the Ancoats neighborhood of Manchester, but it's actually Morrissey's own voice slung up a couple of octaves.[16]

The doubling produces an uncanny effect, in part because the texture of Morrissey's croon is so unmistakable: velvety and wrung out with vibrato, itself a feminine affectation in the context of pop music. The spectral, feminized Morrissey lends dimension to the song's drama. He empathizes so deeply with Joan of Arc—a woman executed, in part, for the crime of dressing in men's armor—that his voice vaults upward to her imagined range. It's a bathetic melodrama, given that the speaker in "Bigmouth" is only facing repercussions for being an ass, a consequence he twists around so he might imagine the flames at the stake licking his ear and melting his anachronistic Walkman. If he's the victim of the encounter, he must occupy a passive position relative to the aggressor, and using a bit of studio trickery, he comically emphasizes his relational femininity.

The Smiths never quite adopted the goth rock uniform of black clothes and black hair—Morrissey instead accessorized with an antigravity quiff and bouquets of daffodils—but much of their music slides in neatly beside that of their more somber-looking peers. Perhaps their best-known track, 1985's "How Soon Is Now?," crescendos with one of the most daringly self-pitying lines in rock history: "I am human and I need to be loved / Just like everybody else does." Between lines about being too shy to pick up anyone at the club, Johnny Marr's guitar duets with Morrissey, producing an elephantine whine that hits the ear like a wordless, feminine voice. It's one of the more marvelous examples of the chemistry between the two musicians. Morrissey complains, and so Marr teases his guitar into complaining. Together, the two voices try their best to out-whine each other until the song collapses in a long, echoing outro. The spectral production aligns to some degree with the sound of the Cure, but Morrissey's lyrics don't conjure visions of spiders or grim reapers. He locates a much more subtle horror: the bottomless chasm of queer self-loathing.

Like "How Soon Is Now?," Placebo's 1998 single "Pure Morning" revolves around a single chord ringing out into a storm of reverb. Both drum patterns land heavy on the snare, which echoes into what sounds like cavernous space. But if the Smiths crystallized abject alienation in their song, Placebo, a three-piece post-punk band formed in London in the mid-1990s, speak to the sort of union that hovers just outside convention. Lead singer Brian Molko sings of a "friend who's dressed in leather"—a woman, given the pronouns he uses, but certainly not a girlfriend. She's a combination weed hookup and BDSM partner, up for bloodplay and deep conversation, maybe at the same time.

In the '90s, Molko wore his hair in a wavy bob and slathered on black eye makeup and black nail polish. He flowered in the space left open for him by the goth subculture of the '80s, adorning himself with darkly feminine markers. His androgyny also saturated his tinny, nasal voice. Placebo tended to tune down their guitar and bass, which made Molko's voice sound even higher by contrast. They modified the reference points of the rock-and-roll power trio, tweaking the tools available to them just enough to project a queerer vision of guitar rock.

In the video for "Pure Morning," Molko stands on the ledge of a tall office building, morosely deciding whether to jump. A news crew gathers below him while the cops race to pull him back from the edge. A man with a megaphone seemingly implores him to live, to no avail. He jumps, but it's not a suicide. As he falls, gravity pulls him horizontally, and he stands safe on the side of the building. Barefoot and transcendentally femme, he hesitates for a moment in this field of gravity that exists only for him. Then he walks back down to earth. The narrative everyone expects, of a queer, gender-defiant person ending his own life, gets ruptured by an instance of magic. Gravity shifts for Molko. Reality bends, and in his warped pocket of the real, he lives.

5

SOFT MACHINES

Women, Cyborgs, and Electronic Music

While working on the soundtrack to Stanley Kubrick's 1971 dystopian film *A Clockwork Orange*, composer Wendy Carlos fed the voice of her creative partner, Rachel Elkind, into a spectrum follower, a technology that had previously only been used for telephone communications.[1] By the '70s, Carlos had already enjoyed considerable success adapting classical music to the Moog synthesizer, a relatively new musical technology at the time. Her 1968 album *Switched-On Bach* sold exceptionally well and ultimately became the first classical LP to go platinum. The flexibility of electronic music, its ability to mimic existing instruments while also forging entirely new sounds, enticed Carlos. Much of contemporary music's sound owes a considerable debt to her early experiments with Elkind and Robert Moog, the American engineer who invented the first commercial synthesizer. "Sixteen-track and twenty-four-track recorders came to be widely used after the release of *Switched-On Bach*, and then digital synthesizers, hard disk recorders, and computer-based music production systems. Wendy's contributions to this evolution cannot be overstated," wrote Moog in the digital liner notes to the 1999 Carlos compilation *The Switched-On Boxed Set*.[2]

The protagonist of *A Clockwork Orange* loves Beethoven, and so reworking the composer's famous Ninth Symphony became a focus of Carlos and Elkind's original soundtrack. The Ninth prominently features the voice, an instrument so complex and enigmatic that it could not at that point be synthesized from scratch. Wanting a voice that sounded electronic, even if it partially originated from a human throat, Carlos decided to repurpose the vocoder. She had first encountered the device some years earlier: "I got a chance to try one at the NY World's Fair of 1964–65, at the Bell Labs pavilion," she recalled. "I was hooked! When I figured how to make it not just speak, but sing, it earned an assured place in a forthcoming new album."[3]

In Carlos and Elkind's rendition of the Ninth's fourth movement, the processed voice sounds singular and pure. It's hard to separate Elkind from the machine into which she's singing; unlike in earlier experiments with electronic vocal processing—including the Doors' 1967 song "Strange Days," in which Jim Morrison's voice is shrouded in a Moog filter—there's no seam between the organic and the electronic, no way to tease out what's "real" and what's not. The vocoder voice is not a union of two discrete elements. It's a third entity, the likes of which had never been heard before. The ambiguity of the new sound prompted a strong response among listeners. "We got a lot of uncomfortable reactions," Carlos said. "People looked at us and said, 'Oh, my goodness, what is this?' They were scared by it. They were scared hearing a chorus of artificial voices."[4]

While Carlos was busy training her monophonic synthesizers to articulate new sounds one painstaking note at a time, she was also working to articulate her own embodiment in the world. Assigned male at birth, Carlos had always maintained a strong sense of her own femaleness; she recalled in her 1979 coming-out interview with *Playboy* being confused as to why her parents didn't see her as a girl when she was very young. She started experimenting with electronics while she was still in high school, and she studied music and physics while pursuing her undergraduate degree at Brown. In 1962, the composer moved to New York for graduate school. Experiencing intense dysphoria and thoughts of suicide, she concluded that if she were to survive, she would have to transition—a path that had been taken by only a handful of public figures at that point.

Carlos began hormone therapy early in 1968, just months before *Switched-On Bach* was released. It would be a full decade before she came out in public; she began to transition before she told even her closest friends about her gender identity. Elkind worked on the album and negotiated its release with Columbia Records without knowing that Carlos was a woman, though Carlos confided in her shortly after Elkind had secured their record deal. The two musicians' names do not appear on the initial pressing of *Switched-On Bach*. Instead, they dubbed their production company Trans-Electronic Music Productions Inc., a sly, anonymized name that hinted at the truth years before Carlos was ready to tell it.

"At the time that I was working with Wendy I did not know about her gender problems," said Elkind. "In other words, I sort of accepted her just as she was, a wonderful human being. And it was really after I had made the deal with Columbia that she told me about this problem, which was why the album cover really was done the way it was with 'Trans-Electronic,' because she really didn't want to have a name like the Beatles or the Rolling Stones."[5]

After Carlos came out to Elkind, the singer served as her closest confidante and helped protect her privacy. The overwhelming success of *Switched-On Bach* launched the pair into the public eye, forcing Carlos to make a handful of strained public appearances as Walter. She dressed in masculine clothing and used eyeshadow to create the illusion of stubble, having already undergone electrolysis to remove her facial hair. Hormone replacement therapy had feminized her appearance, which was androgynous to begin with, so Carlos found her attempts at male drag not especially convincing. Some gossips even speculated she was a cis woman pretending to be a man so that the music world would take her seriously.

The two musicians moved in together in a brownstone on West Eighty-Seventh Street in New York that housed their studio. Elkind fielded requests from pop musicians to visit Carlos, turning away prog keyboardist Keith Emerson, who had bought a Moog immediately after hearing *Switched-On Bach* for the first time, and Beatle George Harrison when they showed up at their doorstep.[6] Only the blind soul star Stevie Wonder was invited up to play Carlos's synths; Carlos, fearing her voice would give her away, said as little as possible during the encounter.

The forced solitude took a toll on Carlos. "The fact that I couldn't perform publicly stifled me," she told *Playboy*. "I lost a decade as an artist. I was unable to communicate with other musicians. There was no feedback." But, alongside Elkind, she worked in private to deepen the link between body and machine, tracing new forms of sound on an unexplored piece of technology. In the late '60s and early '70s, the synthesizer was an emergent body, a musical instrument capable of surprising the ear with previously unheard sounds. Carlos's work with Moog refined the way the machine could be played. She suggested that they add velocity-sensitive keys to the instrument, creating a tactile response that reinforced the idea of the synthesizer as a responsive body. "The weighted keys of the Polymoog have a 'friendly' feel, a pleasing tactile quality quite beyond anything that the keys do to the sound," Carlos said.[7] She also suggested that Moog add a portamento control to the machine, allowing one note to slide smoothly into another. This responsiveness helped transform the synthesizer from a looming, sterile studio appliance into something more like a prosthesis—an extension of the body that enhanced the player's ability to create complex, textured sound.

The softness of the synthesizer's response reiterated the softness of the human body, its malleability and adaptability, its willingness to take on new forms in response to stimulation. By developing the synthesizer as a musical instrument capable of creating new forms of the voice, Carlos preempted the work that she would do by coming out as a trans woman. "*Switched-On Bach* in 1969 was a good musical barometer, while transsexuality in 1979 is a fairly good sexual and attitudinal social barometer," she said in her *Playboy* interview. "When *Switched-On Bach* was new, it stimulated strong reactions. Those who were comfortable in all forms of music, those who were open to novel variations, loved it. Transsexuality, too, is an emotional, action-prone situation, in that it tends to polarize people, depending on the attitudes one brings to sexuality and human rights. In both cases, there's no middle ground."

When it hits the ear, the voice conveys information about the body from which it issues. Voices have gendered associations, but they also connote metadata such as age, health, and emotional state. The voice is a loaded sound, and so to hear a voice created anew with the help of a machine is a startling experience. Carlos and Elkind's cyborg voice frightened certain listeners, no doubt due to its ambiguity. The Ninth calls for multiple voices, and so multiple pitches with identical timbre weave together in Trans-Electronic's rendering, making the vocoder difficult to gender. The voice that courses through the *Clockwork Orange* soundtrack seems to embody multiple genders at the same time. It lies in the uncanny valley at the exact middle of multiple dualities: male and female, human and machine, real and unreal. By distorting the listener's ability to perceive a fixed body at the other end of a voice, the vocoder threw the practice of listening into delightfully productive confusion.

Ambiguous sound thrived in Carlos's compositional work, which didn't seek to reproduce acoustic instruments and "natural" voices so much as to refract them through a new and futuristic mode of listening. The synthesizer—a black box whose method of producing sound waves is invisible to the naked eye—supplied the perfect template for the articulation of alien environments, places where the meaning of any given sound could be in flux, open to definition for adventurous listeners. In her *Playboy* interview, Carlos challenged the conventional notion that gender followed irreversibly from one's assigned birth sex, suggesting instead that the body was a malleable palette that could be reshaped according to inner narratives and desires. With her music, she offered a parallel challenge, inviting the ear to shed its presumptions of sound and voice and join the composer on an open plane of possibility.

In the introduction to her 2002 collection of interviews *Pink Noises*, journalist and musician Tara Rodgers proposes that it was in fact a woman performer who initially gave rise to electronic music, not the male Futurists who usually get credit for the genre's birth. The Futurists, a group of early-twentieth-century artists based in Italy, entertained the idea that mechanical noise could have value as music, but Clara Rockmore, a Russian-American classical musician, was the one who popularized the theremin, one of the first purely electronic instruments to be played live for an audience.

The thereminist plays her instrument without ever touching it. Antennas detect the position of the thereminist's hands and the instrument produces a pitch accordingly. Because there's no tactile feedback, playing the theremin requires incredible precision. The thereminist cannot emote like a violinist or pianist might. She has to adapt her movements to the perception of the machine, which cannot tolerate even a slight slippage from the exact position in space that produces a given note.

"Rockmore's performances, including a showcase of the instrument at Town Hall in New York in 1934, helped to establish electronic and experimental music as a viable art form in the public imagination," wrote Rodgers. "The spellbound audiences were presented with a performance of electronic music as embodied, affective engagement with technology, characterized by nuance and care."[8]

By becoming a virtuoso of the theremin, Rockmore mastered one of history's more enigmatic and subtle instruments. She would shake her hand to achieve vibrato, making the theremin sound almost human—a voice crying out from an untouchable body. To her audiences, she must have looked as though she were playing a ghost: gripping the air and teasing out a sequence of uncanny notes that rose and fell with her careful hands.

Electronic instruments, like all machinery, tend to be associated with masculinity. Machines signify precise and important labor, the kind that women are thought, in patriarchal mythology, to be physically incapable of performing. But electronic instruments attached themselves to the soft science of music, an area where women could at least be performers. Women populate the origins of electronic music, a field that, at its incipience, was too new and too strange to be guarded fiercely by patriarchal gatekeepers. By the mid-twentieth century, electronic music technology had not been entirely masculinized, and so women stepped in to create their own meaning in its emerging sphere.

On the opposite coast from Wendy Carlos, the California-based musician and academic Pauline Oliveros worked to devise her own system for making music from machines. In 1962, she cofounded the San Francisco Tape Music Center alongside fellow electronic composers Ramon Sender and Morton Subotnick. The center was an independent organization that collaborated with many other arts initiatives in San Francisco, staging collaborative live events throughout the city that aimed to "blur the boundaries between art and life." Influential minimalist composers including Terry Riley and Steve Reich would perform at Tape Center events; the organization was an incubator for some of the mid-twentieth century's most imaginative musical minds.[9]

Portable synthesizers were not yet commercially available in the '60s, so Oliveros made her own machines. She fed the sounds of her accordion through a series of tape players and oscillators she strung together herself, manipulating the sound until it took on a strange new life of its own. "I created a system that was quite unstable, but very interesting, and I could use it to create a vast variety of sounds," she said.[10]

Oliveros's 1965 recording "Bye Bye Butterfly" weaves together a sequence of playful, high-pitched electronic trills, played in real time at the San Francisco Tape Music Center. About halfway through the composition, an aria from Puccini's *Madame Butterfly* enters the mix like a ghost intruding on the present from the past. The sound of Oliveros pressing play on the recording reverberates through the piece like percussion, and then the opera itself appears. Women's voices course through the nest of electronic whine, like they're straining to be heard. They echo and throb alongside the electronic wails, two voices in conflict. Sometimes the machines match the pitch of the singer; more often, the tones clash. There's something irrepressibly sad and strange about the piece. Even though the sampled aria is taken from the beginning of the opera, it sounds as if Butterfly might already be dying, crowded out by bizarre new sounds from well beyond her time. The electronics ultimately drown out the voice, burying her in noise. An old model of femininity—the perfectly pitched soprano playing out a tragedy—sinks underneath a new vision of how women can articulate sound.

The provocative composition "bids farewell not only to the music of the nineteenth century but also to the system of polite morality of that age and its attendant institutionalized oppression of the female sex," Oliveros wrote.[11] The chaotic notes she coaxes from her electronic studio seem to lacerate the nineteenth-century opera. Eventually, the chaos swallows it whole. With "Bye Bye Butterfly," Oliveros introduces and then clears away her source material, an opera whose young protagonist commits suicide after learning her husband has left her and married another woman. She samples Butterfly's entrance aria, in which she, a fifteen-year-old Japanese girl, meets the American man intent on marrying her. He does, then impregnates her and leaves her, only to return once she has given birth to their son to introduce her to his new American wife. Distraught, she decides to take her own life rather than live with the pain of his rejection.

Oliveros welds Butterfly's aria to the squeal of her oscillators, letting the young girl announce herself and then wiping away the music before Pinkerton, the man she'll marry, can get a word in. "Bye Bye Butterfly" throttles the opera's plot, cinching it shut underneath electronic noise before its tragedy can unfold. In the wake of the sampled opera, machines echo, connoting futurity but also a new form of freedom. In the world of the composition, women do not have to sing their way to their own deaths. They do not have to marry terrible men and then die for them. They can issue their own ugly, challenging screams from the belly of a tape machine and carve a way forward that does not necessitate the subjugation of their bodies. Oliveros, a lesbian, upends the tragic heterosexual procession of *Madame Butterfly* and forges her own narrative. Unlike the opera singer's, her sounds do not emanate from the body. She produces a voice in tandem with machines, a cyborg musician rewriting the role of the woman performer.

In the decades that followed her early tape experiments, Oliveros would develop a philosophical structure she called "deep listening," a way of calibrating the sense of hearing so that the listener consciously absorbs all ambient sound. "You can in a way defocus your ears so you're taking in all of the sounds around you, inside of you, in your memory or imagination all at once," she said.

> The best image or metaphor I can give for it is a tapestry of sound: threads of sound that come and go and some that stay. Trying to expand oneself to include more and more of the field, I call inclusive listening. And then when something attracts your attention to focus in on, that's exclusive listening. You can do both at once, actually. I have a lot of

> exercises and pieces that try to expose these different forms. And this is what we do in the Deep Listening retreat. Deep Listening is a process. I guess the best definition I could give is listening to everything all the time and reminding yourself when you're not listening.[12]

Attending to the practice of listening was not, for Oliveros, just an artistic tool. It had psychological and political utility as well. "How you're listening is how you develop a culture, and how a community of people listens is what creates their culture," she continued. Listening to music and to environmental sound could be more than a passive process. It could create reality, opening the human ear to new forms of being.

Working separately on opposite coasts, Carlos and Oliveros both laid the theoretical groundwork for the genre that was soon to expand rapidly into mainstream popular culture. Both queer women, they had a deep personal investment in creating the new. At the periphery of mainstream social narratives, they made use of machines to reorder the world of sound and carve out a habitable space amid a largely uninhabitable landscape.

In 1980, the American sculptor-turned-performance artist Laurie Anderson released an eight-and-a-half-minute single called "O Superman" on the New York–based independent label 110 Records. With no percussion and no traditional instruments, just Anderson's voice and a throng of electronics, the song made an unlikely candidate for a pop hit, and American listeners largely ignored it. But the uncanny electronic epic found unexpected success in the United Kingdom the following year. The influential BBC DJ John Peel caught wind of the song and played it on his *Radio One* show in 1981; almost immediately, his listeners wanted to know who this strange new voice belonged to. UK record stores were inundated with requests for copies of the single. Looking to cash in on the hubbub around Anderson, Warner Bros. Records offered a deal to release the single in the UK, where it climbed to number two on the pop charts.[13]

It's not the sort of song that would become a mainstream hit today, but the cyborg sound struck a chord with British listeners, who would go on to embrace synthpop fully as a phenomenon in a few years. In lieu of a drumbeat, Anderson keeps time across all eight minutes with a single looped vocal syllable, a "ha" that seems to challenge the ear with its insistence. The sound's bare structure indicates laughter, but there's no mirth in the delivery, just light boredom or maybe detached bemusement. "O Superman" also makes abundant use of the vocoder, the voice processing technology that Wendy Carlos and Rachel Elkind first applied to music in the early '70s. With her strange, fractured, overdubbed robot voice, Anderson uses her half-sung, half-spoken lyrics to unravel the bizarre state of living as an individual under militarized Cold War capitalism in the United States.

"Well, you don't know me / But I know you," Anderson sings, her voice multiplied and partially deepened, like a chorus of different ranges. "And I've got a message / To give to you." It's a panopticon voice, a television voice, the voice of everyone at once; its multiplicity invokes the feeling of other people watching. But inside that paranoia hides a sincere yearning to be loved—a contradiction with a similar emotional resonance to that of the jokes people make about whispering "Good night" to the FBI agents watching them from their laptop cameras.

In the last lines of "O Superman," the speaker calls out for a maternal embrace, but the only mom she knows is the motherland. "Hold me mom / In your long arms / In your automatic arms / Your electronic arms," Anderson sings, "Your petrochemical arms / Your military arms." The mother she knows is the nation that shelters her from the oblique threat of other countries, the surveillance state that keeps her, supposedly, safe. Even through the electronic effects, Anderson's voice sounds earnest and vulnerable, like that of a child seeking protection from an obscure power they don't quite understand: a benevolent yet unknowable omnipotence.

In the video that accompanied "O Superman," and in live performances throughout the '80s, Anderson wore her hair short and spiked while dressed in a suit and tie. Her clothing often looked laminated, shiny, not a "real" suit but a stage show getup, a suit meant to convey both authority and pizzazz. It matched her laminated voice, which often simulated the pitch in which power speaks—a cis man's voice—without obfuscating the mechanism of the illusion; the electronic voice was never meant to sound "real." Anderson has called the artificial deepening of her voice "audio drag," an auditory accompaniment to the sartorial drag she performed simultaneously. The point of drag is more often than not exaggerated play, not realism. Anderson dressed up as a facsimile of a man in order to toy with and deflate the symbols that enable men to wield power over others.

In a piece called "Mach 20," which she performed live as a musical guest on the NBC sketch program *The New Show* in 1984, Anderson uses her deepened voice to dramatize the trajectory of human sperm post-ejaculation. Behind her, green cartoon sperm swim across a projection screen. Her voice is comically low, and she speaks haltingly, like a game show host trained to pause frequently for dramatic effect or William Shatner playing Captain Kirk on *Star Trek*. In this absurd voice, she romanticizes the plight of the sperm. "Generation after generation of these tiny creatures have sacrificed themselves in their persistent, often futile, attempt to transport the basic male genetic code," she says. "But where is this information coming from? They have no eyes, no ears, yet some of them already know that they will be bald. Some of them know that they will have small, crooked teeth. Over half of them will end up as women. Four hundred million living creatures all knowing precisely the same thing—carbon copies of each other in a kamikaze race against the clock."[14]

Here, Anderson's drag character imagines sperm not as cells participating mutually with eggs in the process of human reproduction, but as bold, noble agents struggling tirelessly to make more men. She uses militarized language ("kamikaze") to describe their journey. She positions femaleness as an unwanted defect, akin to baldness or bad teeth but even more shocking, the third item in an intensifying list of undesirable traits. She then goes on to imagine sperm cells the size of sperm whales, traveling coast to coast at a heroic speed of fifteen thousand miles per hour, or "Mach 20," another snippet of military lingo. By scaling up the sperm, she emphasizes the absurdity of imagining them as creatures with will, agency, and purpose. The sound of her processed voice, the "voice of authority," as she would call it, deepens the irony of the piece.[15] As her drag persona recites a patriarchal creation myth, Anderson punctures its power by mimicking a secondary sex characteristic popularly imagined to belong solely to men. With the aid of technology, she playfully usurps those features used as tools in the subjugation of women and other targets of misogyny.

Though she used electronic processing (and a keen sense of humor) to imitate the vocal affectations of men, Anderson also occasionally positioned technological prowess as the domain of the teenage girl. She performed a piece called "The Language of the Future" on a public television special called *Good Morning Mr. Orwell*, conceived and curated by the video artist Nam June Paik and aired across the United States on the first day of 1984. In the performance, Anderson plays a man who has survived a plane crash and on subsequent flights must distract himself from his anxiety by talking to other passengers.[16] He chooses a fifteen-year-old girl across the aisle to be his in-flight companion, only to realize suddenly that she is not speaking the same language as he is. Instead, she speaks "computerese: a kind of a high tech lingo. Everything was circuitry, electronics." Anderson, cloaked in vocal drag, mimics the girl's feminine slang as she describes a tumultuous relationship: "'Man, oh man, you know, like, oh *man*, it's so *digital.*' And she just meant the relationship was on again, off again, always two things switching." Toward the end of the piece, the spotlight on Anderson darkens, but she continues speaking. "Jump out of the plane," she says. "There is no pilot. You are not alone. This is the language of the on-again, off-again future, and it is digital."

Anderson's quasi-musical transmissions tended to be purposely enigmatic. "I have the right and the responsibility to make images that make people wonder and think. It's confusing for a lot of people because they're thinking: 'Well, this is sort of political sort of sexual, but she's not telling us what to do next,'" she said in a 1987 interview.[17] It's difficult to attach a single concrete meaning to any of her performance pieces, but in many ways, Anderson's work was prophetic. America is still a cruel and absent parent with long military arms. And young people do use the language of computer technology to describe their reality, though they aren't talking about on-again, off-again relationships.

Instead, millennials and members of Generation Z use the word "binary" to talk about gender, mapping the system of sexual categorization onto the binary used in digital technologies. Inside the gender binary, there is male and there is female, a one and a zero, just as there is in computer code. Anderson, in her work throughout the '80s, was already glitching this duality. In "The Language of the Future," she's a woman playing a man imitating the futuristic lingo of a teenage girl. The gender of her performance flips back and forth until it's hard to trace where the one ends and the zero begins. The ironic, playful future Anderson constructs is a prismatic one, where identities can flit from body to body, and where the sanctity of preordained identity falls into flux. Her performance about binary modes of being foreshadowed the contemporary articulation of nonbinary identities: ways of moving through the world that strain against sex-essentialist dualism.

"Now, I'm no mathematician, but I'd like to talk about a couple of numbers that have really been bothering me lately," Anderson says in her deepened voice in the 1986 concert film *Home of the Brave*.[18] "And they are: zero and one." She has just introduced the show by dancing in silhouette in her suit, letting the masculine edges of her clothes flash against a blue screen. The lights come up, and she, like the other performers onstage, is wearing a mask: a stocking that fits over her face, adorned with cartoonish indications of eyes, nose, and mouth. She picks up an electronic violin and begins to play, but the sound that comes out does not sound like that of a violin. It's more like a wolf howling through a digital filter, a mournful, futuristic sound that doesn't seem to correspond to any particular instrument. It's difficult to imagine a body, human or otherwise, that could make that noise.

"Nobody wants to be a zero," Anderson continues. "To be a zero means to be a nothing, a nobody, a has-been, a clod. On the other hand, almost everybody wants to be number one. To be number one means to be a winner, top of the heap, the acme. There seems to be a strange kind of national obsession with this particular number."

It's not difficult to transmute this schematic to gender, which gets sorted into two discrete types: marked and unmarked, as Deborah Tannen argued in a 1993 *New York Times* magazine essay, "Marked Women, Unmarked Men." Women, she wrote, are marked as "other" to the default, neutral state of maleness. One gender has value only to the extent of its usefulness to the neutral position; the other can be considered inherently valuable. Women are zeroes, marked others, while men can enjoy the privileges of being ones.

"Now, in my opinion, the problem with these two numbers is that they are just too close," says Anderson in *Home of the Brave*.

> Leaves very little room in there for everybody else. Just not enough range. So, first, we need to get rid of the value judgments attached to these numbers, and realize that to

be a zero is no better, no worse than to be number one. Because what we are actually looking at here are the building blocks of the modern computer age. Anything that can be expressed in words or numbers in any language can be communicated using this simple, foolproof system. It's all here in a nutshell, the entire alphanumerical system: A to Z, the zero to infinity of digital intelligence.

The use of binary language supplies infinite range, and yet most people grow up encouraged to sort everyone they see into one of two categories: male or female, one or zero. By using multiple digits, markers compounding markers, the eye can see to the vanishing point on the horizon, eluding reductive dualities. With a little creativity, the binary itself can transcend its base components. Anderson finishes speaking, and a zero appears on the screen, then a one. Each number is accompanied by the annoying blare of a horn. Then the numbers disappear, the horn quiets, and the musicians remove their masks. The lights come up and the music begins.

As voice processing technology grew cheaper and more accessible, more and more artists started wrangling their voices through machines. In 1998, the actress and former folkie Cher released one of the most distinctive singles of the turn of the millennium. The dance pop smash "Believe" made use of Auto-Tune—a pitch-correcting technology formerly used to gently nudge off-key notes to their proper place—as a form of robotic flair. Her voice curdles throughout the song, jumping from note to note artificially, as if she were a cyborg goddess with an augmented throat. Since then, vocoder and Auto-Tune have appeared across the spectrum of popular music genres. Rap mogul Kanye West used it as an emotional intensifier on his weepy 2008 album *808s & Heartbreak*; his frequent collaborator, the folk-rock musician turned electronic experimentalist Bon Iver, laced his falsetto through Auto-Tune even before he traded his acoustic guitar for a suite of synths.

In 2006, the Swedish synthpop duo the Knife released *Silent Shout*, a dark, icy dance record that makes extensive use of voice modulation. Though mostly unknown at the time, they had previously enjoyed an indirect bout of success: their 2002 single "Heartbeats" was covered in 2003 by the folk singer José González, and Sony used his version of the song in a popular ad for flatscreen TVs, netting the duo considerable royalties. But with *Silent Shout*, the Knife was able to enjoy success on their own terms.

It's a dense and thorny record, latticed with ghosts and yet so tuneful that it gets stuck in your head. *Silent Shout* calls back to the goth-pop pioneers of the '80s such as Siouxsie and the Banshees and the Cocteau Twins, but in singer Karin Dreijer's voice, it also offers something new. With the exception of one duet, "Marble House," there's only one singer on the album, and yet voices cascade across a multitude of ranges, both those generally heard as male and those considered female. Karin corrodes and mutates their voice throughout the record, constructing characters that play off each other in wiry dramas about sex, desire, and power. They'll inhabit an artificially shrill soprano on one song, then play a throaty baritone on the next. Often, these voices harmonize with each other, creating density and dimension against intricate synthesizer patterns.

Together with her brother Olof, Karin destabilized the traditional arrangements of electronic pop music. Because the Knife comprised a man and a nonbinary performer then perceived as a woman, certain male critics assumed that Karin's role was confined to the vocal booth while Olof handled the tricky man's job of working the machines. The "dean of American rock critics" Robert Christgau described Olof's synthesizer work as "cunning," while affixing the word "wacky" to Karin's "kiddie screech."[19] A

Pitchfork review of *Silent Shout*'s deluxe edition read, "Olof Dreijer worked his sister Karin Dreijer Andersson's vocals through sickly FX, making her nursery rhyme delivery sound like it was coming from the bottom of a slimy well."[20] It was easier to imagine a man modulating Karin's voice than to believe they were the one pitching themselves across octaves; tellingly, both writers consider Karin and not Olaf to be childlike, a passive and impulsive voice playing inside their brother's deliberate sound worlds. Then, in 2009, Karin released their debut solo album as Fever Ray. The first vocal note on the first track, "If I Had a Heart," vibrates at an artificially low pitch against a swampy drone of synthesizer. Karin, it seemed, was perfectly capable of shifting their own pitches and producing their own backing tracks.

Throughout the aughts, the Knife were notoriously press-shy, conducting few interviews and wearing theatrical masks to photoshoots and concerts. Few fans really knew what they looked like. But for the tour around their 2013 album *Shaking the Habitual*, a longer, looser record about deprogramming the subconscious habits that sustain capitalism, Karin and Olof shucked their masks. They recruited nine other band members, took singing lessons together, and worked with choreographers to put together a dance routine. All eleven members of the group costumed themselves in bright, shiny jumpsuits and glittery face paint, a mix of glam rock's irreverent getups and the colorful uniforms on *Star Trek*. In lieu of an opening act, the Knife booked queer performance artists to introduce the night, leading the crowd in an aerobics warmup and pep talk.[21] The show stood in stark opposition to the austere performances the two siblings had done as a duo. Suddenly, the Knife was in full color.

In 2014, I went to one of these shows at the Aragon Ballroom in Chicago. There was no indication at any point during the performance that Karin or Olof were unique among the performers. The group had no hierarchy. They moved fluidly, playing enormous, bizarre custom-made instruments and singing live or lip-syncing. Often, they danced without pretending to vocalize at all. The line between "live" musical performance and canned tracks blurred to the point that the former was no longer prioritized over the latter. The show left no space for us to fetishize a "real" voice. Any one of the performers could be emitting a sound at any time, or they could be making no sound at all. The point was not the construction of music in real time. The point was holding space with the audience, drawing them into the glittering world of the show.

Because the members of the Knife wore unisex costumes and similar makeup, the eye's urge to gender each individual body relaxed. The ear, having been trained on the band's electronic vocal treatments, had already let go of the impulse to assign genders to lungs and diaphragms and larynxes. The band, like the audience, was populous enough that discrete pitches bled together into a mass similar to the one Karin liked to simulate in the studio. And then the band stepped away from the microphones, and the chorus of voices remained, hovering above and around the performers' bodies.

The Knife did not play an encore. Instead, the house lights came up, and one member of the band stayed behind to play a closing DJ set. There was no hard snap back into the reality that lurked outside the venue. The audience danced, lingering in the glow left by the performance, holding space with each other, and slowly, eventually, trickling out into the night.

6

NOT A WOMAN, NOT A MAN

Prince's Sapphic Androgyny

It helped that he was short, with that forever-young face and those big doe eyes. He was short even for a woman, five foot two, well under the contemporary human average, this writer's exact height. It meant that he could wear heels and stand next to his female bandmates without towering over them. He wore heels not to achieve a domineering stature, not for power, and not for comedic effect. The shoes became him effortlessly, with grace, as if they were a natural extension of his skeleton, as if they had always been there.

Few artists have sustained such a totalizing androgyny for so long as Prince. The Minneapolis artist began making records at age eighteen, and even then he knew he needed total control over his sound, his look, his entire world. Prince Rogers Nelson signed a record deal with Warner Bros. when he was still a teenager, but he was hardly a baby wunderkind primed for exploitation. He knew what he wanted, and he would fight the industry's sleazy control tactics every step of the way to get it.

In the first seconds of his 1978 debut album, Prince launches his voice skyward to an incandescent femininity. While many male singers at the time used falsetto for emphasis, as a momentary break from a "normal" range, Prince flipped the template, casting falsetto as the primordial state of his voice. Drop the needle on *For You* for the first time, and Prince comes to you as an ethereal being—not a boy, not a girl, but something else.

When he signed a three-album deal with Warner, Prince insisted on complete creative control over his work, and the label gave it to him—a rarity among artists in general, to say nothing of a teenager from Minnesota who had yet to cut his teeth in the music business. Prince produced the minute-long opening title track of *For You*, layering his falsetto in waves, turning his delicate, expressive voice not just into a choir but into a full band. His bass notes wobble like a bass guitar would, and his trebles coalesce into what could pass for a celestial synthesizer. He introduced himself to the world not as a singer and songwriter but as a whole environment of elastic sound.

Throughout his prolific career, in the way he dressed, the way he held himself, and the way he sang, Prince chased androgyny. He called upon a rich tradition of black dandyism in the music business. Soul stars James Brown and Rick James both donned flamboyant, gender-defying outfits onstage throughout the '70s, wearing shiny, skin-tight jumpsuits or brightly colored blazers as they sang. George Clinton, Bootsy Collins, and other members of the funk ensemble Parliament-Funkadelic similarly took to the stage in fabulous getups, strapping on glittery angel wings and luxurious headdresses that complemented their music's Afrofuturism (during many of their shows in the '70s, a spaceship descended from the ceiling to escort the members of the band off the planet toward a brighter, funkier world). But these outfits were clearly costumes, breaks from reality enabled by the stage. Prince, by contrast, seemed to integrate femininity deep into his own reality, seemed to carry it with him wherever he went. His androgyny wasn't something he could toggle on and off. It seemed to be a part of who he was, reflected not only in his clothes but in his voice, mannerisms, and presence.

On the title track to his 1982 breakthrough album *1999*, Prince waits to sing. His bandmate Lisa Coleman issues the first line, followed by guitarist Dez Dickerson. Prince emerges as the third singer, and his voice synthesizes the voices of the woman and man who have gone before him. It has both the crimped strain of Lisa's delivery and the sulky grain of Dez's; it's not a man's voice or a woman's voice but a fusion of the qualities often associated with each. In every aspect of his career, Prince delighted in that fusion. He found spiritual and artistic transcendence in letting himself be two or more things at once, and he followed that multiplicity into some of the most arresting pop songs of the past fifty years.

In 1981, Prince opened for the Rolling Stones and the audience did not understand him. He took the stage at the LA Coliseum in a black bikini bottom and studded trench coat, the same getup he sports on the cover of the 1980 album *Dirty Mind*. He sang the way he sings: effeminately, with a bratty edge. Perhaps forgetting that Mick Jagger had worn a dress onstage some years back, the crowd threw bottles at Prince and screamed homophobic slurs. He got booed off the stage.[1]

The '80s, it seemed, had less room than the '60s for gender ambiguity. By that point, the Rolling Stones had already been folded into the catalog of acceptable masculinities; no longer androgynous provocateurs playing the blues in long hair and flamboyant clothing, they were simply men who played rock and roll the way men were supposed to. The stage, their stature, and their whiteness shielded them; they had lost all their danger. Prince, an effeminate black man who was fond at the time of wearing thigh-high stockings with half his ass out, made the Rolling Stones' fans squirm to the point of violence.

Prince was no stranger to slurs. Being small and effeminate all his life, and getting along more readily with girls than with boys as a kid, he had suffered homophobia through his childhood and teen years. His elementary school classmates were apparently fond of calling him "princess."[2] It seems he knew, even as a boy, that the only reason he was met with hostility was because there was a certain quality of power to his androgyny. Instead of shoring up masculinity, he doubled down on what made him feminine. Throughout his songs, he relates to women not as objects of conquest or distant points of yearning, but as kin: people whose femininity reflects his own. He is not drawn to women because they are different from him, because their gender accentuates his own by contrast. He gravitates to women because he feels he shares something of their essence.

In the 1979 single "I Wanna Be Your Lover," Prince enumerates the roles he would like to play for the woman to whom he's singing: "I wanna be your brother / I wanna be your mother and your sister, too," he offers. Perhaps unintentionally, he echoes a line from *My Antonia*, the 1918 novel by the queer and gender-blurring author Willa Cather, who in college went by "William" and dressed in men's clothes. "I'd have liked to have you for a sweetheart, or a wife, or my mother or my sister—anything a woman can be to a man," says the narrator of *My Antonia* to the eponymous character.[3] By listing the titles the English language offers for intimacy, both Prince and Cather reach for an intimacy without a name, a closeness too vast and elusive for a term such as "lover" or "sweetheart," both of which imply a union across difference. Heterosexual on its face—both the speaker of "I Wanna Be Your Lover" and the narrator of *My Antonia* are straight men—this desire ruptures the capsules into which human affection is typically forced. It's an intimacy beyond title or structure, a love that supersedes the words available to describe it.

This sapphic expression would permeate Prince's music and the visuals that accompanied it. In the 1984 film *Purple Rain*, the artist's theatrical debut, Prince plays the Kid, a character who struggles to reconcile the toxic masculinity he has inherited from his father with his feminine slant. The Kid has grown up watching his father physically abuse his mother, and so when he becomes involved with an aspiring singer named Apollonia, he lets his pent-up anger get the best of him. Apollonia, wanting to jumpstart her career, gets romantically involved with the manager of a local venue where the Kid also performs. Upon learning she has courted the manager's affections in order to join a girl group, the Kid hits her. It's not the movie's first scene of violence. There's a throw-away joke, shocking in its casual misogyny, where two men toss a woman in a dumpster because she is annoying them. Earlier, the Kid comes home after a show and walks in on his father beating his mother. He tries to separate them, and his father knocks him to the ground. In another movie with another star, the Kid might have leapt up and fought back. Instead, he lies where he lands, contemplating his pain. It's a feminine position, the same one we see Apollonia take later in the movie. In one encounter, the Kid is the feminized recipient of violence; in the next, he's the masculine perpetrator.[4]

The Kid's competitiveness and jealousy mark him as male throughout most of the film, but his movements and affect are ineffably girlish. He likes to peer coquettishly over huge sunglasses and strut around in high heels. He seems possessed of two opposing forces: the masculine, which tells him to dominate women and edge out other bands on the Minneapolis circuit, and the feminine, from which his music springs. Onstage, he physically mirrors his female bandmates in the Revolution, often wearing outfits similar to those of Wendy and Lisa, the guitarist and keyboardist who keep urging him to let the band perform a number they've written called "Purple Rain." Though they've undeniably penned the Revolution's best song, he shuts them down, fearful of ceding control over the band.

In one of *Purple Rain*'s more moving sequences, the Kid walks in on his father playing an original composition on the piano that had previously stood silent in their home. He had no idea his father wrote songs; he asks if he's written any down, and his father stubbornly asserts that he doesn't need to. Later, the Kid witnesses his father attempting suicide. The elder man survives a gunshot to the head, and after he has been taken to the hospital, the Kid throws a tantrum in the basement, smashing glassware and ripping up sheaves of paper. Then he realizes what's on the paper: music staves, dozens of them, signed with his father's name. There has been music in his father all along, bottled up and hidden under the masculine barbs he showed the world.

During the Revolution's first performance after his father's suicide attempt, the Kid plays "Purple Rain." He dedicates the song to his father, then launches into the emotional ballad, stunning the crowd. The moment subverts the trope of the rock star winning back the girl by expressing his true feelings in song. The Kid is not singing to Apollonia, and he has not even written the music that accompanies the film's climax. Instead of righting his narrative by seizing control and taking what's his, he lets himself slip, falling back into the collective instead of following his ego. He has already seen where that brittle road leads. By finally letting Wendy and Lisa get their shine, and crediting them with composing the song in his preamble, he loosens his clutch on the Revolution and himself. He lets go of his masculine impulse to use the band as a bolster and softens into feminine collaboration, one part of a greater whole. This transformation is reflected in the first lines of the song the band plays after "Purple Rain"—"I Would Die 4 U," which begins with a triplet that has since become emblematic of Prince's androgyny: "I'm not a woman / I'm not a man / I am something that you'll never understand." The Kid falls into neitherness and frees himself.

Prince embodied sapphic desire (wanting across sameness, not difference) throughout his career, but Wendy and Lisa's presence in the Revolution—the real band with the same name as the movie band—helped make that thematic lesbianism literal. Friends since childhood, the two women were girlfriends during their time as Prince's collaborators. Their butchy femme presence onstage in *Purple Rain* offered a glimpse of the Kid's genderfucked future, and their seductive exchange at the beginning of "Computer Blue" made subtext text. "Is the water warm enough?"

Lisa asks. "Yes, Lisa," Wendy responds. "Shall we begin?" "Yes, Lisa." Their voices are similar in pitch and timbre; whatever they are about to begin, they are beginning it as equals. Then the two women disappear, and Prince jealously butts in. "Where is my love life? / Where can it be? / There must be something wrong with the machinery," he sings, as if he's overheard Wendy and Lisa and wants a love life built on the same model.

In 1986, Prince released "Kiss," the lead single from his eighth album, *Parade*. It soared to number one on the *Billboard* Hot 100 and burned a hole in pop radio. Nothing else sounded like "Kiss." The song had no bassline, and the guitar sounded shredded, clipped, full of lacunae. Compared to its contemporaries, "Kiss" was only half a song, and yet it held together on the strength of Prince's indelible vocal melody, delivered in a tight falsetto.

The video for "Kiss" shows Prince dancing in the same buttoned crop top he wears on the cover of *Parade*, along with matching side-snap pants and high-heeled boots. Wendy sits on a stool in the same room playing a hollowbody guitar, an instrument that barely seems to correspond to any sound that appears in the mix. The two musicians sport the same haircut, a slicked-up pompadour, which unifies them visually, although gender signifiers scatter across the two bodies. Prince has the heels, the exposed midriff, and the patchy mustache; Wendy wields the phallic guitar and is fully clothed, but also wears bright red lipstick and dangling earrings.

There's a third figure in the video, a woman in a black bikini, dark glasses, and a sheer black veil who dances with Prince. When the singer drops out of falsetto to issue a low "yeah," she's shown lip-syncing it, a moment that at first causes Prince to look at the camera in mock confusion. Hers is the low voice and his is the high; in the last shot of the video, the woman approaches Prince from behind and kisses his shoulder while he sings the word "kiss" in his lower register. It's as if the two figures, who have danced around each other for the whole video, have merged, like they've stopped singing to each other and begun singing in the same voice.

Like Laurie Anderson, who performed the masculine alter ego Fenway Bergamot by electronically lowering her voice, Prince developed a gender-swapped character through the use of pitch shifting. Her name was Camille, and Prince recorded her debut self-titled album in 1986, intending to release it without any indication that he was the one behind the microphone. Like much of Prince's work, the project was ultimately scrapped, though a few of the album's songs later appeared on the 1987 LP *Sign O' the Times*. "Housequake," "Strange Relationship," and "If I Was Your Girlfriend" all boast Camille's voice, which features the texture of Prince's baritone transposed up to a pitch that might have come from a throat unaffected by testosterone.

In the album's liner notes, Prince credited lead vocals on those songs to Camille. She also appeared on a newer track, "U Got the Look," where she playfully duets with Sheena Easton. "I never seen such a pretty girl look so tough," sings Camille, and Sheena enthusiastically responds: "Baby!" Their voices intertwine, circling each other at a similar pitch. Though Camille's voice sounds technologically manipulated—a little compressed, a little mousy—it negotiates a sisterly relationship with Sheena's. "U Got the Look" is not the story of a man singing to a woman, but two women singing to each other, closing the space between their voices and their bodies, appreciating both each other's beauty and each other's strength. As Prince's feminine alter ego, Camille could say and do the things that were closed off to him as a man.

Prince's sapphic genderplay crystallizes on "If I Was Your Girlfriend." "If I was your girlfriend / Would you remember to tell me all the things you forgot / When I was your man?" Camille asks in her lithe mezzo. "If I was your best friend / Would you let me take care of you and do all the things / That only a best friend can?" By crediting the song to an unknown performer with a female name, Prince entertained the idea of Camille traversing genders: she was a woman who at some point could have claimed to be "your man." But "man" hides in the past tense in the song's lyrics, an identity abandoned for its limitations. As a male lover, Camille was excluded from certain rites of intimacy she deeply desires throughout the song: helping her girlfriend get dressed, crying at movies together, bathing and tickling each other. She craves both sisterhood and romance with her lover, a kind of intimacy that strays from heteronormative scripts. Being half of a straight couple is not enough. She wants to participate in her girlfriend's whole world, not just the parts deemed suitable for consumption through a male lens.

For Prince, a male identity was a barrier to complete intimacy. In his music and his stage presence, he softened himself, closing the space that separated him from women. Androgyny marked a channel of free expression and free love, a liquid space where Prince could not only desire women but adopt those features he desired at the same time. "Prince posed himself as a human question mark, a mystery creature who could not be contained by conventional categories, someone whose very being transgressed and transcended any division or boundary that stood in the way of total emancipation," wrote critic Simon Reynolds after the star's death in 2016.[5]

Prince adopted a symbol much more apt than the question mark. It appears in an early form in *Purple Rain*, adorning the Kid's purple motorcycle (and occasionally appearing as ambient graffiti): a Venus symbol mixed with a Mars one, a circle and an arrow and a cross all in one. Though the beginning lines of "I Would Die 4 U" suggest an identity constructed by negation—not a woman and not a man—the symbol implied a way of being that combined both male and female attributes. Prince wanted it all. Later, he would add to the symbol, crossing it at the center with a horn. "The new identifier was a combination of male and female signs. The horn part suggested a kind of fusion through music," wrote critic Joseph Vogel.[6]

Copyrighted as "Love Symbol #2," the glyph would, for fourteen years, serve as Prince's unpronounceable name after a dispute with his record label edged him into a combative corner. Warner Bros. wanted Prince to slow down his release rate so as not to oversaturate the market with his albums. Prince had no interest in toning down his output, and so to troll both the label and the world, he rescinded his lifelong moniker in favor of a symbol that could not be spoken or typed. By taking the glyph as his name, Prince insisted on the challenge of his presence. He was not just male and female at the same time; he was both and then some, a third category whose abundance spilled over the binary.

He frequently displayed the symbol onstage. It popped up in his lighting rigs in the '90s, and when he performed at the 2007 Super Bowl halftime show, he played a custom-made purple guitar in the shape of his glyph—an overt symbol of androgyny searing into the most masculine entertainment event in America. Prince floated the idea that a third-gender identity could be a form of plenty, not failure or lack. The horn crossing the Venus and Mars symbols resembles a cornucopia as well as an instrument. By refusing to box himself in, Prince let himself explore a creative field far broader than the space he would have been allowed if he had conformed to just one gender. His gender transgressions were inseparable from his creative profusion. He made music in order to refuse all possible limitations.

Unlike Bowie, who switched costumes from album to album and distanced himself from his stage characters by naming them, Prince drew no hard line between his stage presence and his inner self, to the extent that the public was allowed to know him. When he wasn't going by Love Symbol #2, he used the name his parents gave him. He wore purple so devoutly that he has become synonymous with a particular shade. He was singularly and resolutely amorphous, layering himself in plain view, building a mythos rather than adopting and discarding personae. Bowie had many names and faces, but Prince was always Prince.

In her poem "Minneapolipstick," Rachel McKibbens recounts watching *Purple Rain* covertly on TV with her cousins at 3:00 a.m. In the Kid and Apollonia's relationship, she sees a window into her own budding queerness; finally, there's a name and a face to reflect her forbidden desires, a couple marked by their matching eyeliner and doe-eyed naïveté. "Your / falsetto gospel rang our young / queer souls awake," she writes.[7] The poem is split into numbered quarters. The most concise and most resonant, truest to its subject, is part three, which in its entirety reads: "Boys will be boys, unless they aren't."

7

THE FAKE MAKES IT REAL

Synthpop and MTV

At the end of Sally Potter's 1992 film *Orlando*, a young girl sees an angel through a camera lens. She is running around a field with a camcorder while her mother, the eponymous character, sits beneath a tree. Hearing music, Orlando looks up. She begins to cry quietly, and her daughter runs over to ask why she's sad. "I'm not," Orlando replies. "I'm happy. Look. Look up there." Her daughter points the camera to the sky and sees an angel hovering in a gold lamé gown, aloft on gleaming, motionless wings, singing. "I am coming, I am coming / Here I am / Neither a woman nor a man," the angel announces in a celestial falsetto. We only ever see the angel through the child's camera. Then there's a cut, and Orlando, played by Tilda Swinton, shifts her gaze from the angel to the viewer, acknowledging our presence in this moment through joyful tears.[1]

During the first act of the film and the 1928 Virginia Woolf novel on which it is based, Orlando is a young nobleman. One day, the character wakes from a long sleep to discover she has transformed into a woman, and, unbothered by the development, sets about reordering her life accordingly. Possessed of an incredible longevity, Orlando drifts through centuries somewhat apart from the world, living outside its usual narrative cycles. She has miraculously changed genders and does not seem to age or die, so society's scripts become irrelevant to her. In the movie's closing moment, it seems she has at last found another like her, a being whose androgyny marks them as holy, at once part of the world and above it. That the angel is only seen through the lens of a video camera implies that technology plays a key role in the androgynous apparition's presence.

The voice of the angel belongs to Jimmy Somerville, the Scottish singer best known for fronting the synthpop group Bronski Beat, whose debut single "Smalltown Boy" became a global hit (top ten in the UK and number forty-eight on the Billboard Hot 100). On the only album he made with the band, 1984's *The Age of Consent*, Somerville uses his powerful falsetto to articulate queer desire and the threats from the straight world that follow it. The album begins with a syllable launched skyward with tremendous force: "Tell me *WHY*?" Somerville asks in the song "Why." "Contempt in your eyes when I turn to kiss his lips / Broken I lie, all my feelings denied, blood on your fist / Can you tell me why?" A fast disco beat pulses anxiously behind his words, and between lines a square-wave synthesizer squeals. Throughout the song, Somerville never breaks from his falsetto, the "false" voice above what's considered a typical male vocal range. Even as he's singing about violent homophobes, he maintains his femininity. At the bridge, he turns the focus of the "you" from the homophobic aggressor to the lover for whom the aggressor seeks to punish him: "You and me together / Fighting for our love" he repeats eight times, then projects a wordless vowel, a blissful "ooh!," at the very top of his range—a moment of temporary triumph.

No longer a novel accessory draped over rock arrangements, synthesizers saturated pop music in the 1980s. They were the only instruments heard on certain albums, thanks to the pioneering efforts of artists such as Wendy Carlos, Bob Moog, Giorgio Moroder, and Kraftwerk, who saw the future in computer music. Expressions of vocal androgyny similarly abounded on the pop charts, many coming from queer musicians. Bands including Soft Cell, Erasure, and Frankie Goes to Hollywood built gay phantasmagorias atop disco's liberatory backbeats, while women singers including Annie Lennox and Grace Jones asymptotically approached masculinity both in how they sounded and how they looked.

Many of these bands hailed from the United Kingdom, maybe because Europe was more eager to embrace the strange new sounds of the synthesizer. Musicologist Louis Niebur theorized that American audiences were skeptical of synths in the '70s; they "considered electronic sound queer, other or European—as opposed to the electric guitar, which is the male sound."[2] The synth-based subgenre Italo-disco was popular in the United States toward the end of the '70s, but it also caused remarkable backlash among people—mostly men—who considered computer music to be "fake" since it didn't come out of a recognizable instrument. You can watch a guitarist's fingers on a fretboard and see, more or less, where each individual note comes from. It's harder to look at someone twiddling knobs on a Moog and make the same connection between movement and sound.

Disco, new wave, and synthpop embraced artifice, rejecting the rockist assumption that music needed to be authentic to be good. By embracing the artificial sounds of the synth, these genres supplied the perfect staging grounds for queer and gender-blurring performances. As a primary instrument, the synthesizer confounds the ear. The listener cannot locate a body behind the sound of a synthesizer. Its music does not result from vibrations rumbling through a wooden hollow, a brass tube, or a human throat; the synthesizer instead transforms electricity or data directly into sound waves. The artificiality of the instrument colors the human voice, dislodging it from its usual acoustic setting and placing it in a futuristic dreamscape. Hearing a voice singing inside a synthesized environment throws the provenance of the voice into question: If nothing in the song emanates from a body, is the voice still real? Does it come from a person with a gendered body, or has it been untethered, like the synthesizer, from traditional systems of meaning?

In 1978, a German singer named Klaus Nomi performed at an event called New Wave Vaudeville at the Irving Plaza theater in New York. Amid a lineup of comedic and outrageous acts by members of the local club scene, Nomi showed up in a clear plastic cape and slashes of glittery eye makeup to sing the mezzo-soprano aria "Mon cœur s'ouvre à ta voix" from Camille Saint-Saëns's 1877 opera *Samson and Delilah.* His voice, a poised countertenor, shocked the crowd, who had been primed on lip-synced sets and comedy sketches throughout the night. It was as if a woman were singing through the body of a man; Nomi's bone structure and receding hairline marked him as someone who had lived through a testosteronized puberty, but the voice sounded like it issued from unchanged vocal cords. The evening's MC "had to come out and say, 'This is not an electrical recording. He's actually singing,'" recalled songwriter Kristian Hoffman, who would go on to compose many of Nomi's original pop songs. "People didn't believe it."[3]

Initially trained as a tenor, Nomi developed the higher end of his stunning range while taking voice lessons in New York. "We worked really on his tenor voice, which was lovely. And I used the falsetto, which was obviously *there,* to help the top of the tenor voice," said his instructor, Ira Staff. "But he was really interested in working the falsetto, and I just thought he'd end up brokenhearted because there was no context for using your falsetto voice those days. There was no countertenor career, which is huge now in baroque opera. There was no way really to use it except for private sport and fun."[4]

On New York's underground performance circuit, Nomi's voice took on a life of its own. He garnered a cult following; no one else could sing like him, and his unique, otherworldly stage presence set him apart from the rest of the new wave, though he shared the movement's predilection for retrofuturist aesthetics. He loved plastic clothes, sharp angles, and dramatic stage lights, all of which contributed to his extraterrestrial presence.

Not long after the New Wave Vaudeville performance, David Bowie caught wind of Nomi's astonishing talent and hired him as a backup singer and dancer for his 1979 appearance on *Saturday Night Live*.[5] Bowie played "TVC-15" that night, dressed in a purple skirt suit. He also revisited an older song, the title track from his 1970 album *The Man Who Sold the World*. For that performance, he donned a stiff plastic suit with a single conjoined leg, a garment so restrictive he could not walk in it. Nomi and his frequent collaborator Joey Arias instead carried the star to the microphone at the beginning of the song and removed him from the lip of the stage at its conclusion.

The costume suits the song. Bowie sings "The Man Who Sold the World" from the perspective of someone meeting a man who has become completely alienated by power. The speaker thinks the man "died alone / A long, long time ago," to which the eponymous character responds, "Oh no / Not me / I never lost control." The song's lyrics are sparse enough to be ambiguous, but the man's thirst for money and power implies a brittle masculinity. He has faded to obscurity, and no one even knows he is still alive, but he has held on to a sense of domination over the rest of the world, which sustains him.

Bowie's plastic suit fleshes out the character; he wears a symbol of masculinity so rigid and well defined that it immobilizes him. His voice—a firm, authoritative bark that stands in contrast to the sly nasal delivery heard on the 1970 studio version—completes the effect. Behind him, Nomi and Arias sing high harmonies, their voices as flexible as their bodies are in high-necked dresses and leggings.

Nomi loved the dramatics of Bowie's plastic suit so much that he tried to buy one of his own. He found he could only afford half of the getup, so he commissioned the stiff, triangular tuxedo top that would become his trademark costume. The outfit restricted his movement to some degree—he would wear it to TV interviews only to find he could not sit down in the provided seat—but it left his legs untethered. He wore black leggings under the garment, which emphasized the contrast between the organic curves of his body and the hard angles of the tux. The leggings also feminized him, making the distended masculinity of the suit top look all the more absurd.

Nomi wears the tux in the video for "Lightning Strikes," a cover of a single released by Lou Christie in 1966. The original song features Christie singing with a handful of female backing vocalists, who emphasize intermittent words throughout the verse. At the chorus, Christie leaps up to meet them in harmony; he's singing high for a man and straining to maintain his true voice instead of breaking into his falsetto. The speaker has become so enamored of a woman that he must sing as high as he can, mirroring his heightened emotional state with a taxing physical feat. The high voice does not come naturally to Christie; he has been pushed there by extenuating circumstances.

In his cover, Nomi alters the song's vocal narrative. He has no backup singers—he performs the occasional interjections himself. In the verses, he sounds restrained, almost deadpan; he's half-speaking, half-singing the words, making no attempt to mask his German accent. Instead of sounding comfortable and easy in the lower part of the melody like Christie, he sounds bored, sometimes petulant. The chorus is where things get exciting. With no strain and no difficulty, Nomi vaults into his countertenor, singing the notes with indulgent vibrato. The lightning that strikes does not mark the consummation of a heterosexual flirtation—no woman sings with Nomi—but the opportunity for him to flaunt his own femininity. He ends each pre-chorus section with a growl or a scream, like he's ready to cast off his stuffy lower register and soar through the high notes. His tenor sounds claustrophobic, but his countertenor is liquid and free.

Like Bowie did during the Ziggy Stardust years, Nomi tethered his androgyny to an extraterrestrial fiction. His stage name referred to an imaginary alien species of whom he was a member; a song he wrote himself, "Keys of Life," declared the aliens' benevolent intentions. "We came from outer space / To save the human race / From lies and from corruption / From death and from destruction," he sings in a 1979 live performance of the track.[6] His own prerecorded vocals repeat the song's title behind him, as if he were not a singular Nomi but the leader of a whole squadron of angelic-voiced visitors. "The future has begun," he asserts. Behind him, a synthesizer squiggles chaotically, calling to mind the machine's history as a producer of sci-fi sound effects before Wendy Carlos and Bob Moog helped adapt it to music. No acoustic instruments can be heard in the performance, only a drum machine, a synth or two, and Nomi's multiple voices. He and his cohort rise from an alien landscape, promising humanity's salvation.

Nomi tended to perform wearing angular black lipstick and streaks of eyeshadow across his browbone. His face was whited out and his thinning hair spiked. If he didn't appear in his plastic tuxedo, he would appear in another alien approximation of human dress, like a clear plastic cloak with a comically high collar. In 1982, an interviewer on a French talk show asked why Nomi liked to hide behind such striking makeup. The singer responded: "I'm not really hiding, I'm showing out, because the way I am it's hard to look like a normal person. . . . When I was a kid, people always said I looked strange, and it made me feel very unhappy. And all of a sudden I go on stage, and people like me for that."[7]

Onstage, Nomi played up his strangeness. He looked wide-eyed around the room while singing; never smiling, he moved his head and arms robotically, as if scanning for some indication of how he should behave as a visitor on earth. He played his alien persona with moving innocence. In contrast with David Bowie's knowing, savvy rock-and-roll star from outer space, Nomi embodied a vulnerable outsider who wanted to assist humankind but couldn't quite find a way into their ranks. "His level of androgyny [was] not just the androgyny of the sexuality, but the androgyny of . . . whether you're human or not," said photographer Anthony Scibelli.[8] "This was an androgyny beyond androgyny, where he became robot-like." Ann Magnuson, a performance artist working in New York at the same time as Nomi, added, "He really seemed like a creature from another dimension."[9]

"It was said about you that you were either the eighth wonder of the world, or a tragic accident of nature," said the French interviewer. "What do you think of this definition?" Nomi smiled. "Well, that sounds wonderful," he replied. "It sounds extraordinary. I hope it's true."

In 1984, Nomi became one of the first publicly known figures to die from complications from AIDS, a disease that had been ravaging gay communities in the United States for years but was still poorly understood by doctors and the public alike. He died completely isolated, as no one yet knew precisely how the disease was spread and his friends feared contagion. By the time of his death, the camp and artifice of new wave had already begun to reverberate on the pop charts. Nomi's musical inclinations—androgynous vocals leaping through electronic sound environments—outlived him. A handful of like-minded pop musicians had seized on the freedom offered by flexible, outlandish vocalizing and wholly synthesized instrumentation. They carried his otherworldly and beautiful sound through the rest of the decade and beyond.

The falsetto had precedence in pop music by the time synthpop began to frost the radio with its utopian sheen. Singer Freddie Mercury had used the upper edge of his abundant range to connote flights of fancy and melodrama with Queen, though his voice rode the heft of its rock band setting, the sole otherworldly figure in an otherwise worldly scene. His voice implied queerness without confirming it; his stage presence rested on the rock front man's established position as a flamboyant provocateur, a role that insinuated a break from heterosexual norms without necessarily pinning the singer as gay (he was, in fact, bisexual). But, unlike Mick Jagger or David Bowie, Mercury had the range. He slung himself toward the upper reaches of the atmosphere, exploiting all the comedy, thrill, and drama of his multi-octave voice.

Michael Jackson, who had released solo albums throughout the '70s and whose first album of the '80s, *Thriller*, became the world's best-selling LP within a year, used his own falsetto to negotiate an uneasy truce between his history as a child star with the Jackson Five and his overwhelmingly popular solo act. Though he was twenty-four when he released *Thriller*, Jackson still often sang like an adolescent, a boy with a high, gentle voice trying on masculine gruffness for size, the inverse of Mercury's breaks from manliness. His full-grown childlike demeanor complicated Jackson's gender; as Francesca T. Royster wrote in *Sounding Like a No-No*, "through his cries, whispers, groans, whines, and grunts, Jackson occupies a third space of gender, one that often undercuts his audience's expectations of erotic identification."[10] Though both artists sowed gender-confounding vocal expressions into the pop charts, Jackson and Mercury consistently bounded the feminine edges of their range with retreats into their lower, coarser registers. Many synthpop front men, by contrast, tended to sweep themselves up into a high, delicate voice without apology, grounding, or excuse.

An early synthpop hit came from the UK duo Soft Cell. "Tainted Love," a cover of an obscure B-side originally recorded by Gloria Jones in 1964, married the original's soulful melodies to the neon-stained and futuristic sounds of synthesizers. The song shot up to number one on the UK charts and hung around for nearly a year on the *Billboard* Hot 100, where it peaked at number eight. "Tainted Love" stood out as one of the tamer offerings on Soft Cell's debut album *Non-Stop Erotic Cabaret*, which included such kinky numbers as "Sex Dwarf." Curiously, the duo's lead singer, Marc Almond, got involved with the UK's industrial scene after he had already become a pop star. He collaborated with Coil, the band made up of Throbbing Gristle's Peter "Sleazy" Christopherson and his boyfriend, John Balance, on their 1984 debut EP *How to Destroy Angels*. In 1985, Almond appeared in the video for Coil's own demonic cover of "Tainted Love," which took Soft Cell's poppy flourishes and transmogrified them into haunted tubular bells and tortured, buzzing synthesizers. Coil's "Tainted Love" was the first record whose proceeds were donated to AIDS research. Gay communities were being ravaged by a plague that people in power preferred to ignore, and the gut-quaking sounds of the cover spoke directly to the chronic feeling of terror that hung in the air at the time.

Coil's version of the single, released on their own imprint Force & Form in the UK and on the Chicago-based industrial label Wax Trax! in the US, didn't touch the charts. The two versions of "Tainted Love"—the danceable hit and the soul-crushing dirge—highlight the duality of gay experience during the synth-pop era. On one hand, more openly gay musicians were sending euphoric pop hits to the top of the charts than ever before. On the other, gay men were dying of a hellish disease for which there was no cure. Mainstream synthpop supplied an avenue of escape from the fear that hounded gay communities at the time.

The heightened, unreal feeling that synthesizers poured into pop songs enabled a certain levity and playfulness among 1980s songwriters, despite all the horrors that were going on in real life. In what critics dubbed the Second British Invasion, a legion of UK pop bands started conquering the American charts. The Human League's "Don't You Want Me Baby?" and A Flock of Seagulls' "I Ran" both enjoyed huge success across the pond from the bands' native England, no doubt due in part to their outlandish music videos. The music channel MTV launched on August 1, 1981, and its video jockeys (VJs) soon picked up on the outrageousness of British new wave bands.

"Next to the prosaic, foursquare appearance of the American bands, such acts as Duran Duran seemed like caviar. MTV opened up a whole new world that could not be fully apprehended over the radio," wrote Parke Puterbaugh in a 1983 issue of *Rolling Stone*. "The visual angle played to the arty conceits of Britain's young style barons, suggesting something more exotic than the viewer was likely to find in the old hometown."[11]

Many UK bands also found that they could provoke and delight US listeners by poking at good old-fashioned sex taboos. Frankie Goes to Hollywood was one band that found success with such a strategy. The group's 1983 debut single "Relax" centers front man Holly Johnson's mischievous voice as he sings about the joys of bringing oneself to orgasm. A pounding, slapped bassline keeps the beat on a single note; the song doesn't move through chord changes so much as it gradually increases the intensity of a sparse arrangement punctuated by a three-note guitar riff and splashes of synthesized horns.

In the more scandalous of the song's multiple videos, set in a gay fetish bar, the synthesizer sound is accompanied at one point by the image of a man blowing a giant fanfare trumpet. The comically large horn obviously does not produce the electronic tone heard on the track, but the dissonance between sound and sight accentuates the strangeness of the video's setting. A gay bar represents a break from mundane reality. Johnson enters the space in an oversized suit and tie, a square among kinksters. As the video progresses, he's eventually thrown onto the stage inside the bar; freed from his usual context, he sheds the suit jacket and joins an orgy, using his tie to leash a man crawling on all fours. The unreality of the synth sound provided an escape hatch for people watching these taboo acts unfold. Because this gay orgy was not "really" happening—because the presence of artificial music detached the scene from even a filmic reality—Frankie Goes to Hollywood could visibly indulge in flamboyant kink and (more or less) get away with it. (The song and its videos were ultimately banned in the UK after somebody at the BBC realized what Johnson meant by the word "come.")

The success of synthpop songs like "Relax," which leapt to number one on the UK singles charts in January 1984, made room for a plethora of glittery, high-voiced expressions of queerness, many of them more utopian than deliberately provocative. Erasure's 1988 single "A Little Respect" begins, like "Tainted Love," with a dysfunctional relationship. But instead of gritting his teeth and weathering the storm or pledging to leave the couple like Almond did, singer Andy Bell makes a bid for mutuality. He asks his partner for "a little respect" at the chorus, and as he does, his voice lifts off into his falsetto, as if modeling the relationship's potential for change. He wants freedom and joy within his partnership, and he knows it's possible: just listen to how free his voice can get. With his dazzling falsetto, Bell hollows out a pocket of reality where the straight world can't get to him.

MTV marked a sea change in the way music was consumed in the '80s. Unlike performance programs such as *Top of the Pops*, music videos aired on MTV did not need to situate their performers in front of a microphone. They could be fantasies in miniature, four-minute dramas divorced from the conceit of the live show but softer and more liquid than narrative-based short films. They could open windows into a reality more colorful and faster-paced than ordinary untelevised experience.

In the video for their 1982 single "Time (Clock of the Heart)," UK pop band Culture Club (led by lifelong androgyne Boy George) playfully exposed the artifice of the synthpop song and its accompanying videos. The band tracks the song in the recording studio, then performs the single on television, cameras and technicians in full view. Boy George's made-up face flashes on a wall of TV screens tracking the performance. Finally, the band waits eagerly in a living room decorated for Christmas to see themselves on TV. Their video comes on-screen, and each member of the band clicks his own remote to see his face glowing from the tube. Each musician, having seen himself broadcast, drinks gleefully from a mug printed with his name. By appearing on television, the members of Culture Club have been made real: transmitted, amplified, named.

British rock band Dire Straits released a single in 1985 that would similarly dramatize the transportive effect of the music video. Though it's not a synthpop song, "Money for Nothing" is one of the few '80s hits to call out MTV by name. The lyrics stage an exchange between two men working in an appliance store, balking at the spectacle of the music videos spangled across their television displays. "That little faggot with the earring and the makeup / Yeah, buddy, that's his own hair / That little faggot got his own jet airplane / That little faggot, he's a millionaire," stews front man Mark Knopfler in character as a blue-collar laborer bitter at the apparent ease of the androgynous musician's job. "That ain't working," he scoffs—as in that's not a real job that real men do; that's singing, a girl thing. All the pop star does is show up, sing into a microphone, and play guitar, work that demands little compared to the physically taxing job of installing microwaves, fridges, and TVs. The musician performs feminized labor in public, earning "money for nothing / chicks for free," and earning the scorn of men performing more traditional masculinity off-screen.

If Knopfler's character is loudly disgruntled, then a secondary vocal character played by Sting, the front man of the UK new wave band the Police, voices the magnetism of the music video's glamour. "I want my MTV," he repeats in falsetto during the preamble of "Money for Nothing." With thin, high harmonies, he serves as Knopfler's foil: a man who doesn't dismiss the musicians on TV, but feels viscerally drawn to them. The music videos he sees offer escapism from his boring everyday work, and he willingly submits to their flash. Sting's enthusiasm turns out to be contagious. Even Knopfler, in all his laconic gruffness, makes it through his slur-filled tirade and admits pangs of envy: "I should have learned to play the guitar / I should have learned to play them drums," he concludes wistfully.

The video for the song itself makes use of early computer animation to highlight a stark existential contrast between the televised existence of the musicians and the mundane lives of the manual laborers. The two men speaking to each other in an appliance store appear as low-polygon animated characters: blocky, awkward, and crudely rendered. The band on TV, played by Dire Straits, gets to enjoy photorealism, though their appearances are slashed through with animated color, as if heightened by their presentation on a screen. The rich, famous musicians splashed across the store's TVs move and look like people. The two workers are bound by the limits of the nascent technology animating them.

Within the frame of the video, the workers are the ones who exist in "real" space versus television space, but their existence is obviously the flimsier of the two. TV is where people look real, whole, and powerful, with a full range of motion. No wonder Sting wants in. His and Knopfler's voices even lilt at the chorus when they mention the appliance: "We've got to move these color TVs," they sing in harmony, their voices rising together as if realizing the magic potential of the heavy box in their hands.

In 1980, a year before the French philosopher Jean Baudrillard published his influential text *Simulacra and Simulation*, arguing that for all intents and purposes material reality had been replaced by a copy of itself, Jamaican singer Grace Jones removed a lifelike mask of her own face in the video for her single "Private Life." A cover of a song from British-American rock band the Pretenders' first album, Jones's rendition rehomes the reggae composition. Pretenders' front woman Chrissie Hynde sang the tune as an outsider to reggae, a white American trying on the genre for size. Jones, having grown up in Jamaica's Spanish Town, knew reggae well. The cover fit, even though the song's lyrics were hostile to authenticity. "I'm very superficial, I hate everything official," sneers Jones. "Sentimental gestures only bore me to death." At the start of the '80s, the open embrace of artificiality held more intrigue than baring one's soul—thus the mask, which in the video Jones takes off to reveal an unfeeling, mask-like expression underneath. Of the two faces she wears, the literal mask is ultimately the more convincing.

As early as 1977, Jones, a former model, made it clear that she had no investment in the "naturalness" of her performance. During an appearance on the Dutch music program *TopPop*, similar to the UK's *Top of the Pops*, she lip-syncs like a drag queen, making no effort to convince the audience that she's really singing. Instead, she relishes the artifice of the show.[12] Her hair cropped close, wearing a shiny pink gown, gleaming lipstick, and bracelets that wrap both her forearms in metal, she mouths along to "La Vie En Rose," an Édith Piaf cover that became one of her first hits. The microphone is a little too short for her, and she frequently throws her head back without affecting the volume of the voice heard through the speakers. Her body clearly does not produce the voice, but she is animated by it. She enjoys the sound of herself just as her audience might; she's just as detached from the voice as anyone else who can hear it.

Many of the songs Jones has recorded throughout her career are cover songs. She has never treated her position as a singer as an opportunity to share her inner life with the world, but as a chance to perform fabulously, to put on a show for the sake of a show. Her androgynous voice and appearance accentuate her music's sense of artificiality; she often looks not like a woman but like a tall, thin robot, a genderless being imported from science fiction.

In reality, Jones has felt deeply androgynous since childhood. She was close to her brothers as a kid, and she identified more with their masculinity than with the femininity she was told she should carry. One brother in particular, Chris, was especially feminine for a boy, and their complementary gender mismatch deepened their bond. "I was born a little more masculine, a girl with some of the boyness Chris lacked," wrote Jones in her 2015 memoir. "And he had some of the girliness I didn't have."[13] Jones recalled going with her brother to gay clubs once they were both adults, spaces where she adopted mannerisms she would later use in her work. She felt at home there. "I'd go with him to the clubs. Being tangled up, having some of the man in me, I loved that. The man in me—as well as the girl—loved men!" she wrote. "I felt I was among my own even as I was so far removed."[14]

After navigating a rocky but ultimately successful career in modeling, Jones tried her hand at music, even as she felt alienated from the way her voice sounded. "I never believed in it as a voice," she wrote. "It was very deep and manly—it sounded like it was coming from another person."[15] In time, she warmed to how she sang and recorded three disco albums at the end of the '70s. Her debut single, originally released in 1975 on the French label Orfeus, was "I Need a Man," an original song that "became an unofficial gay national anthem."[16] As a masculine woman, Jones could sing explicitly about wanting to have sex with a man, opening up a channel of identification for gay men who felt the same desire but had a harder time saying it out loud. Her deep voice and physical androgyny made her a perfect avatar for subterranean queer sentiment at a time when there was still a strong taboo against homosexuality.

Jones's first album of the '80s, 1980's *Warm Leatherette*, was also the first to feature a record cover shot by her boyfriend at the time, photographer and graphic designer Jean-Paul Goude. Goude would go on to produce many of the most iconic images of Jones. On the cover of the 1981 album *Nightclubbing*, she wears a sharp flattop and a suit jacket with exaggerated shoulders; a cigarette hangs at a perfect right angle down from the line of her mouth. She's all straight lines and hard geometry, the organic curves of the human body obscured. Her 1985 album *Slave to the Rhythm* distends her image even further. Goude created the striking cover by cutting up and stacking multiple photos of Jones's face, extending her open mouth into a carnivorous yawp. She looks genderless and then some; neither a man nor a woman, she might not even be human. Her stiff, robotic physicality mirrored Klaus Nomi's, though Jones's manifestation of science fiction androgyny had more barbs. She may have been an alien like Nomi, but she never once proclaimed herself the savior of the human species.

If Nomi and other male synthpop artists used androgyny to fixate on utopianism, then Jones saw gender-blurring performance as an opportunity to interrogate masculine authority. As an androgynous woman, she could parody masculinity from just outside its borders. She enjoyed covering songs originally recorded by men; the title track to *Nightclubbing* initially appeared on Iggy Pop's 1977 album *The Idiot*, a collaboration with David Bowie. Pop's version is a sleazy, humorous romp through the mind of a disaffected partygoer, who encounters all kinds of stimulation out in the clubs but whose voice never expresses an inkling of excitement. In her cover, Jones exaggerates the speaker's sense of detachment. She introduces a regular vibrato to the vocals and sings over a sparse dub beat, pronouncing every word as if in all caps. She's a more technically proficient singer than Iggy, but she uses that skill to remove herself further from the nightlife she describes.

If "Nightclubbing" is a song about roughing it through the underbelly of a thriving city, then vibrato makes for a strangely formal vocal strategy. Jones recounts the evening's events cleanly, with skill but without emotion, a robot among ghosts. As a woman, she might be expected to use a pop song as a conduit for raw feeling. The week *Nightclubbing* came out, pop singers Kim Carnes and Juice Newton had singles in the top ten of the Hot 100 with "Bette Davis Eyes" and "Angel of the Morning," respectively—both love songs centered on dynamic, sincere, emotional vocals. Instead, Jones used "Nightclubbing" to bask in and intensify the apathy Iggy Pop and David Bowie got to enjoy as men. She wasn't a female avatar for emotional outpourings, but an androgynous beacon of cool, gathered power.

In the video for "Demolition Man," a song written by Sting that also appeared on *Nightclubbing*, Jones wears a suit similar to the one on the album's cover paired with low-heeled pumps. At first, she moves inhumanly fast, like a wind-up toy, dancing in circles under a spotlight on an empty stage to a smattering of cheers. Presumably this is a concert—the video was assembled using footage taken from Jones's 1981 *A One Man Show* tour—but the viewer is not shown an audience, and Jones's dance appears to be possible only through the illusion of time-lapse photography. She picks up a trombone, readies it, aims it at the ceiling. She blows into it, but the only sound that comes out is like a car skidding off a highway at ninety miles per hour. The lights kick up fiery. The clamor dies down, and the bass comes in.

Jones posts up on a large staircase, crouching and still. "I'm a walking disaster / I'm a demolition man," she sneers in a guttural voice, jerking her head around and glaring at her audience. From nowhere, a whole army of Grace Joneses begin goose-stepping across the stage, all wearing the same suit and heels, all in sunglasses and gleaming lipstick. The moment she declares herself a man armed with the capacity for destruction, Jones multiplies. She becomes a uniform, like a cop or a soldier. She is not an individual but a mass made powerful by bulk and repetition, turning her idiosyncratic appearance into a repeatable stamp. By mimicking the mechanism of dominance used by the state and its militia, Jones opens a peephole into its workings. Cops aren't individually powerful, but serve as symbols of the weight of the machine behind them. The point of cops is that a cop always looks like a cop, never like a person. Copying herself by the dozen, Jones conjures up her own mechanism of masculine power. "I'm nobody's friend," she bellows. "I'm a demolition man!"

In the video for "My Jamaican Guy," collected with "Demolition Man" on the 1982 *A One Man Show* video compilation, Jones enjoys a more intimate encounter with one of her clones.[17] The camera closely frames the singer's face in full makeup: the sort of colorful and dramatic look that a drag queen might wear to a show. Jones shouts, and then the camera cuts to a second portrait shot of Jones in no makeup, with just a slash of white paint over her left eyebrow. The two shots oscillate: Jones in high-femme makeup, Jones without makeup. There's a profile shot where both versions of the performer seem to face each other. The un-made-up Jones kisses the Jones in full lipstick. The camera zooms out, and the two iterations of the singer are dancing close, both wearing the *Nightclubbing* suit. The femme Jones is played by a performer in a mask; only the masculine Jones can move her face as she enthusiastically kisses her double.

A One Man Show includes a performance of "Walking in the Rain," the first single to be released from *Nightclubbing*. The song was written and originally recorded by the Australian new wave duo Flash and the Pan, and released on their self-titled debut album in 1978. "Feeling like a woman / Looking like a man / Sounding like a no-no / Mating when I can," Jones sings. She has not changed the lyrics from the original, in which George Young whispers the same lines against sparse, atmospheric instrumentation. It's a little dubby, the original song, characterized by a thin bassline and minor chords played on a synthesizer. There's no percussion, just a beat kept by what sounds like fingers snapping through a filter.

Jones's version fleshes out the original's reggae roots, lacing in a drum kit and occasional distorted guitar while retaining the song's lonely, wistful mood. In her voice, the gender ambivalence in the lyrics takes on a different cadence. In his version, Young seems to be offering up the secret of his inner femininity. He looks and sounds like a cis man, his voice coarse and unpoised, like he's sloughing stray thoughts into a handheld tape recorder. He pronounces the words "feeling like a woman" as if uttering a private confession. Jones, by contrast, issues the same line in a tight, controlled bark. That she looks like a man is obvious in the video; that she feels like a woman is only surprising in that she feels anything at all behind her painstakingly constructed veneer. Because her appearance is so artificial, the line hits the same nerve as it does in Young's voice, just via a different trajectory. A female performer playing a masculine robot, Jones assures the audience with her tongue in her cheek that she feels just like a woman beneath that hard, shining facade.

"I have a very strong male side, which I developed to protect my female side," wrote Jones in her memoir.[18] Her performances also have a male and a female side, and yet her work does not simply project her interior experience of gender. Jones's music is not an opportunity to know her. It revels in its own artificiality. She sings lyrics she has not written and wears stage costumes that render her unapproachable. Her androgyny manifests as gleeful irony, answering the many paradoxes that accompany performing as a woman with a new set of paradoxes all its own. She looks like a man, feels like a woman, is neither, and is both. She means and doesn't mean what she sings. She puts on a one-man show with an army of her own clones. On the stage and behind the lens of a video camera, all these contradictions can stand without resolution. There is no real body behind the show, just an image multiplying itself, creating room enough to hold the unstable question.

In a dark suit and cropped hair, Annie Lennox stands at the head of a boardroom table slapping a cane into a gloved palm. A projection plays on a screen behind her, a video of businessmen hurrying to work. Were it not for the heavy black eyeliner and red lipstick she's wearing, the singer might look just like one of them: stoic, possessed, sure of her own power and its clear expression through her clothing. Her bandmate, David A. Stewart, types away on a keyboard at the other end of the table. He, too, is dressed in a dark suit, but the typing feminizes him. It's as though Lennox were running a meeting and Stewart were the secretary feverishly taking notes in a corner while the men talk shop.

This scene plays out in the video for the breakout hit of the UK synthpop band Eurythmics, "Sweet Dreams (Are Made of This)." The band, which consisted solely of Lennox and Stewart, formed after the pair had played together in a series of rock bands and decided to strike out on their own, armed only with their synths and Lennox's magnetic voice. Like Jones, she often sang with little emotion, deliberately eschewing vibrato from her vocal technique. Eurythmics supplied something of a counterpoint to the glut of effeminate men who dominated synthpop. She was a masculine woman singing with a lower and more restrained voice than many of her male peers.

In the video for "Sweet Dreams," Lennox mingles masculine power with feminine glamour, using each to accentuate the other. Throughout the verses of the song, released in 1983 on the album of the same name, her voice oscillates between two primary notes. It's stoic rather than expressive, robotic like the instrumentation around her, which, aside from intermittent sprays of piano, is entirely synthesized.

In one shot of the video, Lennox and Stewart mime playing the cello along to what is obviously a synthesizer solo. Both musicians are blindfolded in this sequence, and Lennox wears a long curly wig and a red ball gown. They sit outdoors, among trees and cows, a bucolic setting in sharp contrast to the dark boardroom. The ultrafeminine getup fits Lennox as strangely as the image of the cello fits the electronic music that is heard. The moment echoes the horn player in Frankie Goes to Hollywood's "Relax" video, who blows into a big piece of metal as a sound obviously made by a computer rings out.

The videos that accompanied singles from Eurythmics' second and third albums, both released in 1983, see Lennox putting on a show of different heightened genders. Throughout "Love Is a Stranger," she repeats a gesture from early-twentieth-century drag shows: pulling back her wig to reveal her real, short hair. Before Eurythmics broke out into mainstream popularity, Lennox would wear wigs to the band's performances at small club gigs. One audience member apparently noticed that the singer's long brunette locks were not her real hair, and reached up onstage to steal her wig. "Suddenly, in strobe-lit slow motion, a strange new head was revealed," wrote Kurt Loder in a 1983 profile of the duo for *Rolling Stone*. "This one—which Annie hadn't counted on unveiling quite so soon—was anything but ladylike. The startling, carrot-colored hair was cut cell-block short on the sides and greased straight back on top, and the crowd's collective jaw hit the floor."[19]

The moment was shocking enough to throw Lennox's gender into question for years. "No one knew who Eurythmics were at the time," Stewart said. "So the whole audience must have thought, 'What's goin' on?' And ever since then, people have been sayin', 'Is Annie really a man?'" The thought of a cis, white woman covering her real, short hair with a long wig was apparently alien to UK concertgoers in the early '80s. Many people primarily associated wigs with drag queens, and the idea of a cis woman behaving like a drag queen onstage was enough to scramble the brains of more than a few onlookers.

The video for "Love Is a Stranger" repeats and satirizes that intrusive moment of audience participation. Lennox moves from place to place via a limousine driven by Stewart, and in each new location, she tries on a new character. She leaves an apartment in a blond, curly wig, dangling earrings, and fur coat; then, as she's about to exit the limo for apartment number two, she pulls off her wig to reveal slicked-back orange hair. Suddenly, she's a brunette in black leather with a beauty spot on her chin. She pulls off that wig, too, in the same ecstatic gesture of the drag queen revealing her act. The second time she enters the limo, she's dressed in her power suit, with no makeup and no wig, aggressively combing back her short hair. Dawn begins to break, and Stewart deposits Lennox in an outdoor scene with trees. Her movements become robotic, like those of a wind-up toy that has started to run down.

Lennox introduces a more sympathetic drag character in the video for "Who's That Girl?" Instead of moving from a feminine presentation to a masculine one, she plays both a man and a woman simultaneously, doubled in the same setting thanks to a little studio trickery. Her primary character is a singer at a nightclub with coiffed blond hair and pale pink lipstick. As she sings, Stewart enters with a girl on his arm, then another girl, then another. "Who's that girl / Running around with you?" Lennox mouths accusingly. As more and more of Stewart's paramours realize his duplicity, they join her in lip-synching the question.

Seated at one of the nightclub's tables is a man in a suit with sideburns and stubble, also played by Lennox. Unlike her snakelike businessman, he has a quiet demeanor. He stands in contrast to Stewart's flash, too; while Stewart wears a white suit, carries a cane, and pops bottles of champagne, this second man surveys the scene contemplatively, never drawing attention to himself. When she has finished her performance, Lennox in the blond wig leaves with Lennox in sideburns. The video's final shot shows the two personae kissing each other, framed almost identically to Grace Jones's encounter with herself in "My Jamaican Guy."

Throughout Eurythmics' surreal visual narratives, the strongest relationship Lennox cultivates is with the camera. She tends to fix the lens with a startling gaze, implicating the viewer while making it clear that she is putting on a show. After she withdraws from kissing her masculine persona in "Who's That Girl?," she aims a coy look at the camera, as if acknowledging the physical impossibility of the kiss: it's a green screen trick, not a direct documentation of intimacy. She keeps her eyes locked on the camera throughout "Sweet Dreams" and "Love Is a Stranger"; the latter is made all the more bizarre by the fact that Lennox is singing about a romantic infatuation. "I want you / And I want you / And I want you /

So it's an obsession," she sings high up in her head voice. Yet no one in the video serves as the object of her desire like you might expect. The only other person in the scene with her is Stewart, her driver, whom she steadfastly ignores.

Stewart wears sunglasses throughout the band's videos, which obscure his eyes and tend to obliterate him. Next to Lennox's fierce, commanding gaze, he barely seems present. He does, however, add a layer of complexity to the act of watching each video; in most of the narratives, he watches Lennox on a screen of his own or, in "Here Comes the Rain Again," follows her around with a video camera. While sitting in the limousine in "Love Is a Stranger," he pulls out a portable television screen and observes Lennox rolling around wigless on the floor in her leather getup, a shot the viewer has already seen. In "Sweet Dreams," a screen attached to his keyboard displays a shot that will come up later in the video of Lennox and himself meditating. In both cases, the screen bores through time, showing what has already happened or what is about to occur.

With the presence of the time-hopping screen, sequential time disintegrates. These self-conscious music videos do not follow a familiar narrative. As favorites on MTV, they were meant to be looped, meant to happen and then happen again as VJs replayed them. They moved, but they didn't allow time to pass normally. As opposed to feature films, which use music to support their narrative action, music videos use action to support their songs. Movies avoid excessive repetition, but music videos rely on it; the pop song lives and dies by the chorus, so the music video, which follows the music, may repeat itself. It's a visual product that follows the logic of music, not drama, and so it allows for a looser interpretation of material reality than most movies.

As the music video garbles time, it also scrambles relational power. While characters in movies rarely acknowledge the camera—to them, the camera as an object in space does not exist—performers in music videos tend to treat the camera as an audience member, an eye into which they may gaze. The music video's fourth wall is a thin membrane. It does not require the same deference as the fourth wall that bounds a film. The performer may look at the camera. She is not displaying herself for an unperceived voyeur. Whether she dresses in suits and ties or wigs and heels, the music video is her show.

"In a world ordered by sexual imbalance, pleasure in looking has been split between active/male and passive/female," wrote Laura Mulvey in her seminal 1975 essay "Visual Pleasure and Narrative Cinema." "The determining male gaze projects its phantasy onto the female figure, which is styled accordingly. In their traditional exhibitionist role, women are simultaneously looked at and displayed, with their appearance coded for strong visual and erotic impact so that they can be said to connote *to-be-looked-at-ness*."[20]

As Annie Lennox stares down the camera and brandishes a man's cane, an obvious phallus, she ruptures her own meaning as a woman singer. She is styled to be looked at in her lipstick and eyeliner, but she is also the one doing the looking. Not only does she wear short hair and masculine clothing, she fixes the viewer with an aggressive gaze, reflecting their own voyeurism back at them. The camera serves as her accomplice as she throws gender's ciphers into disarray.

In the video to her 1986 hit single "Control," Janet Jackson—sister to Michael and the youngest of the Jackson siblings—acts out a similar rupture. The video begins with a brief non-musical narrative of Jackson leaving her parents' house for her very first gig. Her mother has just cooked dinner and is disappointed that Jackson is heading out so soon; her father, meanwhile, shuts down Jackson's plans to move into her own apartment. Standing in the doorway of their house, the two parents visually represent a traditional gender arrangement: the dad in shirtsleeves, vest, and tie, the mom in a pink housedress and white apron. On their stoop, eager to leave, Jackson mixes gender symbols, wearing a white men's shirt buttoned all the way up with a black leather jacket slung over her shoulder—visual nods to masculinity that offset her long hair, hoop earrings, and full makeup.

"This is a story about control," Jackson says. She is onstage now, speaking to the audience before the lights have come up. "My control. Control of what I say and control of what I do. And this time, I'm gonna do it my way." She pivots her gaze to look directly into the camera. "Are we ready? I am," she says. "Cause it's all about control. And I've got lots of it." The camera pans out. Jackson, wearing a black double-breasted suit and mock black turtleneck, is sitting on a swing, which descends to the stage from the ceiling. Her hair is done up so it resembles a flat-top from the front but spills long down her back. The synthesizers start playing, and Jackson starts dancing, thrusting her hips like a man might. In the world of the video, she is perfectly androgynous, perfectly self-contained, and completely in charge of her own meaning.

I'll leave you back beneath that tree where Orlando sits with her daughter, watching the angel sing. Note, again, that the angel only appears through the viewfinder of the camcorder. Note that both a child and a lens are necessary to bring the ethereal genderless person into being. The viewer does not see what Orlando sees, is not given the view of the singer through a simulation of the organic eye. The viewer sees what the daughter sees, encoded in lines of data. This new and androgynous flesh appears in the cybernetically enhanced eye of the child, the new generation, looking up through her camera to witness whatever it is that has made her mother weep with joy—and, weeping, turn boldly to the viewer to fix them in her gaze.

8

INFINITE UTOPIA

Queer Time in Disco and House

There was only one clock at the Loft, an old wooden timepiece with a single hand, and soon enough it broke down, as if it had buckled under the weight of what was transpiring around it. It was a fitting enough symbol: the ad hoc dance club in New York's Greenwich Village didn't acknowledge time. David Mancuso, DJ and presider over the space, which doubled during the week as his home, sent out invitations to his weekly dance party illustrated with Salvador Dali's *The Persistence of Memory*: melted watch faces slipping across a surrealist landscape. Time was a construct and it had no sway inside the walls of the Loft. "Once you walked into the Loft you were cut off from the outside world," said Mancuso. "You got into a timeless, mindless state."[1]

At a time when gay clubs were still illegal in New York (for every three men in a club, there legally had to be one woman, so as to discourage "all-male dancing"), the Loft broke ground as one of the first underground dance spaces in New York. A minor discotheque craze, imported from Paris, had bubbled through the city in the '60s, but it wasn't until the '70s that DJing emerged as an art form in its own right, popular first in primarily gay spaces and then across urban America as a whole. The Loft helped set the mold for the subterranean dance party. Intended as a site of utopian gatherings, it had no bar, though it did offer partygoers free, organic food. Mancuso charged an entry fee to help pay for rent and overhead, but he never turned anyone away for lack of funds. The point was the music, which played loud enough to melt away the outside world.

Frankie Knuckles did not have an invitation to the Loft the first time he attended one of Mancuso's parties, but he knew Larry Levan, and Levan knew the woman working the door. The two friends skipped the line, walked in, and found themselves transported. "It was unlike anything I'd ever seen before in my life," Knuckles said. Not only was the music "the absolute best," the crowd seemed unfixed and permeable.[2] Like Levan and Knuckles, many dancers at the Loft were black and gay, but revelers of all stripes mingled there. The markers that distinguished individuals in the world outside the Loft seemed to soften and fall away within its walls. People were no longer differentiated and siloed, but part of something larger than themselves. "Unable to avoid body contact on all sides, individual dancers had little choice but to dissolve into the amorphous whole, and, as the distinctions between self and other collapsed, they relinquished their socialized desire for independence and separation," wrote Tim Lawrence in *Love Saves the Day*.[3]

Levan and Knuckles had met through the Harlem drag community, introduced by a drag queen named Gerald. Levan sewed dresses for the House of Wong, one of many drag ball collectives named for fashion designers that would compete against each other on the dance floor. Levan adopted the drag moniker Laurence Philpot after his mother's maiden name, while Knuckles went by Setter. Before long, the two friends' flamboyant presences earned them a reputation among New York's nightlife scene. "We were club kids before the term was invented," said Knuckles.[4]

That two of electronic music's most important pioneers met through drag is not surprising: the history of dance music in the United States is inseparable from the history of queer black survival. Dance clubs offered sanctuary during decades when the rest of the country was not so welcoming. Though the discotheque in its original configuration came from France, the style of DJing that emerged in New York depended on the reactions of the primarily gay crowds that composed the DJ's audience. Early disco pioneers such as Mancuso, Francis Grasso, and Steve D'Acquisito played with dancers, not for them. Unlike a live band, whose members might feel separate from and superior to their audiences given the literal amplification of their voices and instruments, a DJ communed with the crowd. They didn't talk over them. The goal was to get people moving, and DJs would select their records based on dancers' direct and indirect feedback. As Lawrence wrote:

> Loft dancers . . . weren't simply permeated by sound but also used their bodies to produce their own waves. Percussion instruments—whistles, tambourines, maracas—functioned as prosthetic extensions that enabled dancers to generate sound and rhythm. Boots, shoes, and sneakers flickered across the wooden floorboards as if they were a continuation of the sound system. Vocal cries combined with the vinyl to produce a hybrid mantra. And inaudible physical gestures—arm movements, facial expressions, sweat—sent signals to the ever-watchful Mancuso. Dancers, in other words, didn't just embody the music in their dance. They also produced music as part of a vibrant circuit.[5]

Mancuso and his contemporaries would spin rock, soul, funk, Motown, and R&B tracks on 45 RPM vinyl records. These songs might play on the radio in the daylight, but they took on a different cadence when woven into the flow of the after-dark set. Blended together with songs of a similar tempo, singles from soul singers Marvin Gaye and Diana Ross adopted new meanings. Even songs by the Beatles would pop up here and there. They were no longer discrete music products but parts of a larger whole, not promotional snippets intended to consolidate the consumer base of a given band but music bleeding into music, with little relation to anything outside the living moment.

Though DJs controlled the music that played in a given space, their reliance on the energy of the crowd democratized listening and dancing. DJs did not look or behave like rock or pop musicians; they camped behind the turntables, but they also belonged to the crowd, who tended to be the real stars of the show.

"An untheatrical anonymity . . . is extremely important to successful dance music," wrote music critic Ken Emerson in 1975. "This lack of personal identity on the part of disco performers allows unawed dancers to assert their own identities—through their dress, through their partners and through the steps they execute. Such a dance-floor democracy has been alien to white rock, which promotes a superstar elite and generally subordinates the music to the mystiques of its makers."[6]

The unceasing beat of the disco dance floor also upended the power dynamics of rock and pop. "The fact that disco was foregrounding rhythm to such an extent that it was sidelining the key symbols of rock's authority—the lead vocalist and the lead guitarist—constituted a significant challenge," wrote Lawrence. "The ideological nature of this conflict was reflected in the contrasting identities of the two constituencies. Whereas white heterosexual men dominated rock, disco was teeming with African Americans, gays, and women."[7]

Unlike the start-and-stop jolt of the jukebox, the automated record-playing machine that by the '70s was beginning to grow passé, the DJ set offered an organic and meticulously crafted music experience that would last for hours on end. No clocks disrupted the Loft, and so the Loft supplied an escape hatch from normative time, allowing dancers entryway into a queerer way of being.

Disco enabled an alternate reality for dancers seeking refuge from capitalism's rigid structures. Not only did the environment suspend the illusion that time was not passing as it normally did, but disco clubs, as primarily queer spaces, were also dislodged from the usual succession of straight life. If people found intimacy on the dance floor, if they went home with their dance partners after the set, it wasn't a preliminary chapter in the long-form narrative of marriage, pregnancy, and child-rearing. Sex didn't have to serve as the prelude to a prewritten story; sex could just be sex.

As theorist Jack Halberstam wrote in *A Queer Time and Place*, "queer subcultures produce alternative temporalities by allowing their participants to believe that their futures can be imagined according to logics that lie outside of those paradigmatic markers of life experience—namely, birth, marriage, reproduction, and death."[8] Because encounters on the dance floor didn't fit into heterosexual chronologies, they came loose from dominant conceptions of time. Like an acid trip, whose peaks and valleys inspired the flow of Mancuso's DJ sets, a night at the club could spool away toward infinity. Each moment held boundless lateral feeling, and each fellow dancer could feel like a lifelong friend even if you never said a single word to them.

Dance subcultures countered the straight shape of a life in its entirety, but disco frayed straight time on a microcosmic level too. The art of mixing bristled against the way pop songs typically functioned as a preordained unit of time. While each song played at a disco club in the '70s might have originally followed familiar patterns of tension and release, verse and chorus, DJs would elongate certain sections of their picks to keep the crowd moving. Looping a song's outro gave the DJ more time to sync up the next track, allowing for a seamless flow of music. The more adventurous DJs soon began extending sequences from the middles of songs too. In the careful hand of a talented mixer, the pop song became flexible and amorphous, no longer imposing its prerecorded chronology according to an unchanging, predictable progression but bending and swelling in time with the movements of the crowd.

The house DJ at the Gallery in SoHo, Nicky Siano spun on the cutting edge of DJ technique. He was one of the first selectors to toy with the speed of the records he played. He manipulated the club's sound system, turning speakers on and off to emphasize just one section of a drum solo at a time—the snare, the bass, the hi-hat—and then grouping the sound back together into a cohesive beat. He found a way to deepen the break, a technique originally used in gospel where every instrument but the drums would fall silent, then one by one come back into the mix.

"David Mancuso was into the vinyl as pure sound. I was into making it what I wanted it to be, and I always wanted something more sensational," Siano said. "I would turn everything off except the tweeter arrays and have them dancing to tss, tss, tss, tss, tss, tss, tss for a while. Then I would turn on the bass, and then I'd turn on the main speakers. When I did that the room would just explode."[9]

Siano's precision beatwork and outgoing, flamboyant personality established him as one of disco's premier mixers. He presided over a predominantly gay crowd, whose tastes he catered to by spinning tracks with primarily female vocalists. "The Gallery was gayer than the Loft," said fellow DJ Michael Gomes. "It was women singing songs."[10] A space suffused with the sound of women singing was more likely to draw a gay male crowd, as if Patti LaBelle or Diana Ross could animate queer men's femininity with their voices. The activating power of the diva remained in place even when she was physically absent, heard but invisible. Her voice coursing through a dance club was enough.

Disco's growing popularity on the underground circuit caused record companies to sit up and take notice, and by the mid-1970s the music had become a studio genre in its own right. In an attempt to cater to DJs' blending needs, singles came out extra long, ending with extended strips of four-on-the-floor drumbeats. New acts mimicked the sounds DJs favored, chasing after the dance room success of Philadelphia soul and Motown.

"The DJs understood how to turn a good song into a great song," said Joe Cayre, one of the record executives who chased the disco gold rush. "They were experts in reconstructive surgery."[11] His choice of metaphor is telling. It positions the song as a body: not a rigid body remaining static through time, but a soft, malleable body, open and changing and alive. You might even say the disco song had a trans body, marked by its movement from one state of being to another but undeniably freer and truer in its changed form. With a deft hand and a scalpel, the DJ could transform an ordinary pop song into a vessel for sublime experience.

Donna Summer, an emerging American singer who had teamed up with the Italian producer Giorgio Moroder while living in Berlin, released her second studio album *Love to Love You Baby* in 1975. Its entire A-side comprised a seventeen-minute cut of the title track, which ebbed and flowed in a silky progression accentuated by the intermittent sounds of orgasmic moaning.

Summer's voice acted as a perfect cipher for the gay disco crowd, and "Love to Love You Baby" soon entered the rotation at the Gallery. Her singing stood out from that of the other female voices that rang out in the space. Unlike many Motown singers, who harmonized in powerfully projected voices, Summer sang with a light touch. The gentle grain of her head voice approached a male falsetto; she glided across the peaks of her notes rather than sinking into them with the full weight of her breath. When she sing-speaks the verses to "Love to Love You Baby," she barely rises above a whisper, and the chorus—the soft repetition of the song's title—floats in her gossamer delivery.

As one of the first songs specifically tailored to the disco club, which required a sustained mood, rather than the radio, which demanded concision, density, and constant novelty, "Love to Love You Baby" reoriented popular music's relationship to sexuality. Instead of building up tension across the verse and then letting loose at the hook, Summer's first hit lets tension and pleasure comingle. The quick orgasmic thrust of the traditional pop song gets subsumed into a steamy session of extended play. No male voices appear on the record, so "Love to Love You Baby" offers a vision of completely feminine sexuality: one focused on the slow rise and fall from the brink of orgasm, rather than a race to the finish.

Throughout the song, Summer repeats the title steadily. The words themselves contain a percussive moment of repetition. Her pronunciation of "love to love" hits like a brushed cymbal, and the soft loop of enclosed sound spirals outward. More than any song recorded by the time of its release, "Love to Love You Baby" maps the logics of the dance floor. It's in no rush to get to a pleasurable, sugary chorus. The song is all pleasure, feminine pleasure ebbing and flowing in a spacious rhythm, simmering patiently over Moroder's steady beat.

Summer's voice multiplies over the course of the extended track so that by the final hook, she no longer sounds like just one woman enjoying herself but a whole chorus of women luxuriating in their own sexuality. The trajectory from individual to multiple voicings reflects the interior experience of stepping out onto a dance floor. At first, a dancer might be hyper-aware of her own presence as an individual, different from everyone else around her. As the music works, the boundaries of discrete personhood begin to soften, and the dancer feels increasingly porous, part of the circulatory system that is the club. The dance ritual doesn't bludgeon away individuality in order to force normativity, but it does allow the individual to become part of a collective, amoebic organism. The dancer is both herself and beyond herself, a contradiction that requires no resolution within the dance floor's magic circle.

In the spring of 1977, Donna Summer released *I Remember Yesterday*, a mostly nostalgic album that looked back at the genres that preceded and informed disco. Moroder thought that the record should "conclude with a futuristic song." "I decided that it had to be done with a synthesizer," he said.[12] Using a Moog, he composed a rippling bassline and synthesized the sound of a snare and a hi-hat. (The Moog's limited percussive ability was no match for the punch of an acoustic bass drum, so Moroder rounded out the beat with an overdub on the kit.) He presented the beat to Summer, who developed a descending vocal melody to complement the upward bubbling bass riff. With a few space-age Moog leads, the song coalesced into "I Feel Love," a mesmerizing track that became the first successful attempt to sneak a totally synthesized song into the discotheque.

While "Love to Love You Baby" frames "love" within an explicitly sexual context, "I Feel Love" opens the word to encompass something more ethereal. Summer sings the first verse as a single voice, a soprano delivered in her head register with no backing tracks. By the first chorus, she's joined by a second version of herself that sings an ascending countermelody. This shadow voice trails her throughout the rest of the song, which yawned past eight minutes on its twelve-inch release. Slowly, Summer multiplies; one voice becomes two, two become three. If the lead vocal seems to be nearing the upper boundary of Summer's range, then each additional voice soars past that edge until Summer's one voice transforms into a choir of impossible, unearthly femininity. The bassline, which Moroder doubled on a delay across the left and right channel to create a three-dimensional stereo effect, remains in place, grounding the song, but Summer floats higher with every chorus. By the finish, there are so many ascending voices that even her primary descending melody sounds like it's lifting into the air. This love, which takes several beats to pronounce, is no earthly love. It's a love beyond the body, beyond sex, beyond gender and time and power.

"Gloria Gaynor might have been the first queen of disco, but Summer, blending with Moroder's technology, had become its first cyborg princess," wrote Lawrence.[13] It's true that Summer sounds at one with the atmosphere on "I Feel Love." Moroder adds some reverb to her voice at the end of certain lines, which makes it sound as though she's evaporating into the space around her. But disco was already a cyborg endeavor; the presence of the Moog just codified its futuristic bent. DJs were musicians that did not play instruments, negotiating with a playback machine to create live music from prerecorded audio. Technology birthed the music; the specific quirks of the turntable assembly gave rise to the way disco sounded. From the start, disco DJs were cyborgs by design: technologically aided beings who unstitched time and grew new bodies in the limbo.

In Summer's wake, another angelic-voiced singer started filtering electronic disco records onto the radio. The San Francisco–based artist Sylvester had his first single enter the *Billboard* Hot 100 in 1978, after years of stifled bids for success as the leader of the funk-rock group the Hot Band. His skillful falsetto had won him a famous fan in David Bowie after he opened for the British star during a 1972 San Francisco gig, but the Hot Band struggled to gain traction across the United States. Sylvester was an androgynous, gender-fluid performer who had belonged to drag troupes throughout his teens and twenties. As a member of the LA-based teen drag queen collective the Disquotays, he gleefully broke the California law that still prohibited public cross-dressing. After moving to San Francisco and fronting his own band, Sylvester often took the stage in full femme, which prompted significant homophobic and racist backlash when he and the Hot Band toured the American South. The group ultimately tanked, but the disco craze of the late '70s gave him an opening. His voice was perfectly suited to the new genre's transcendent rhythms, and with the song "Dance (Disco Heat)," Sylvester had a hit.

With a chorus of women's voices joining Sylvester's throughout the song, "Dance (Disco Heat)" highlighted the disco dance floor as a site of feminine collectivity. If the world outside the club tried to abrade difference, insisting on compulsory masculinity for those considered to be men, then the world inside the club let those boundaries dissolve. No laws restricted expression there, and there were no homophobes allowed. Even if many Americans weren't fully ready for the utopian promise of the disco club, they were eager for the sounds that came out of it. "Dance (Disco Heat)" peaked at number nineteen on the *Billboard* Hot 100 toward the end of 1978. A follow-up single, "You Make Me Feel (Mighty Real)," cemented Sylvester's sound on the charts.

Produced by Patrick Cowley, who, like Sylvester, was gay, "You Make Me Feel (Mighty Real)" broke away somewhat from the Italo-disco template set by Giorgio Moroder and Donna Summer. It both upped the tempo of disco, creating a bridge to the genre that would come to be known as high-NRG, and tethered it to the ground. If Summer's voice always sounded like it was about to float away into the stratosphere, Sylvester's managed to be at once celestial and rooted, promising utopia not in some distant future but in the here and now of San Francisco's queer spaces. Both sung and produced by gay musicians, "You Make Me Feel (Mighty Real)" solidified disco's queer sound. "[Cowley] was gay, Moroder is straight, and I have to say that comes out in the sound," said Josh Cheon of the archival record label Dark Entries.[14]

Sylvester improvised both the melody and the lyrics to "You Make Me Feel (Mighty Real)" atop Cowley's strobing beat. His words "said exactly what was going on," the vocalist asserted, conveying what it meant "to dance and sweat and cruise and go home and carry on and how a person feels."[15] This simple, direct expression of queer joy turned "You Make Me Feel (Mighty Real)" into a long-lasting pride anthem. Cowley and Sylvester continued to work together on the 1979 album *Stars*, whose glistening ten-minute title track stands apart as one of the most transcendent songs of the disco era. They fell out not long after but reconnected in the early '80s, by which time Cowley was dying. Sylvester drove Cowley back and forth from the studio on his moped as they worked on their last collaborative song, 1982's "Do

You Wanna Funk." That same year, Cowley died at age thirty-two, an early victim of AIDS.[16]

In 1987, Sylvester's husband, Rick Cranmer, died of the same unabating plague. A year later, on December 16, 1988, Sylvester also passed away from AIDS at his home in San Francisco. He had performed at that summer's Pride festival in a wheelchair, singing with his queer community for as long as he possibly could.[17] In the records he released up until his death, he left behind traces of a world better than the one he had to live and die in, a world that appeared to him and his family in glimpses, in the fleeting dance floor bliss that could unspool in the moment toward infinity.

Disco died a fiery symbolic death in July 1979, when a crowd of rockists gathered at Comiskey Park in Chicago to watch a box full of records explode. Tens of thousands of people attended the stunt, which was staged between two baseball games (just in case there was any doubt that it was a spectacle intended for straight assholes) but attracted more than double the White Sox's usual pull. Attendees brought their own disco records to hurl onto the field, chanting "disco sucks" while the vinyl burned.[18]

Disco Demolition Night had an immediate effect on the perception of the genre among club owners and DJs. "After they blew up all the records in the park . . . the very next day, a host of clubs, big superclubs across the country, went from disco to either country and western or R&B," Frankie Knuckles said in 2012.[19]

Anti-disco sentiment had simmered among rock fans ever since the genre first broke out of underground clubs. In 1976, John Holmstrom took to the pages of *Punk* magazine's first issue to torch dance music. "The epitome of all that's wrong with Western civilization is disco," he wrote, dismissing it wholesale as "canned crap."[20] In all likelihood, he and other anti-disco rockists were spitting not on what was actually playing in the clubs they never attended, but on the straight and whitewashed disco that had begun to take hold of the radio alongside the real thing.

"Unaware of its gay underground origins, most punks saw disco as the mass-produced, mechanistic sound of escapism and complacency, uptown Muzak with a beat for the moneyed and glamour struck," wrote Simon Reynolds.[21] The Bee Gees and *Saturday Night Fever* had brought a vanilla take on the genre to the masses, and the masses struck back against a form of music they considered, likely with some degree of homophobia, to be sugary, brainless pap. Severed from its utopian origins by opportunistic record executives, disco had become passé.

By the time angry white rock fans enacted the symbolic murder of disco, Knuckles had relocated from New York to Chicago, plucked from his home city by Robert Williams, who planned to open a new club called the Warehouse in the Second City. Williams also hailed from New York; born in Queens, he first met Knuckles and Larry Levan while he was working at the Spofford Juvenile Center. The club kids were in trouble for skipping school, and he was their juvenile officer. Williams would later see them around at gay clubs, including the Tamburlaine in Midtown. "They were much better dancers than I was," he said.[22]

Knuckles and Levan cut their teeth behind the turntable at New York's Continental Baths, a gay bathhouse in the basement of a hotel on the Upper West Side. Levan got the gig first, while Knuckles tagged along to work lights, stepping in to play music whenever his friend overslept. When Levan moved on to another residency, Knuckles took over his station at the Baths. He DJed there until the space went bankrupt and closed in 1976. Initially, Williams wanted Levan for the Warehouse gig, but Levan had committed to working the tables at the Paradise Garage, a new club opened specifically with his talents in mind. The club owner passed on the invitation to Knuckles, who in 1977 agreed to pack up and start over in the Midwest.

While disco had made its way to the Windy City, Chicago's nightlife paled in comparison to New York's in the late '70s, so Knuckles' deft command of the turntables and deep collection of records supplied a breath of fresh air. Keeping a steady supply of the soul music that was disco's lifeblood, he also mixed tracks imported from Europe, where electronic beats and basslines had caught on in Giorgio Moroder's wake. The combination of classic, soulful vocals and cutting-edge electronic sounds would become Knuckles' signature.

An all-night juice bar with a predominantly young, gay, and black clientele, the Warehouse blended the spirit of the New York underground with the religious fervor of a South Side Chicago church. "The feeling, the feedback that you get from the people in the room, is very, very spiritual," Knuckles said in 1995. "For most of the people that went there, it was church for them. It only happened one day a week: Saturday night, Sunday morning, Sunday afternoon."[23]

As disco entered its latter-day era and fell out of favor among labels, Knuckles had to develop new techniques to keep his disciples worshiping. "By '81, when they had declared that disco is dead, all the record labels were getting rid of their dance departments, or their disco departments, so there were no more up-tempo dance records," he said.

> Everything was downtempo. That's when I realized I had to start changing certain things in order to keep feeding my dancefloor, or else we would have had to end up closing the club. So I would take different records like "Walk the Night" by the Skatt Bros. or stuff like "A Little Bit of Jazz" by Nick Straker, "Double Journey" [by Powerline] and things like that, and just completely re-edit them to make them work better for my dancefloor. Even stuff like "I'm Every Woman" by Chaka Khan, and "Ain't Nobody," I'd completely re-edit them to give my dancefloor an extra boost.[24]

His creative edits earned him an enthusiastic fan base. Many Warehouse dancers, thinking they had heard a prerecorded remix instead of a live one, tried to buy the music Knuckles played. "They would rush to the record stores the next day looking for that particular version and never find it. It used to drive the record stores crazy," the DJ said.[25] Unable to purchase Knuckles' remixes, Warehouse attendees and other dance music listeners began distributing bootleg tapes of the sets among their friends and acquaintances. Many of the tapes were simply labeled "Warehouse music." Over time, the epithet got shortened to "house music," and the burgeoning genre had its name.

Knuckles got ahold of his first drum machine after he left the Warehouse and opened his own club, the Power Plant, in 1983. Derrick May, a young clubgoer who would go on to pioneer Detroit techno, sold him a Roland TR-909 after watching him spin, and soon enough Knuckles started integrating synthesized drum patterns into his sets. Just as Moroder's Moog had transformed disco into a futuristic fantasy, the addition of the drum machine to house music lent the emerging genre a cyborg sheen. It punched up the beat of a song, intensified the energy of a crowd, and drew disco's successor further away from its pop origins.

Because a drum machine could produce a beat indefinitely, DJs didn't have to worry about looping drum breaks or outros on vinyl. A house song made with a TR-909 contained theoretically infinite time, which loosened selectors' reliance on the shapes of prerecorded tracks. "Those songs didn't have structure, but the beats were killing," said fellow DJ and house producer Farley "Jackmaster" Funk. "We brought our drum machines to the club and created electronic four/four. It just made disco sound very thunderous."[26]

Knuckles debuted the TR-909 on a track that would become one of his signature songs, a collaboration with a young songwriter whose home demo tapes Knuckles liked to play at the Power Plant. "The first time I used [the drum machine], I used it on a version of 'Your Love' that I did with Jamie Principle," he said. "And I would use it live in the club. I would program different patterns into it throughout the week, and then use it throughout the course of a night, running it live, depending on the song and playing it underneath, or using it to segue between some things."[27]

What began life as a poem Principle wrote for his girlfriend, a hushed confession of romantic love, transformed into one of the many community anthems that would come to define house music in the '80s. Though the singer was an unknown at the time that Knuckles started spinning his tracks, the anonymity of his voice infused his music with a mysterious appeal. He sang in a high, androgynous register, making it hard for listeners to gender him. "Nobody knew who Jamie Principle was, and everybody loved this record," said Wayne Williams, a fellow Chicago DJ who had helped introduce disco to Chicago's South Side.[28]

Built atop a three-note arpeggio and a simple, sturdy bassline, "Your Love" adapted the strategies Moroder had used with Donna Summer on "I Feel Love" to house music's soulful electronic sound. During the verse, Principle sings on a single track, his voice gently cloaked in reverb. At the chorus (which, in the Knuckles mix, happens only once) a second voice enters, singing the same melody simultaneously on a higher octave. The higher version of the melody, sung by Adrienne Jett, coils around the lower one. The two voices do not harmonize; unlike traditional mixed-gender duets, in which the man's voice is intended to accentuate the woman's femininity by contrast and vice versa, Jett and Principle bleed into each other, becoming a single voice. The love they both call for is not suspended across irreducible difference, but instead channels desire through a porous, morphing body.

With the founding of the local Chicago label Trax Records in 1984, house became not just a club genre or a bootleg phenomenon, but, like disco before it, a commercially viable form of original music. The transcendent experience of dancing to a Frankie Knuckles set was parceled out and distributed on vinyl. In their lyrics, many original house singles explicitly codified the utopian streak of the venue that gave the genre its name, as well as the womblike spaces where disco had first grown. House, like disco before it, aspired to erase artificial boundaries between people, dispel capitalistic mechanisms of power and control, and unify communities under the banner of the groove.

"During the Reagan era, the dance floor was a place to escape," said Principle. "You could stay out all night and not worry about what was happening here. When Frankie had his Power Plant club, it was like going to church and letting yourself be free without worrying about all the craziness that was happening in the streets and in the world. The music took you away for an amount of hours. You'd get out of the Power Plant club and the sun was shining. It was a totally spiritual kind of thing."[29]

Rhythm Controll's 1987 track "My House" solidified the connection between the club and the church with an ad hoc sermon by Chuck Roberts, whose frenetically preached words would serve as something of a house manifesto. "No one man owns house," he says, "because house music is a universal language spoken and understood by all." His statement reflected the operating principles of house producers and labels, who played fast and loose with concepts of authorship.

Jesse Saunders's 1984 track "On and On," commonly cited as the first twelve-inch house record, was not quite an original composition but a layered pastiche. Saunders's DJ sets revolved around a megamix he owned on bootleg vinyl, which included sections from the novelty disco track "Space Invaders" by Australian duo Player One. When the disc was stolen, he decided to re-create it from memory on a Roland TR-808 drum machine and a pair of synthesizers, adding original flourishes and bratty spoken vocals to the sections he knew by heart. "I just wanted another version that I could play in my DJ sets," he said.[30] "On and On," a musical Frankenstein's monster, became a hit, selling thirty thousand copies. Those looking for house in Chicago's record stores finally had something to take home.

If rock music stamped original songs with a name, a face, and a brand, cultivating the illusion of authentic individual genius, then house positioned its DJs more as conduits than composers. They were artists, but they used preexisting songs as raw materials, complicating the question of attribution within the context of a label release. The concept of music as private property never held much water in dance subcultures. House was a language, and an entire language can't be restricted by copyright.

This loose, free approach to music making produced a spate of tracks with utopian messaging. On Joe Smooth's 1987 cut "Promised Land," Anthony Thomas sings of a future when "we walk, hand and hand / Sisters, brothers / We'll make it to the promised land." The song carries an anxious beat, as if Smooth were trying to hasten the eventuality of paradise. "Bring Down the Walls," a collaboration between vocalist Robert Owens and producer Larry Heard, similarly calls for the triumph of love over power across an itchy, hi-hat-heavy beat. "We're gonna bring down the walls / Let 'em fall," Owens sings, his voice rising to a silky falsetto.

The persistent presence of synthesized instruments pitched house's gaze toward the future, even as its lyrics and vocals drew upon the history of gospel music. House singers often appeared as cyborgs, not naturalized voices rolling through the immediate present but technologically augmented beings from a time just out of reach. Many songs accentuated the artificiality of the house voice with cyborg language. Steve "Silk" Hurley's 1986 single "Jack Your Body" repeatedly glitches its vocal sample, turning the consonants in the word "jack" into a percussive element in their own right. The phrase, a snippet of slang that proliferated in house lyrics, calls to mind the orifices studding a synthesizer or an amplifier. In three words, body and machine join together into a new, ambiguous form.

House furthered disco's complex relationship to time. Because the groove lives or dies with the crowd, dance music gives rise to a spontaneous present in which the DJ and the dancers engage in constant subliminal communication. Though disco DJs spun prerecorded tracks, invoking the voices of physically absent people lodged in the recent past, they made active, dynamic live edits to their chosen songs. A disco set drew upon the sounds of the past to reinscribe the living now. House added another temporal dimension to this arrangement. Prerecorded voices and live edits mingled with live drum machines and synthesizers, whose transparent roboticism tugged dancers to the precipice of the future. The past, the present, and the life yet to come all converged on the house floor, inflating the moment with time that blazed in all directions.

House, which like disco shook the walls of forbidden, transient spaces while the straight world slept, bloomed while a plague took hold of America's gay communities. Though the devastation of AIDS affected Chicago far less than San Francisco or New York, the disease still represented an existential threat to queer liberation. Gay men were dying young of an incurable and mysterious illness, and the conservative presidential administration did nothing. Ronald Reagan didn't mention the disease until 1985, and even then he had to be prompted by a reporter's question. By then, AIDS had claimed nearly six thousand lives in the United States.

House's vision of queer utopia promised safety and acceptance at a time when many straight people actively feared gay men as disease vectors. In 1985, Chicago's Howard Brown Memorial Clinic started getting calls from anxious heterosexuals worrying about their chances of infection. One woman reportedly called in to ask if her young daughter, who had skinned her knee on the sidewalk in a predominantly gay neighborhood, was at risk of contracting the disease.[31] In the paranoid straight imagination, gay people and gay spaces had been marked for death.

"Queer time perhaps emerges most spectacularly at the end of the twentieth century, from within those gay communities whose horizons of possibility have been severely diminished by the AIDS epidemic," wrote Jack Halberstam. "The constantly diminishing future creates a new emphasis on the here, the present, the now, and while the threat of no future hovers overhead like a storm cloud, the urgency of being also expands the potential of the moment and . . . squeezes new possibilities out of the time at hand."[32]

House was indifferent to the established structure of the pop song. While radio music looped through chorus after chorus, supplying pleasure and release to daytime listeners, house songs featured few choruses or eschewed them entirely. The point was not the resolution, the tidy bow on the end of a story. House let the moment grow until it spilled over the horizon. On the dance floor, nothing was more important than the eternity of the now.

The gentle, searching voices of house's singers flouted both conventions of gender and conventions of time. Normative gender, after all, relies on its own strict chronologies. There is no phrase more telling in the cis vocabulary than "born a man/woman," a refrain used to indicate a trans person's gender assignment at birth. Every human being on earth is born a baby, but the sex marked on a birth certificate spells out a vision of an eventual puberty and its accompanying social role. There is never any guarantee that a baby will become a man or a woman, but the lie still circulates. Those three words collapse eighteen years into a handful of syllables, ironing out a person's whole childhood in service of cisnormativity.

If the straight world collapsed time in the '80s, marking even healthy gay people as already dead, then house music helped queer communities reclaim the present tense. In the now of the dance floor, gender and sexuality have no eventualities. The music does not break for hours on end, and it has no interest in consolidating its pleasure into a hook. The timekeeping of a normative life—birth, puberty, marriage, childbearing, death—falls away to the glow of the infinite moment. A room full of strangers turned family pulses to an unceasing beat.

9

FUNKY CYBORGS

Time, Technology, and Gender in Hip-Hop

By the 1970s, the Bronx was on fire. Compounding civic neglect left residential buildings derelict in the New York borough, and some landlords figured they could make more money from insurance collected after a structure fire than from renting out their dilapidated properties. Amid a landscape hollowed out by corruption and poverty, a new music culture would branch off from early disco.

At 1520 Sedgwick Avenue in the Bronx, in the recreation room of their apartment complex, DJ Kool Herc and his sister Cindy hosted a back-to-school party that would go down in legend as the site of the birth of hip-hop. The family had moved to New York from Jamaica when Herc was twelve; as a kid in Kingston, he would watch workers loading huge sound systems into nearby dancehalls, where DJs spun bass-heavy tracks to local crowds. Herc was too young to attend these parties, but their presence in his neighborhood left an impression. While still in high school, he learned to DJ on a sound system his father bought that Herc had rigged up to sound louder than life. He had been attending house parties and local disco clubs such as the Puzzle and Disco Fever, so he learned from the dance floor how a DJ could work a room. When his sister needed money for new school clothes, he agreed to help her throw a party to raise funds. On August 11, 1973, Herc and Cindy hosted a "Back to School Jam" that would turn out to be one of history's most monumental high school parties.

Like his contemporaries west of the Harlem River, Herc used his turntables to perform reconstructive surgery on the tracks he played, singling out the section of a song that prompted the most enthusiastic crowd reaction and looping it to keep his partygoers dancing. He teased out the percussive breaks in the funk and soul records he favored, looping drum and bass sections for minutes on end. "In a technique he called 'the Merry-Go-Round,' Herc began to work two copies of the same record, back-cuing a record to the beginning of the break as the other reached the end, extending a five-second breakdown into a five-minute loop of fury," wrote Jeff Chang. "Before long he had tossed most of the songs, focusing on the breaks alone. His sets drove the dancers from climax to climax on waves of churning drums. 'And once they heard that, that was it, wasn't no turning back,' Herc says. 'They always wanted to hear breaks after breaks after breaks after breaks.'"[1] The music played continuously until the most percussive section of a prerecorded song had transformed into a new song of its own.

Unlike disco DJs in Manhattan, Herc used a microphone along with his turntables. He would call out to his friends over the PA, adding his voice to the songs he was pulling apart and rewriting in real time. "I just was saying a few little words," he said. "If the party was rocking, I'd say, 'Yeah, right about now I'm rocking with the rockers, I'm jammin' with the jammers. Young ladies, don't hurt nobody. So remember, it ain't no fun unless we all get some.'"[2] These improvised vocalizations called back to a Jamaican vocal technique called toasting, where DJs would sing rhythmically or chant over reggae and dancehall tracks. Herc's friend Coke La Rock joined him on the mic, talking up his friends in an attempt to catch the attention of the girls in the audience. "Our friends Pretty Tony, Easy Al, and Nookie Nook were all at the party," La Rock said in 2008. "At first I would just call out their names. Then I pretended dudes had double-parked cars; that was to impress the girls."[3]

Both Herc and La Rock were just sixteen when they threw that first party, but the formula they spontaneously adopted—rapping over breakbeats—turned out to spawn one of the twentieth century's most innovative and disruptive new genres. In a room full of teens enjoying the last days of summer, hip-hop was born. "Afterwards, everybody attempted to re-create the energy of that night," said Grandmaster Caz, a rapper and DJ who was one of the partygoers in attendance.[4]

Though initially an expression of straight masculinity, hip-hop, like house, grew from the margins of normative society, in a black and Latino borough feared and neglected by the rest of New York, and so it developed its own rebellions against standard progressions of time. Straight time and normative gender both take root in whiteness, whose dominant ideologies press against every expression of otherness in the United States. Black men, whether gay or straight, were marked for death just as gay men of all races were: not an emblem of creeping disease but a cipher for violence and urban decay in the minds of white Americans.

From that racialized margin, new strategies for making art and music thrived throughout the '70s. In addition to Herc's "Merry-Go-Round," early hip-hop DJs developed the "scratching" technique, rubbing a record back and forth against the needle so it would produce a distinctive skidding sound. In an interview with Mark Dery, science fiction author Samuel R. Delany noted that the hip-hop techniques of "scratch and sampling begin . . . as a specific miss-use and conscientious desecration of the artifacts of technology and the entertainment media."[5] The turntable carried with it a specific logic of time as a unidirectional phenomenon. By looping, scratching, and sampling records, hip-hop DJs defied that baked-in ethos. They would delete music from the flow of a song via direct physical intervention (scratching and looping) or insert tangential sounds into a track (sampling). With a careful hand on the needle, DJs imposed their own authority over the sequentiality of a prerecorded piece of music.

In some of its earliest incarnations, hip-hop defied the structure of the pop song to carve out a space where a vision of utopia could unspool without interruption. Largely regarded as the genre's breakout single, though it came from artists with shallow roots in the New York subculture, Sugar Hill Gang's 1979 record "Rapper's Delight" was released on Sylvia Robinson's new indie label Sugar Hill Records as a fifteen-minute track, based on the bassline to Chic's 1979 disco single "Good Times" and extolling the joys of summer in the city. Since live rap sessions often stretched for hours at a time, the very notion of releasing a hip-hop single—a contained, replayable unit of rap—startled the genre's early participants. "Record? Fuck, how you gon' put hip-hop onto a record? Cause it was a whole gig, you know? How you gon' put three hours on a record?" Public Enemy's Chuck D asked Chang. "Bam! They made 'Rapper's Delight.' And the ironic twist is not how long that record was, but how short it was. I'm thinking, 'Man, they cut that shit down to fifteen minutes?' It was a miracle."[6]

Despite its oversize length for a commercial single, "Rapper's Delight" caught the ears of radio DJs, who played it in its entirety on their shows. Bill Adler, the music critic for the *Boston Herald* at the time, said, "Boston had one Black music radio station and it was an AM station called WILD. Whenever they played 'Rapper's Delight'—which was all the time—they played the entire fifteen-minute version, which was unheard of."[7] At the same time that graffiti artists were reclaiming New York's public space with colorful spray-painted tags, rappers and DJs reoriented the radio's relationship to time. "'Rapper's Delight' crossed over from New

York's insular hip-hop scene to Black radio, then charged up the American Top 40, and swept around the globe," wrote Chang. "It became the best-selling twelve-inch single ever pressed."[8]

In the early '80s, as house music was beginning to build cyborg paradises in Chicago, hip-hop began its own era of technological utopianism. One of the many Bronx DJs to emerge in Kool Herc's wake, Afrika Bambaataa took inspiration from pioneering electronic bands across the Atlantic, such as Germany's Kraftwerk and Japan's Yellow Magic Orchestra. In 1982, he released "Planet Rock," a futuristic rap single formed around a Kraftwerk sample and the first 808 beat to appear in hip-hop. Aided intermittently by a vocoder, Bambaataa positions the dance club as a site of escape from temporal structures. "No work or play, our world is free / Be what you be," he raps. In the world of the song, time is no longer bifurcated into labor and leisure. Instead, it flows as a continuous whole, not demarcated by external power but internally, individually defined.

Hip-hop arose from a landscape of pervasive unemployment, especially among young people of color, and its relationship to time reflected the absence of the factory or office clock. "If we understand the machine as a product of human creativity whose parameters are always suggesting what's beyond them, then we can read hip-hop as the response of urban people of color to the postindustrial landscape," hip-hip scholar Tricia Rose told Mark Dery. "Electro-boogie took place in a historical moment . . . when factory production and solid blue-collar work were coming to a screeching halt in urban America."[9]

Early hip-hop artists flocked to cyborg imagery to reconcile the American Protestant insistence on work as a moral good with the lack of available work in a neglected borough. "What Afrika Bambaataa and hip-hoppers like him saw in Kraftwerk's use of the robot was an understanding of themselves as *already having been robots*," continued Rose. "Adopting 'the robot' reflected a response to an existing condition: namely, that they were labor for capitalism, that they had very little value as people in this society. By taking on the robotic stance, one is 'playing with the robot.' It's like wearing body armor that identifies you as an alien: if it's always on anyway, in some symbolic sense, perhaps you could master the wearing of this guise in order to use it *against* your interpolation."[10]

By using robotic signs in their music, hip-hop pioneers resisted their racial and class positioning as disposable laborers. Robots—machines invented to perform work for human benefit—ironically allowed these artists to navigate a third path away from work and play, toward a space where no such distinctions were necessary.

Later in the '80s, the New York group Public Enemy further honed hip-hop's relationship to time. Flavor Flav, rapper and hype man with the ensemble, took to wearing oversize clocks as necklaces, visually cementing the presupposition of "Planet Rock" that time did not have to be an external force bounding the body of the individual. It could instead originate in the individual and fan out to the wider world, contradicting the way structures of social power use time as an organizing principle. Clocking in and clocking out had no meaning when the individual, untethered from traditional labor, owned the clock himself.

In Public Enemy's video for "Fight the Power," Flavor Flav repeatedly flashes his clocks at the camera while Chuck D lyrically orbits the potential for revolution and eventual utopia. Part of realizing such a utopia relies on the rewriting of popular sequential narratives, and Chuck starts by unraveling colonialist stories of "progress" within popular music. "Elvis was a hero to most / But he never meant shit to me, you see / Straight up racist that sucker was / Simple and plain / Motherfuck him and John Wayne," he raps. By aligning Elvis, the symbolic figurehead of rock music, with Western actor John Wayne's cowboy characters, Chuck identifies the settler logic underpinning the music industry. Elvis didn't revolutionize or improve the music developed by black artists, music that had strong social value in marginalized communities but lost its specificity and its soul when transformed into a white commercial product. He simply conquered that music, a cowboy pioneer crossing a cultural frontier to extract value from black art.

On a microcosmic level—disrupting the prerecorded song via scratching—and a macrocosmic level—lyrically reframing history to cut through colonialist myths—hip-hop slashed back at straight white time and reordered sequentiality to fit its revolutionary ethos. While the genre also made claims on its surrounding landscapes, filling the streets with music, it left certain spatial distinctions mostly untouched. In the video for "Fight the Power," one shot shows a mother and young child watching the parade proceeding outside their window. There are women among the dancers and revelers in the streets, but only men have access to the mic and the turntables, and the crowd is predominantly male. Women might join men on the hip-hop streets, but mothers with kids, it seems, have to remain behind glass.

Though women were present at every stage in the genre's evolution—Kool Herc played his first party with the help and initiative of his sister; Sugar Hill Records was founded by a woman; B-girls danced alongside B-boys in breakdance crews; women wrote graffiti alongside their male peers; and South Bronx rapper MC Sha-Rock, the first female MC, helped develop the cyborgian vocal technique of beatboxing—hip-hop's reputation as a masculine cultural form soon became entrenched, in part due to the expectations of white consumers, and in part due to its physical settings and competitive bent. "[Hip-hop] emerged in the streets—outside the confines of a domesticity shaped and informed by poverty, outside enclosed spaces where young male bodies had to be contained and controlled," wrote feminist author bell hooks in her 1992 essay "Eating the Other." "In its earliest stages, rap was 'a male thing.' Young black and brown males could not breakdance and rap in cramped living spaces. Male creativity, expressed in rap and dancing, required wide-open spaces, symbolic frontiers where the body could do its thing, expand, grow, and move, surrounded by a watching crowd. Domestic space, equated with repression and containment, as well as with the 'feminine' was resisted and rejected so that an assertive patriarchal paradigm of competitive masculinity and its concomitant emphasis on physical prowess could emerge."[11]

Hip-hop, like rock, emerged as a predominantly masculine art form, a space where boys could be loud at each other. In order to participate in such an arena, women MCs generally had to adopt a certain measure of masculinity to prove they could keep up with the boys. "In keeping with young women's experiences in graffiti and breaking, strong social sanctions against their participation limited female ranks. Those who pushed through found that 'answer records' (rap battles between the sexes records) were the most likely to get airplay and club response," wrote Tricia Rose in her 1994 book *Black Noise*.[12]

Hip-hop's female masculinity manifested both in the way women dressed and in how they sounded on the mic. In the late '80s, the all-female New York group Salt-N-Pepa broke into the mainstream with the 1987 B-side "Push It," which saw re-release as an A-side single in 1988. It was one of the first singles by women rappers to become a nationwide hit, and it owed its success in part to Salt-N-Pepa's conscious decision to rap the way men did.

"It's hard to be a rebel when you're a girl because people want to hear that gruff LL Cool J voice or that Run DMC voice, not these high girl voices," Salt said in a 1987 interview with *Melody Maker*. Pepa concurred: "The female rappers I've heard, I don't want to be anything like them—funny little squeaky mouse voices."[13]

In the video for "Push It," Salt-N-Pepa underscore their gruff, gravely voices with the way they look and move onstage. Both rappers wear their hair short in asymmetrical swoops; both wear oversized bomber jackets, red leather boots, and gold chains. They dance playfully with each other, gently roughhousing and sneering into each other's faces. Behind them, DJ Spinderella scratches records in her own matching jacket, setting up shop behind the turntables, where you would usually have seen a man. The song's production also inverts a more typical gender dynamic in hip-hop music, wherein men rap and women whisper or sing. On "Push It," Salt-N-Pepa rap, often intensifying their words into a shout, while a man, the group's producer Hurby Azor, whispers the name of the song intermittently. In their universe, only women are allowed to be loud. This dynamic didn't keep Salt-N-Pepa from climbing up the charts: "Push It" peaked at number nineteen on the *Billboard* Hot 100, and its success ultimately helped the group's 1986 album *Hot, Cool & Vicious* go platinum, marking the first time a female hip-hop group had sold at such a volume.

The first woman to put out a full-length hip-hop LP on a major label, fellow New York rapper MC Lyte laced her 1988 debut album, *Lyte as a Rock*, with plenty of gruff-voiced barbs, including a dis track aimed at female rapper Antoinette. "10% Dis" was recorded, ironically enough, at the behest of Audio Two, a male duo who felt that Antoinette had ripped off the beat of their song "Top Billin'." They sent their friend Lyte out to air their grievances, not wanting to engage in a rap battle against a woman themselves.

The cover of *Lyte as a Rock* depicts MC Lyte hanging on the arm of her bodyguard, Big Foot, who's more than a full head taller than her, tall enough to break the cover's top frame. Another man crouches at their feet, gesturing to a second woman who has just walked out of the cover's left frame in a black dress and red heels. The woman, whose face cannot be seen, provides a physical foil to Lyte, who wears a tracksuit and sneakers. To Lyte's right, an anonymous, full-femme woman accentuates the MC's relative masculinity. To the rapper's left, her bodyguard towers over her, emphasizing her small frame and relative femininity. Lyte lands somewhere between the two figures, not an object of desire like the femme woman but also not entirely a masculine subject. As a female rapper, she lands between worlds.

In the '90s, following the success of superstar rap groups including New York's Public Enemy and Compton's N.W.A., who both had smash albums in the late '80s, more and more female rappers held their own space within the now-mainstream genre. The New Jersey rapper Queen Latifah, who released her first album, *All Hail the Queen,* when she was still a teenager, signed to the storied label Motown Records for her third full-length release, 1993's *Black Reign.* The album, which would end up going gold, spawned the charting singles "U.N.I.T.Y.," a feminist song decrying misogyny, and "Just Another Day," a semi-melancholic ode to Latifah's hometown of East Orange, New Jersey. In the video for the latter track, Latifah raps in the streets amid a crowd of black men, women, and kids. Unlike in the "Fight the Power" video, mothers with young children join her outside. She wears oversized T-shirts and hoodies under overalls, a tomboyish look that would help cement her as a longstanding queer icon. (Despite persistent rumors that she dates women, Latifah has never publicly come out as gay, bisexual, or queer.)

The same year that Queen Latifah released *Black Reign,* she shared space on the *Billboard* Hot 100 with the Detroit rapper Boss, whose debut album *Born Gangstaz* came out on Def Jam West in 1993. Boss also had two singles chart that year: "Deeper" and "Recipe of a Hoe." In the videos for both, she appears in oversized jackets, black sunglasses, and a black beanie. Her hair is cut short; at a glance, she's easy to mistake for Eazy-E, the high-voiced member of N.W.A. who also tended to don hats and sunglasses in music videos and photo shoots. Stoic, she never smiles, and her voice intensifies the gruffness heard on "Push It," landing in a squarely androgynous register intended to appeal to men as well as women. "I'm the first female gangsta to do stuff men can relate to," Boss said in a 1993 interview. "That's crucial in rap. I talk from a woman's point of view, but I talk hard and tough."[14]

As the decade wore on, a new kind of rap superstar would complicate women's role in hip-hop, not simply adopting masculinity to appeal to a male-dominated market but flickering between gender signifiers in a glitchy, surrealist fantasy world. In 1997, songwriter and producer Missy Elliott stepped in front of the mic for the first time on her debut album *Supa Dupa Fly*. She had worked with Timbaland and the rest of the Swing Mob collective in New York to make music for the R&B group Jodeci, as well as for Elliott's own R&B band Sista. As a solo artist Elliott carved out ample space to play with preconceptions of time, space, and corporeality. In her first video, for her album's lead single "The Rain (Supa Dupa Fly)," she contradicted the notion that women needed to be thin and diminutive in order to appear in front of a camera. Rather than play down her presence as a fat woman, she accentuated it, wearing an inflatable black jumpsuit, shiny and bilious like a trash bag, in front of a fisheye lens. If contemporary logic dictated that Elliott was too big to be a star, she would defy that standard by making herself even bigger. Her strategy worked: "The Rain" became a hit, snaking up to number four on *Billboard*'s Hot R&B/Hip-Hop Songs chart in part thanks to its striking video.

Throughout her music and her videography, Elliott strained against the standards that threatened to cage her. She built upon the ground broken by rappers such as Salt-N-Pepa and Boss, but her music and her presence complicated the idea that women rappers needed to be strictly masculine to succeed. Missy integrated masculinity into her work, but she was also abundantly feminine, seizing as many gender markers as she could to overload the eye and the ear. Her work was and is delightfully confusing, breaking open the expectations levied on it with a keen sense of play and chaos. She made hit songs with unintelligible hooks, scrambling her voice into gibberish. On "Work It," the lead single from her 2002 album *Under Construction,* she throws her voice into reverse. "Put my thang down, flip it and reverse it," she raps at the chorus, and then plays the line backwards twice. It's a hook that dispels any attempts to sing along with it, and it stuck in people's ears all the same, reaching number two on *Billboard*'s Hot 100.

"Work It" flips Elliott's flow at the same time that her lyrics flip gendered expectations of her sexual subjectivity. She's in control at every stage of the encounter she describes, surveying her male partner for his prowess—examining a dick famously cloaked behind a sample of an elephant trumpeting—and then ordering him around: "Go downtown and eat it like a vulture. . . . Sex me so good I say 'blah-blah-blah,'" she raps, reframing the chorus's gibberish as an expression of post-orgasmic daze.

The music video for "Work It" further emphasizes Elliott's inverted relationship to normative femininity. Throughout the video, her dance moves defy physics. She lifts off the crowd from a prone position, as if falling in reverse; she spins on her head without moving her hands, as if animated by something other than herself. In one sequence, she dances through a beauty salon. Her short hair, tracksuit, and chain differentiate her visually from the long-haired, lipstick-adorned women getting their hair cut. The shot's colors flip into the negative, as if to reiterate Elliott's distinct embodiment. She's not a woman playing a man here, but a woman donning an inverted femininity in order to position herself as a sexual subject. In another shot, she raps about shaving her "chacha," then blows a handful of pubic hair into the camera. At once, Elliott performs femininity—grooming her body hair before a sexual encounter with a man—and entirely subverts it, exposing the process and detritus of said grooming in a provocative and hilarious gesture.

The sanctity of the body tends to come undone in Missy Elliott videos, which embrace surrealism in pursuit of an alternative, otherworldly way of being. In "Get Ur Freak On," set in overgrown urban ruins that suggest a postapocalyptic far future, Elliott's neck snakes out from her body, thrusting her face into the camera. In "One Minute Man," she pops her head clean off her shoulders, resting it on a pair of birdcages while her body goes off to flirt with a shirtless, well-oiled man. Again, she delineates a sexual encounter on her own terms and her own timeline. Barring premature ejaculators from consideration ("I don't want no one-minute man," goes the chorus), she lets her own body set the tempo rather than adhering to a man's idea of good, quick sex. If he's done in a minute, she doesn't want him.

Appearing in a room full of clocks, guest vocalist Trina calls back to the work/play division implied by timekeeping instruments: "I put this thing on ya, can you stay hard? / If not, you better keep your day job," she raps. If his body can't keep up with playtime, he ought to get back to work. In "One Minute Man," factories and jobs don't impose temporal demands on the bodies of laboring men. Women do.

In the 2013 video for "The Initiation," rapper Mykki Blanco (the drag persona of the artist born Michael Quattlebaum) also puts a face where it shouldn't be. He stalks the streets in bright blue nail polish. The camera pans up to his shaved head, and a second face juts out from his scalp, rotated ninety degrees from the expected one. The second face is the one that raps. Blanco walks by a group of men who have been lined up by the cops, who are ripping off their hats to look for extra faces. One boy's head reveals a second face like Blanco's; the cops pin him to the hood of their car and arrest him.

Many of Blanco's early videos depict the rapper in two distinct genders: as a masculine performer, shirtless and short-haired, and a feminine one, in a long wig and makeup. A 2013 cover story on the rapper reiterated that duality with a drag cliché, depicting Blanco with one half of his face made-up, wearing half a wig, while the other half remained unadorned.[15] Blanco, it seemed, held two people in one body, a hybrid solution in the cis imagination for reconciling the confusing phenomenon of gender fluidity.

The two-faced people in "The Initiation," who hearken back to the surreal bodies in Missy Elliott's videos, serve as a cipher for this confusion. It's one of the few videos in which Blanco does not wear a wig, and yet his chimeric physicality still speaks to the way cis people think of transness. The cops line up suspects and strip them of their clothing, searching for incongruent body parts, just as trans women suspected of doing sex work are frequently harassed and assaulted by police who punish them for bodily non-comformity. Blanco, long depicted as two people, coalesces into a single person with two faces. But the face that appears on the top of his head isn't an "extra" feature, nor is it an aberration. It's the face that does the rapping, the one that produces the music. The face that speaks becomes as real as the expected face. Blanco, a figure with both masculine and feminine attributes, reconciles his features into a surreal but identifiable whole: a third entity who gets away on his own terms.

"Carpe noctum / Carpe vinum / Carpe diem," Blanco raps: seize the night, seize the wine, seize the day. He speaks Latin and calls upon God, repurposing elements of Catholic mass for his own outsider sermon. He orients himself as a reverse cryptid: "Wolf becomes a man become a wolf," he raps, reverting and then re-reverting the transformation of human into werewolf. He seizes the day only after he has seized the night, rendering time as his for the taking. It's here, on the fringes and out of order, that he survives. "The very words themselves, the very voice itself / Between the living, within the walls / Inconquered, I remain unvanquished." Outside time and space, there's no death to fear. With no death to fear, the body can arrange itself in any order it likes.

10

BUTCH THROATS

Women's Music and Riot Grrrl

In 1969, one month before New York's Stonewall Inn erupted in riots that would go down in history as the turning point in twentieth-century queer liberation, Maxine Feldman debuted a song called "Angry Atthis" at a lesbian bar in Los Angeles. "I wrote it in about three minutes, in a bar in LA," Feldman said in 1998. "Before Stonewall we had Mafia-run bars where you were a fourth- or fifth-class person. It was the only place for dykes to meet; we didn't have festivals, or women's bookstores."[1] The folk musician had moved to LA from Boston, whose coffee houses had begun refusing to book a "big loud Jewish butch lesbian," as Feldman put it, who would draw an openly gay following at shows.[2] Feldman had gotten kicked out of Emerson College in the early '60s for refusing to stay in the closet and had traveled west in search of a more accepting city. But even California sequestered queers in dark bars owned by people who didn't have their best interests at heart.

A briskly strummed and barbed folk song, "Angry Atthis" spat back at the repression enforced on mid-century queer communities. "I hate not being able / To hold my lover's hand / Except under some dimly lit table / Afraid of being who I am," Feldman sings in a husky alto. "We've run half our lives / From that damn word 'queer.'" The reclaimed slur rings out like a klaxon, with a touch of reverb on the vocal take. Feldman strums a guitar faster and faster, as if to indicate the growing urgency of the lesbian community's predicament. The singer's voice frays as the song speeds up, until finally the lyrics reach a point of no return. "No longer afraid of being / A lesbian," Feldman finally proclaims, stretching out the word "lesbian" so it takes up as much space as possible.

Recorded and released in 1972, "Angry Atthis"—a pun on the name Atthis, one of Sappho's lovers—joined Madeline Davis's 1971 song "Stonewall Nation" in a growing movement of lesbian protest music. While disco, as a gay male art form, privileged the aesthetics of the city—its density, speed, and anonymity—contemporaneous Women's Music, a movement founded specifically to highlight the work of often queer women musicians, negotiated lesbian identity through a more pastoral sound. Acoustic instruments and the unadorned human voice reverberated at the core of lesbian folk music, which supplied a new opportunity for queer women to tell each other stories about oppression, community, survival, and joy through their songs.

The association between lesbianism and the open, organic sounds of Women's Music may have been derived in part from certain American myths about liberated women in the Old West. In the nineteenth century, some white women settlers enjoyed more freedom, including the right to vote and own land, in western provinces than they did in America's eastern cities. "The West was the first home of women's suffrage in the US, with nearly every western state or territory enfranchising women long before women won the right to vote in eastern states," historian Virginia Scharff wrote. "Under colonial Spain and newly independent Mexico, married women living in the borderlands of what is now the American Southwest had certain legal advantages not afforded their European-American peers," added historian and author Vicki L. Ruiz. "Under English common law, women, when they married, became *feme covert* (effectively dead in the eyes of the legal system) and thus unable to own property separately from their husbands.

Conversely, Spanish-Mexican women retained control of their land after marriage and held one-half interest in the community property they shared with their spouses."[3]

The mythos of the American West held space for masculine women well into the twentieth century. Lesbians in the '70s found that the rugged aesthetics of country western bars allowed them to present butch in public without provoking violence from straight onlookers. "In the '70s, when lesbianism took androgyny as both principle and style, the country-and-western bar was one of the only welcoming sites outside of the womyn's community," wrote B. Ruby Rich in 1992. "It was there, to those honky-tonk joints, that women could always go in flannel shirts and jeans and no makeup, raise no eyebrows, even dance with a girlfriend alongside all the straight country gals doing the same."[4]

Folk music had also long proved to be a reliable podium for the protest song. While establishing their own space within the genre, lesbian musicians such as Feldman and Davis built on the rich history of politically minded folk singers such as Phil Ochs and Woody Guthrie. But while white men with acoustic guitars could purport to speak to a large contingency of Americans, given the cultural space they were afforded as "neutral" voices, Women's Music had an explicitly closed audience. As part of the lesbian separatist ideological movement, these musicians were women writing and performing songs primarily for other women.

The first explicitly lesbian songs in American history were groundbreaking not just for their lyrical content but also for the way their singers navigated a newly androgynous vocal style. With the lesbian song came the lesbian voice, a way of singing that took on a uniquely butch edge among women folksingers. The way Feldman's voice frayed in "Angry Atthis" suggested a rage and frustration that burned through traditional vocal mannerisms. Feldman's voice hit low and dark, but also sounded ragged and inflamed. In pitch, color, and grain, the singer broke away from expectations of what women should sound like and instead forged a distinct vocal quality that differentiated Feldman from themore feminine folksingers that had broken through to mainstream success in the '60s and early '70s, such as Joan Baez and Joni Mitchell. A group of women performing for women, participants in Women's Music developed their own vocal vernacular as a way of signifying in-group belonging and allying their music to the broader social cause to which they devoted their work.

In 1973, inspired by a comment that singer Cris Williamson made on a local women's radio program, a group of feminists in Washington, DC, founded Olivia Records, a grassroots intervention in an industry overwhelmingly dominated by straight men. "We started with virtually no experience and only $4,000 in donations," Judy Dlugacz, the label's president, told the *New York Times* in 1983. "We had to learn on the job how to make records."[5] By 1974, the label had issued its first single, a split seven-inch featuring one song each by Williamson and Meg Christian. The single pulled in twelve thousand dollars—the equivalent of around sixty thousand in 2019—which allowed Olivia to expand its operations. As the label's flagship acts, the two artists on the single would become the first musicians to release full-length albums on Olivia. Christian put out *I Know You Know* in 1974, and Williamson issued the groundbreaking LP *The Changer and the Changed* in 1975.

Christian, one of Olivia's founders, "decided to use [her] music as a celebration, as a way of talking about the complexities and strengths and the positive parts of who we were as women," she said. "Olivia originated out of a desire to create something useful to women's lives and an organization that would generate jobs and money within our community."[6] As artists, producers, and technicians, women performed all the labor behind Olivia's operations. The label's artists enjoyed little radio play, but their records sold by word of mouth. Williamson's album *The Changer and the Changed* moved 100,000 copies in its first year, a number practically unheard of for an independent label in its first three years of existence, let alone one run entirely by women. "We stopped struggling, trying to fit ourselves in a structure that didn't want us in the first place and created a structure that did," Williamson said.[7]

Though most histories of Women's Music tend to focus on white artists, black lesbians and other queer women of color contributed significantly to the movement. Olivia's third LP release was the 1976 self-titled debut record by the electric rock band BeBe K'Roche, whose main lineup and production team included both black and white women. The album, which veered away from the acoustic folk of Olivia's early records, was produced by Linda Tillery, who would release her own solo LP on Olivia the following year. Tillery also recorded a song for the 1977 Olivia compilation *Lesbian Concentrate,* which spoke out against straight singer Anita Bryant's Save Our Children campaign to relegalize antigay discrimination in the United States. "Don't Pray for Me" called out Bryant by name and railed against her "blind innocence." "Sweet Christian lady preaching hate / I think you need to get your head free," Tillery sang against a funk-rock backbeat, joined by a chorus of her labelmates' voices. "You needn't worry about my soul, 'nita / You need the time to heal your own / We're coming out to walk in the sunlight."

"The radical women's movement of the 1970s held out hope that women of all social, economic, and ethnic backgrounds would be able to measure themselves by their own standards and not those of the dominant male culture," wrote Tillery in the foreword to Eileen M. Hayes's 2010 book *Songs in Black and Lavender: Race, Sexual Politics, and Women's Music.*[8] Women's Music may have been a "predominantly white lesbian social field," as Hayes put it, but plenty of black radical music emerged from under its banner, fighting the inextricably intertwined forces of white supremacy, misogyny, and homophobia.[9]

The Women's Music movement, which had hosted free and accessible concerts in church basements and other queer meeting places, quickly realized the demand for their art, and in 1974 Christian and Williamson, along with Margie Adam, performed at the first National Women's Music Festival in Champaign-Urbana, Illinois. In 1976, the Michigan Womyn's Music Festival, now better known as Michfest, hosted its inaugural performances, which included many Olivia mainstays, including Tillery, Teresa Trull, and Holly Near.

Toward the end of the '70s, Women's Music evinced an ideological fracture that would mark the movement for decades after its peak. Olivia, like many lesbian separatist collectives at the time, welcomed trans women into its fold. A recording engineer living in California, Sandy Stone joined Olivia at Tillery's invitation shortly after her transition. She was out to the other women working for the label, and they accepted her for who she was. "The collective was very clear that they considered me to be a woman," Stone said in a 2014 interview. "We spent a long time—about a year, maybe more—in which we got to know each other and by the time that I actually joined the collective, we felt that we knew all that we needed to know about how we were going to get along together. And so, I joined the collective and went to live with them in [the] Wilshire District of LA, where we had three houses: two next to each other and one across the street."[10]

Stone recorded and mixed Olivia's most successful records throughout the '70s, including *BeBe K'Roche* and *The Changer and the Changed*. No controversy attended her involvement in the collective until the end of the decade, when Olivia received a manuscript of a book soon to be published by Janice Raymond, who accused Stone of interfering in spaces where she didn't belong. *The Transsexual Empire*, published in 1979, outed and smeared Stone; a glut of hate mail and threats of physical violence followed Olivia Records in its wake. "We were being broadsided by hate mail," said Stone. "We'd get a letter and the letter would attack one of our albums because of the way that it was engineered and mixed. There were very clear ideas of what constituted a 'male' mix and a 'female' mix, which nobody had ever heard of before. What it came down to was that 'male' mixes had drums, which was linked back to 'throbbing male energy.'"[11]

The hate quickly intensified. "This was vile stuff. A lot of it included death threats," Stone continued. "The death threats were directed at me, but there were violent consequences proposed for the Collective if they didn't get rid of me." After Olivia organized a nationwide tour, they got word of a lesbian paramilitary group called the Gorgons, who threatened to show up to the tour's Seattle stop and murder Stone. "We did, in fact, go to Seattle, but we went as probably the only women's music tour that was ever done with serious muscle security," Stone said. "They were very alert for weapons and, in fact, Gorgons did come and they did have guns taken away from them."[12]

Faced with increasing antagonism from trans-exclusionary radical feminists, including the later threat of an Olivia Records boycott, Stone left the collective to preserve her own mental health. She moved out of LA and began pursuing her doctorate at the University of California at Santa Cruz. While studying with feminist theorist Donna Haraway, Stone wrote the groundbreaking essay "The Empire Strikes Back: A Posttranssexual Manifesto," in which she grounded gender noncomformity in ancient and recent history and dispelled many of the toxic myths that swarmed the trans community.

The Women's Music movement lost some of its fire in the '80s, though Olivia Records put out albums into the '90s and Michfest continued hosting festivals into the twenty-first century with an adamant "womyn-born-womyn" policy, welcoming only cis women and occasionally ejecting trans women from festival grounds. There was a degree of irony in Michfest's steadfast trans exclusion; Feldman, a frequent MC at the fest whose 1976 song "Amazon" became the gathering's de facto theme song, started going by Max and using he/him pronouns (in addition to she/her) toward the end of his life. One of the feminists who had signed an open letter supporting Stone's banishment from the Women's Music community started questioning his own gender identity. Feldman passed away in 2007; eight years later, Michfest opted to shut down rather than change its transphobic entrance policy.

Though none of the early stars of Women's Music ever quite broke out into the mainstream—pop stardom was a vision of success they never harbored much interest in—the butch voice employed by Feldman and his contemporaries did ultimately make its way to pop radio. In 1983, the low, commanding voice of English singer Joan Armatrading made its way to the *Billboard* Hot 100 by way of the upbeat rock song "Drop the Pilot." It only peaked at number seventy-eight, but it set the stage for another low-voiced singer-songwriter who would experience much more success in the United States. In 1988, two years after she performed as an unknown at Michfest, Ohio songwriter Tracy Chapman released her self-titled debut album on the major label Elektra Records. The warm, intimate, and politically galvanizing record made an unlikely star out of the young singer; by the end of 1988, she could hardly move through public space without being recognized.

The lead single from *Tracy Chapman*, "Fast Car," became a hit in the United States, cracking the top ten of the *Billboard* Hot 100. Like Bronski Beat's "Smalltown Boy," released four years earlier, "Fast Car" tells a story of escape from harrowing circumstances. A transitional song, its setting bounces from the speaker's childhood home to the city and then to the suburbs. None of these places are exactly habitable; the speaker contends with family alcoholism and deeply entrenched poverty throughout the course of the song, but her partner's car signifies freedom. No utopian destination appears throughout the song's lyrics. Chapman's speaker does not get to settle. The closest she gets to paradise is the passenger seat of her partner's car, cruising from a troubled past to an uncertain future. Freedom comes not in arrival but in transition.

Built atop a nimble acoustic guitar riff, "Fast Car" breaks from its folk grounding at the chorus, where the crash of drums and a distant trill of electric guitar turns it into a thrilling rock song. Musically as well as lyrically, the song is lodged between worlds. The pastoral expanses suggested by Chapman's bare voice and acoustic guitar turn sour at the introduction of an alcoholic father the speaker must care for. She feels trapped in her hometown, working for pennies, dreaming of a better life. But then the drums and electric instruments come in to suggest the fast pulse of the highway and the promise of freedom it brings. The way Chapman sings the line "I had a feeling I could be someone" at the end of the chorus is at once one of the most exhilarating and heartbreaking vocal deliveries of the '80s.

Chapman's soulful voice bridges the two worlds that coexist in "Fast Car," the world of quiet suffering under waged labor and the one of boundless potential on the open road. Her alto, warm but gruff at the edges, aligned more closely with the voices of Women's Music artists than with the more traditionally feminine folksingers who had previously found mainstream success. Chapman's music was open but sturdy, argued Steve Pond in a *Rolling Stone* profile of the singer, unlike the "female folkies" who had "been painted as vulnerable, fragile creatures singing about their loves and fears." Chapman pointed out the way that perception aided patriarchy by undercutting the agency of solo female artists. "It seems to me that that image was created for female folk singers because they actually had a lot more control than other women in the music scene," she said. "They wrote their own songs, they played them, they performed by themselves—there you have a picture of a very independent person, and trying to make them seem emotional and fragile and all puts a softer edge on it. As if there was something wrong with being independent."[13]

By 1988, it seemed, US listeners were ready for an independent black woman singer who didn't need to tap into a white patriarchal ideal of femininity to sell records. With her short dreadlocks and her deep, coarse voice, Chapman wasn't afraid to project androgyny in look and in sound. A sexual ambiguity hovered around her lyrics as well: while a woman in the passenger seat of a car might suggest a man in the driver's seat, Chapman never genders the "you" in "Fast Car," and the song's music video never shows a partner. Chapman plays her acoustic guitar alone, her face dipping in and out of shadow against a dusky sky. Deeper cuts on the self-titled album hinted at a taboo romance. On "For My Lover," Chapman sings, "Every day I'm psychoanalyzed / For my lover. . . . Deep in this love / No man can shake." It's not that no *other* man can shake her attachment; it's no man at all. Though Chapman has never publicly disclosed her sexual identity, leading a notoriously private life in contrast to the out and proud lesbians of Women's Music, her songs leave ample space for visions of gendered and sexual rebellions. By 1988, a singer with a butch throat had coursed into the pop mainstream.

The same year that Chapman made her debut, Canadian country singer k. d. lang put out her first solo record, *Shadowland*. The covers of both albums featured monochrome portraits of their singers: Chapman appeared with short hair and a turtleneck in a sepia print, looking downward. *Shadowland*'s cover presented a slightly more provocative image of lang, who also wore short black hair and a black shirt but cast her gaze squarely at the camera. The music inside *Shadowland*'s sleeve similarly bristled at gendered expectations of the voice. Throughout the record, lang luxuriates in the lower end of her range, enjoying the power and confidence it conveys. She brandishes a masculine vocal fry on "(Waltz Me) Once Again around the Dance Floor" and adopts an Elvis-like croon for "Black Coffee." When she does leap up into her head voice, as on "Lock, Stock, and Teardrops," she teeters there as a man might do in his falsetto, indicating that her high-voiced register is not her home, but a brief, temporary flight of fancy taken on for emotional emphasis.

"What gives her vocal artistry a dykish quality is its depth and power, and her remarkable ability to take advantage of many of the conventions of country singing while simultaneously critiquing them," wrote Martha Mockus of lang's voice. "She challenges stereotypical presentations of gender by flaunting a consistently androgynous, if not overtly lesbian, image: nudie suits, short spiky hair, no wigs, and no makeup whatsoever. To dykes, lang's particularly bold vocal and visual styles suggest lesbian identification."[14]

In 1992, lang did come out as a lesbian in an interview for the *Advocate*, on whose cover she wore a blue suit while in a soft, contemplative pose. The same year, she released *Ingénue*, her second solo album, whose lead single, "Constant Craving," crept onto the *Billboard* Hot 100. The video for the song, which depicted lang singing backstage during a stage production of *Waiting for Godot*, ended up winning Best Female Video at the 1993 MTV Video Music Awards. An androgynous-voiced country singer wearing an oversized button-up shirt and short, gelled hair beat out high-femme pop icon Janet Jackson at a time when MTV still categorized its awards by gender. Something was beginning to shift in the popular imagination of what women could be in public.

Soon after Tracy Chapman and k. d. lang broke through as butch pop stars, a revolution started to stir among teenage girls. The '70s vision of women's liberation had largely fallen out of fashion, as "experts" declared in the pages of magazines such as *Forbes* that financial independence and social equality made women miserable, not free. In 1991, Susan Faludi published the book *Backlash: The Undeclared War against American Women*, arguing that the feminist movement of the '70s caused patriarchy to double down on its oppression via media campaigns that claimed women were actually happier as second-class citizens. Only about one in three women and girls self-identified as feminists at the time, but in Olympia, Washington, a group of young women began to strike back at the messaging that painted feminism as passé. Noting that institutional sexism and misogynist violence had not vanished with the rise of second-wave feminism, they saw the need for another women's uprising, and so, concerned that any other message of delivery might not be quite loud enough, they started a band.

"We're Bikini Kill, and we want revolution girl style now!" Kathleen Hanna announces at the beginning of "Double Dare Ya," a song from the band's debut self-released tape. "Hey girlfriend / I got a proposition, goes something like this / Dare you to do what you want / Dare you to be who you will," she taunts. "Double dare ya / Girl-fucking-friend!"

Inspired by all-female punk bands like the Slits, Frightwig, and Babes in Toyland, whose singers' vocal irreverence lent them power and presence behind the mic, Hanna folded Kathi Wilcox and Tobi Vail, fellow students at Evergreen State College, into her musical tornado. Unable to find a female guitarist who jelled with their thorny sound, the three women looped in Billy Karren, a man with feminist sympathies who was content to play a supporting role (and whose presence anyway paled beside that of Hanna, Wilcox, and Vail). Bikini Kill was born in 1990, and its DIY ethos, feminist rhetoric, and ferocious performance style soon spawned a movement.

The music of riot grrrl, like the hand-collaged and photocopied zines exchanged by its participants, favored power and immediacy over polish. While Women's Music artists in the '70s largely sang with practiced skill and played their instruments with dexterity, riot grrrls made a show of their music's frayed edges. It helped that Olympia's music scene was dominated by artists who took amateurism as a guiding ethos, such as the indie pop band Beat Happening and other acts on their label K Records. Wilcox, Karren, and Vail may have been trained musicians, but unlike the hardcore and post-hardcore bands abounding in DC, they felt no need to show off their skill. "What everybody said about us was that we couldn't play our instruments. And we said, '*And?*'" said Wilcox.[15] Shredding was a masculinist construction, and anyway the point of Bikini Kill was Hanna's unabashed scream.

Without shyness and without apology, Hanna sang about sexism with the vicious bite of a woman completely fed up with her own oppression. She sang about sexual harassment and violence, about the massive cultural gaslighting that taught women not to complain about said violence, and about the freedom and power girls could achieve if they banded together. Soon enough, the political messages in her songs coalesced into a political movement. Riot grrrl got its name from Hanna's friend Jen Smith, who wrote a letter to the musician and zinemaker Allison Wolfe saying, "We need to start a girl riot." They started a zine called *Girl Riot*, which allowed other pissed-off young women to connect with each other via snail mail. After moving to DC from Olympia, the members of Bikini Kill (sans Karren) and their friends started hosting riot grrrl meetings for women and girls who, like them, felt that the United States was overdue for a feminist revolution.

The bands that sprang up in Bikini Kill's wake furthered their commitment to ferocity over precision. Wolfe and her band Bratmobile, who befriended Bikini Kill and moved with them to DC, explicitly stated the importance of learning the ropes and playing "badly" in public, to show potential women musicians that everybody starts somewhere. "I think it's important to show people that these structures onstage can be totally broken down. . . . I'm not trying to play bad music, but who's saying it's bad?" said Wolfe. Her bandmate Molly Neuman added, "I think it's really good for bands to go out when they're not ready. Because then, as you do get a grasp on your instruments, people see you in a continuum, as opposed to you just jumped out of nowhere, which is what I always thought: The boy comes out of the womb with a screaming Led Zeppelin guitar, and I feel like I'll never know how to do that."[16]

Though Bratmobile favored surf rock guitar lines in lieu of Bikini Kill's punk power chords, the two groups shared a vocal philosophy. Riot grrrl took the most devalued female vocal affectations—valley girl uptalk, cheerleader chants, girlish squeals of excitement—and gave them teeth. A simper morphed into a growl at the back of Hanna's throat. Her femininity held danger. The way a girl spoke could no longer be grounds for dismissing her when she was the only one in the room with a microphone howling in your face.

Hanna made use of the power afforded to her by her position onstage to reorganize the room at Bikini Kill's shows. She would order men to move to the back of the venue and invite women to congregate at the lip of the stage. "Girls to the front" became a riot grrrl refrain, a long overdue antidote to the scourge of asshole men taking up way too much space at concerts.

Like the first generation of punk performers, riot grrrl musicians folded childlike signifiers into their music and their presence, though their feminist interpolation of girlhood took on a different cadence from that of the brats of the '70s. They weren't flipping off the world in general, just the patriarchy that was strangling the world. With the aesthetics of girlhood, riot grrrls got the chance to reclaim a playfulness and innocence that had been denied many of them by childhood abuse and trauma. Besides, if the infantilization of boys gave them license to act with impunity—white men well into adulthood still get away scot-free with various abuses on the refrain "boys will be boys"—why couldn't an aestheticized girlhood do the same thing? Why couldn't there be freedom and power in a reclaimed feminine innocence? (That riot grrrls had the opportunity to claim innocence at all stemmed from the fact that the movement was largely white, even as it made efforts to practice anti-racism alongside feminism.)

In addition to breaking every rule about how women should look, sound, and behave on a stage, riot grrrl bands encouraged gender deviance among their male fans. Karren was known to wear dresses onstage. The DC chapter of Riot Grrrl, the underground feminist organization that shared a name with the associated music genre, graffitied "REAL BOYZ WEAR PINK" around the city. After their first meeting, the Olympia chapter hosted a Riot Grrrl Extravaganza. The cover charge was two dollars for girls, three dollars for boys, but boys could pay the discounted fee if they showed up to the concert in drag.

Certain male allies took riot grrrl's encouragement to heart, wearing feminine accessories even when it didn't shave a dollar off the cover charge. "They all wore little barrettes in their hair, and they always had our backs," said Michelle Noel, an Olympia resident who for a time played bass in Bratmobile. While certain factions of Women's Music vehemently opposed the involvement of anyone they considered to be men, riot grrrl conditionally allowed even cis boys to the party, so long as they were willing to break down patriarchal assumptions about their own gender. (Le Tigre, the electronic band Hanna founded after the dissolution of Bikini Kill, did play Michfest in 2001 and 2005, implicitly supporting the event's trans-exclusionary policies, but the band's members have since expressed support for trans rights.)

The '90s trend of alt-rock front men wearing dresses in photo shoots likely sprang from riot grrrl's interventions in male gender presentation. Famous dress-wearer Kurt Cobain of Nirvana was a close friend of Hanna's who adopted aspects of riot grrrl in his own music. The open invitation for boys to go femme and girls to do whatever the hell they felt like had a far-reaching impact on performers who felt stifled in their assigned gender.

In 2017, the Venezuelan electronic producer Arca cued up "Deceptacon," an early song from Le Tigre, at a Pitchfork Music Festival DJ set. In a skintight, backless bodysuit and stiletto heels, the trans performer danced gleefully to Hanna's irreverent yelps.[17] In a 2016 interview, queer musician Colin Self noted riot grrrl's foundational influence on their own work: "By the time I was 13/14 years old, I'd seen people like Le Tigre and Sleater-Kinney perform live, all of these riot grrrl bands," they said. "Essentially I remember being like: 'That's what I'm going to do with the rest of my life.'"[18] Two years earlier, in 2014, Mykki Blanco had released "A Moment with Kathleen," a detuned punk ditty that brought Hanna herself on the mic. Riot grrrl's primary goal was to liberate young women, and to some degree it did, though it centered white cis women in its activism. But, for all its limitations, the movement also burned through the boundaries keeping binary genders apart, inspiring transfeminine performers to one day start their own riot.

11

GOD IS GAY

The Grunge Eruption

"Do you think in some paradoxical way the reason you and Kurt connected so much was that he was the female version of you and you were the male version of him?" journalist Kevin Sessums asked musician Courtney Love in 1995, a year after her husband's death.

"That's definitely true," she said. "I am definitely a woman, and he was very much a man, but the qualities were reversed at times, yes."[1]

The star couple of the grunge era, Courtney Love and Kurt Cobain, reached across the aisle of the gender continuum to meet in their own version of the cacophonous middle. When they sang in their respective bands, Hole and Nirvana, they adopted the same ragged, inflamed vocal strategy. They both liked to wear their hair bleached and lank, and they were both known to don black eyeliner and red nail polish. Love's femininity was the more exaggerated of the two, a vintage drag queen cartoon, but she thought of her self-expression as a Trojan horse for her coarse, bristling music.

"When women get angry, they are regarded as shrill or hysterical. . . . One way around that, for me, is bleaching my hair and looking good," she told Simon Reynolds in 1992. "It's bad that I have to do that to get my anger accepted. But then I'm part of an evolutionary process. I'm not the fully evolved end."[2]

Love's anger breached acceptable parameters of femininity, while Cobain's sneering caterwaul made him skew more feminine than his grunge contemporaries. Unlike fellow Seattle groups Alice in Chains and Soundgarden, who channeled metal's technical prowess in their heavy guitar riffs and complex, dynamic vocal melodies, Nirvana never had much interest in shredding. Cobain lacked Chris Cornell's impressive vocal range, and he played guitar like a kid who had picked the thing up on a lark. Nirvana's juvenile affectations endeared, and they supplied the perfect catalyst for grunge's pop breakthrough.

With "Smells Like Teen Spirit," a pop song dressed down in dirty flannel, Nirvana broke off the lid of the underground and forced alternative music into the sunlight. Their second album and 1991 major label debut, *Nevermind*, sold a million copies in eight weeks—four times what Geffen Records had hoped. It landed on the *Billboard* Top 200, and by January 1992, it was the number-one album in the country. Within two months of its release, *Nevermind* went gold—a previously unthinkable achievement for a band of three scruffy punk guys from the Pacific Northwest.[3]

Nirvana sprang up from the same feminist circles as Bikini Kill; the name of the band's breakthrough single came from a phrase Kathleen Hanna drunkenly spray-painted on Cobain's apartment wall while they were both living in Olympia. "Kurt smells like Teen Spirit," she wrote, referring to a deodorant brand marketed to teenage girls.

As a kid, Cobain had identified more strongly with girls and gay boys than with the jocks who tortured him for his femininity. "Because I couldn't find any friends—male friends that I felt compatible with—I ended up hanging out with the girls a lot," he said in a PBS interview. He told the *Advocate* he had a "gay spirit," that he wasn't quite straight, and that if he hadn't ended up with Love, he "probably would have carried on with a bisexual lifestyle."[4]

"I've always been a really sickly, feminine person," Cobain continued. "I've had the reputation of being a homosexual ever since I was 14. It was really cool, because I found a couple of gay friends in Aberdeen—which is almost impossible. How I could ever come across a gay person in Aberdeen is amazing! But I had some really good friends that way. I got beat up a lot, of course, because of my association with them."

Cobain's femininity stayed with him into adulthood, and he cultivated it through his tenure in the public spotlight. "I definitely feel closer to the feminine side of the human being than I do the male—or the American idea of what a male is supposed to be," he said in a 1992 cover story for *Rolling Stone*.[5] He wrote songs about sexual violence; some, such as "Polly," took male aggressors as their speakers, but Cobain's withered delivery made clear that he was not interested in playing rapist as a power fantasy. He played "Polly" on acoustic guitar, accompanied by drummer Dave Grohl on only a handful of cymbal-accented beats. By defusing Nirvana's feral electric sound, Cobain playacted a real life rapist as an abject, hollow man who needed to abuse a young girl in order to feel any kind of power. It's an indictment of crippled masculinity, not a flattering portrait.

In his songs and the videos that accompanied them, Cobain lashed out at the idea of masculine power. Shot in black and white, the video for the *Nevermind* single "In Bloom" reenacts a variety show from the mid-twentieth century, the kind that got the Beatles their big break in the United States. A corny host introduces the "three fine young men from Seattle" to a chorus of screaming girls. Dressed in oversized pinstriped jackets and thick glasses à la '50s singer Buddy Holly, the members of Nirvana barely move as they play their instruments. Cobain in particular looks numbed, casting a dazed glance at the crowd as he weakly strums his left-handed Mustang guitar. The second chorus comes, and the footage slips to a second reel. Suddenly Nirvana's in vintage tea dresses, rampaging around the stage and knocking down the plywood set.

Rather than spin their drag act purely as a moment of comedy, a silly lapse from their "real" gender, Nirvana used femininity as a route to free expression. It's funnier to see them stuffed into an absurd and outdated vision of masculinity than it is to watch them wreak havoc in old-timey frocks. In suits, they're a joke, a trio of stifled, obsequious dweebs putting on a neat show. In dresses, they're Nirvana, a punk band gone rogue, flinging drag and distortion into the homes of MTV viewers. Feminine clothing is liberatory technology, giving the group free license to move as they please and fuck shit completely up.

Cobain wove cross-dressing into his arch, laconic public persona. In a 1991 interview on the MTV metal show *Headbangers Ball*, the front man wore a long, custard-yellow chiffon dress and a matching jacket with a comically high collar. Dark round sunglasses obscured his eyes. "It's Headbanger's Ball, so I thought I'd wear a gown," he said quietly. Nodding to his bandmate Krist Novoselic, who showed up to the interview in a black button-down and olive khakis, Cobain added, "He didn't wear his tux. He didn't give me a corsage, either." "At least I asked you out," Novoselic quipped back.[6] The dress and the gently homoerotic banter set Nirvana apart from the usual *Headbangers Ball* fare. Their music was heavy enough to attract metalheads, but Cobain made sure to poke at his fans' machismo by bringing his femininity onto a TV show specifically marketed toward straight dudes. The dress was a playful provocation, aimed straight at the sore spots of the type of boys who used to throw homophobic slurs in his face.

Though just about every grunge front man wore his hair long in keeping with the subculture's image of unkempt, oily masculinity, Cobain took the look one step further, dyeing his bleached locks pink with Kool-Aid. He wore dresses not just in the safe enclosures of video shoots and television interviews, but to

Nirvana's early concerts on college campuses, before they broke big. Like the barrettes worn by Bikini Kill's male fans, the dresses signaled an open acceptance of femininity and queerness. Cobain was often frustrated with the brittle masculinity upheld by many of his fans, and his clothing was one way to soften Nirvana's image, making it clear that he wasn't just trying to make music for loud, obnoxious boys.

According to Love, Cobain's cross-dressing wasn't just a show he put on for his audiences. "When Love talks about husband Kurt Cobain, which she does with some frequency, it's with affection and slight amusement. Mostly he shows up in benign little anecdotes. Like how she keeps finding him dolled up in women's sweaters from the '50s," wrote Dennis Cooper in a 1994 *Spin* cover story.[7] For a *Vanity Fair* feature that would infamously suggest Love was shooting heroin while pregnant with her daughter, journalist Lynn Hirschberg went thrifting with the couple: "'I got [Kurt] to wear boxers,' Courtney says, helping him to find his size. 'You can't believe how tacky he was. He wore bikinis. Colored. Just a tacky thing.'"[8]

Like many people with uteruses, Cobain suffered mysterious and seemingly untreatable abdominal pain. It was as if the singer were haunted by phantom menstrual cramps. Not only did his sickliness dent his masculinity—the male gender holds little space for chronic illness—his pain clustered in an area associated with womanhood, like the pain of periods and childbirth. Unable to find relief from the medical complex, Cobain started self-medicating with heroin, a habit that quickly became a debilitating addiction.

With the release of their 1992 B-sides compilation, *Incesticide*, Nirvana started draping their music with images of pregnancy and birth. Figurines of unborn fetuses appear throughout the "Sliver" video. The cover of the band's third and final album, *In Utero*, depicts an anatomical drawing of a woman with angel's wings.

In the video for that record's lead single, "Heart-Shaped Box" (written about Love's vagina), fetuses dangle from trees and float in bloody IV bags.

Warmer, angrier, and more visceral than *Nevermind*, *In Utero* articulated pain and frustration with a disarming vulnerability. While *Nevermind*'s rape song inhabited the mind-set of an abuser, "Rape Me" identified with a victim. Cobain repeats the song's title in a corroded yelp as if posing a dare to an imagined aggressor, fantasizing about how the rapist will one day get his karmic retribution. "It's like she's saying, 'Rape me, go ahead, rape me, beat me. You'll never kill me,'" he told *Spin*. "'I'll survive this and I'm gonna fucking rape you one of these days and you won't even know it.'"[9]

Cobain declares himself "anemic royalty" on "Pennyroyal Tea," a song named for an herb historically used to induce abortions. "Distill the life that's inside of me," he howls, as though he had a fetus inside him sapping all the iron from his blood. His stomach pain makes an appearance in the song uncloaked by metaphor: "I'm on warm milk and laxatives / Cherry flavored antacids," he sings, as though the over-the-counter medicines and milk were hard drugs. Loopy on lactose and Tums, Cobain withdraws into an infantile state, at once expectant mother and needy child. "I am my own parasite," he sings on the previous track, "Milk It," in a petulant, tattered whine.

As the one who had actually carried Cobain's daughter to term, Love also penned lyrics about pregnancy, birth, and motherhood for Hole's 1994 album *Live through This*. (Ironically, the two songwriters' overlapping subject matter sparked a rumor among Nirvana fans that Cobain had actually written Hole's songs; no one seemed to entertain the contrary theory that Love, a mother and sexual assault survivor, might have had something to do with the Nirvana songs about birth and rape.) Released seven months after *In Utero* and one week after Cobain took his own life, *Live through This* raged against the media circus that had hounded Love through her marriage to grunge's foremost star. It's a white-hot supernova of a record, wrapping pop melody in fearsome snarls and jagged, scorching guitar work.

"[Love] is the heart of the rock 'n' roll audience," Danny Goldberg, CEO of Warner Bros. Records, told Kevin Sessums for *Vanity Fair* in June 1995. "You meet 14-year-olds and they're all into Hole. It's not just a cult. It's not just colleges. It's not just critics. She's appealing to the heart of the MTV mainstream rock audience. It's not just based on one song. It's her. There are very few women who have ever done that."[10]

"Courtney has that element of danger," said rock journalist Lisa Robinson. "You never know what she's going to do next. We're not used to seeing that in a woman. We're used to seeing that from Jim Morrison, or Iggy Pop, or from Johnny Rotten in the early days of the Sex Pistols. She's a rock star in the sort of unpredictable, volatile way that people voyeuristically expect."[11]

In his profile, Sessums interviewed young fans waiting to see Hole perform in concert. "I'm a Courtney Love fan because I think she's a woman who goes beyond the limits of anything to say what she wants to say and to do what she wants to do," a teen girl named Holly told him.[12]

Love's lyrics and stage presence did in fact rupture just about every preconception of how a tabloid-famous woman should comport herself in public. The *Rolling Stone* review of *Live through This* noted her "corrosive, lunatic wail," as if a woman screaming must be insane rather than justifiably enraged.[13] A more flexible and powerful singer than her husband, Love loaded her words with sparking anger and unruly desire, two emotions largely considered incompatible with a public display of femininity. Hole violently shattered the illusion that girls didn't rage and didn't want. Throughout *Live through This,* she sneers and bellows and riots and begs, so full of hunger that her words seem to be chafing her throat on their way out of her.

Though she presented feminine, a blonde bombshell in a sea of oily boys, Love identified strongly with male performers. "My agent kept saying I was a cross between Bette Midler and Madonna," she told Sessums, recalling her sporadic acting career. "But I kept saying, 'No, I'm not. Fuck you. I'm James Dean. I'm Sean Penn.'"[14] She cited Echo and the Bunnymen's lead singer Ian McCulloch as a foundational influence, claiming in her *Spin* profile "to have copped most of her stage moves from him." When she did point to women who inspired her, she spoke of female performers who had themselves commanded a masculine stage presence: Patti Smith and the Pretenders' Chrissie Hynde. Love channeled all that masculine energy into a high-femme exterior, confusing and enraging those onlookers who expected a demure attitude behind her lipstick and blonde hair.

Like her husband, Love was sexually omnivorous and slept with women, though she ultimately preferred to fuck men—not the way a woman liked to fuck men, but the way a gay man might. "I'm more of a fag," she said. "I've got the same tastes as fags. I like to suck. I go for the rough-trade boys. I'm a total drag-queen fag."[15]

This double inversion floats around Love's quasi-surrealist lyrics, which tend to jam together masculine and feminine imagery. In "Good Sister/Bad Sister," a cut from Hole's first album, *Pretty on the Inside,* Love seems to orbit a scene of sexual violence. "Better burn that dress, sister," she growls, her voice flaring out to its gritty masculine extremes. "I'll be the biggest scar in your back / Run-down and jagged and naked and blind," she taunts at one of the song's breakdowns. "I'll be the biggest dick that you ever had / Hey, want it back?" She not only steals a symbolic phallus; she becomes it. If you want it back, you had better be ready to come take the whole of her, teeth and all.

The dick reappears in the *Live through This* track "Softer, Softest" as a symbol of Love's supposedly corrupted femininity. "Pee girl gets the belt," she sings, speaking to herself as if from the perspective of a childhood abuser. "Your milk is so sick . . . your milk has a dick." While pregnant with her and Cobain's child, Frances Bean, Love felt the full brunt of the media glare on her high-profile marriage. She was, the story seemed to go, wrong for Cobain and unfit for parenthood, both a corruption of the archetypal mother and a corrupting influence on her husband. Her loud, brash persona contradicted the image of the rock star's wife, who is usually neither seen nor heard. She brandished more masculinity than Cobain, an unthinkable violation of her one-sided contract with Nirvana's fandom. She was even worse than Yoko Ono. Her milk—her femininity—had a dick, a betrayal of the silent role she was supposed to play for her husband's devoted following.

Love and Cobain's marriage adhered to certain heterosexual norms: Love was more likely to wear makeup in public, and she did carry the couple's child. But her refusal to fade into the background of her husband's celebrity stained her public image. Something was wrong with her. She was a woman who didn't behave like a woman, who didn't sit down and shut up when asked, who screamed louder and more forcefully than her husband with a band she led herself.

Cobain, for his part, never objected to Love's gender transgressions—they complemented his own. Her position as a woman seemed incidental to their marriage. "I'm just happier than I've ever been. I finally found someone that I am totally compatible with," he told *Rolling Stone*. "It doesn't matter whether she's a male, female or hermaphrodite or a donkey. We're compatible."[16] The line rings as a glib, embryonic take on the pansexual refrain of "I don't see gender," but in the early '90s it was all but unheard of for a pop star to declare that he would still be married to his wife if she were a man—that it was her interior self, not her gender, that drew him.

There were other alternative rock front men who experimented with drag and sang like querulous waifs: Billy Corgan of the Smashing Pumpkins, whose androgynous voice sounds naturally cloaked in a sheet of distortion, and Perry Farrell, who named his band Jane's Addiction after a woman's drug habit. But few asserted their own femininity as both a deeply held personality trait and a site of feminist politics. Cobain repeatedly labeled himself a feminist and told bigoted fans, to little avail, to fuck off. The gay spirit animating him also flooded his music, where his unmanly wail crashed against torrents of badly played guitar, as if polishing his skill would only add to the gendered hierarchy associated with the instrument. There was an innocence to his work, a feeling of unrehearsed candor that haloed even Nirvana's most sardonic songs. The band got labeled grunge, but their ethos stood apart from that of their more technically minded peers.

Before Nirvana barraged the radio, Cobain used to graffiti the phrase "God is gay" on walls around Olympia. He folded the tagline into a lyric on "Stay Away" from *Nevermind*; by the time *In Utero* came out, the refrain had evolved. "What else could I say? / Everyone is gay," he declares on the album's final track. "What else should I be? / All apologies." The change follows biblical logic: if humanity was made in God's image, and God is gay, then all of humankind must be gay too. It's a conceit no doubt originally intended as trollish provocation; as a teen, Cobain also tagged the less theological slogan "homosexual sex rules." But maybe he had a point. Jesus, one of Cobain's visual fixations (he had "Jesus envy," said Love), never did seem much interested in women. Cobain himself was only attracted to women insofar as they were people. Drawn to femininity in others as he incubated it in himself, he reordered the image of the rock star, shrugging off the masculine expectations that attended his fame. In Cobain and Love's messy cosmology, the covenant of heterosexuality started to show its cracks.

12

NO SHAPE

The Formless Internet

In the video for her 1998 dance pop hit "Believe," the singer, actress, and gay icon Cher flits in and out of the material world. She stands in a cage inside a nightclub, a headdress made of fiber optic cables spilling over her shoulders. A rolling drum machine beat twitches beneath airy synthesizer pads, and soon Cher's voice floats into the mix. ". . . After love, after love, after love, after love," she repeats, the two words clearly edited and stitched together from a single take. Her voice, a low, androgynous contralto, bears the artifacts of machine processing. Inside the cage, Cher's eyes glow white.

Before the song's first verse is up, Cher's voice ripples. It has been chopped up, broken, pixelated; it sounds as though she's rolling her Rs, but she's singing "can't break through," and the whole phrase crinkles, even the vowels. The human throat can't physically perform such a vocal act. In the video, as she trills entire words, she teleports from one side of the cage to another, smearing physical space in her wake. Her face, as if issuing from a broken VHS tape, glitches out into lines of visual data. Cher, a cybernetic goddess, no longer adheres to the laws of physics.

By the late '90s, the internet had infiltrated the popular imagination as an open and mysterious frontier. AOL spammed mailboxes with trial CDs, and radio ads began reading off URLs and keywords in addition to phone numbers. Through painfully slow dial-up modems and fat cathode ray tube monitors, many Americans began exploring and creating spaces they did not need to physically enter. Live communication came unbound from the body and the voice; online, it was possible to speak to others in real time without truthfully disclosing your age, sex, or location.

The cybernetic universe and its philosophical connotations slipped into popular media, first via somewhat forced rom-coms such as 1998's *You've Got Mail*, wherein IRL rivals played by Tom Hanks and Meg Ryan fall in love anonymously over email, then in full-blown science fiction phantasmagorias such as the groundbreaking 1999 film *The Matrix*, which adopted the premise that late-century material reality was a giant simulation controlled by a network of artificial intelligences. Written and directed by the Wachowskis, who both came out as trans women years after the release of *The Matrix*, the movie follows a hacker (played with fantastic stoner stoicism by Keanu Reeves) who gets unplugged from the simulation and learns he is a messiah of sorts who, with practice, can manipulate virtual reality at will. It's a deft criticism of capitalism, a system scaffolding reality that is neither natural nor inevitable. It also visually complicates blockbuster ideas of gender, that persistent system underpinning capitalism. Reeves's Neo and his love interest, Trinity, wear practically identical hairstyles and similar black clothing. A minor character named Switch is described in the screenplay as neither male nor female but a "beautiful androgyne."[1] In *The Matrix*, the reality constructed by humanity's oppressors can be warped and remade by those who learn to see its fungibility. Gender, a supposedly natural and inevitable binary system abetting capitalism, can be manipulated, as any trans person knows, in much the same way.

The web's genderfucking potential coursed through pop culture even before the release of *The Matrix*. "Believe" became the first song to use Auto-Tune not as a corrective tool but as an aesthetic one, staggering the contours of Cher's androgynous voice until it became doubly ambiguous—both male and female, both human and machine. In 1997, the first single from Australian pop duo Savage Garden began winding its way up the charts in North America, peaking at number four on the *Billboard* Hot 100. The video for "I Want You" places the band in a dark room filled with futuristic (if ramshackle) electronics. Multi-instrumentalist Daniel Jones tweaks the knobs on an array of nondescript synthesizers and strums a matte black guitar fixed at waist height atop a pole—not a phallus he can pick up and wield, but a piece of static machinery he can approach and manipulate. Singer Darren Hayes fits his face into a machine that scans him with a blue line of light, rendering his features in black, white, and blue on a giant screen flanked by angel statues reminiscent of those in Fritz Lang's 1927 silent film *Metropolis*, one of the first movies to depict an android on-screen.

Hayes's dark, stringy hair hangs to his chin. His face has a beautiful softness to it as in the teens in contemporary boy bands, but his hair does not fall into a perfect symmetrical swoop like that of American pop stars such as the Backstreet Boys' Nick Carter. It is too long to be perfectly masculine. Along with his voice, which rattles out at an auctioneer's gallop swathed in soft falsetto harmonies, his hair glitches him into the realm of androgyny. A face singing in cyberspace just above the expected male range, Hayes, like Cher, flickers between worlds.

Twenty years after Savage Garden released "I Want You" in North America, and a decade after Hayes came out as gay, the songwriter noted the current of queer desire electrifying his early work. "'I Want You' is a song about a dream about being in love with a male energy, and waking up and feeling sad that I knew there was a part of me that was missing," he said in 2017.[2] He was still married to a woman when Savage Garden put out their self-titled debut LP; if he was out to himself, it only came in glimpses cloaked in songs. The band's music, which paired Hayes's high, crimped tenor with sparkling electroacoustic production, told subliminal stories long before Hayes was willing to tell them himself.

The last song on *Savage Garden*, a gentle piano number called "Santa Monica," speaks to the freedom inherent in logging on and acting out, playing with various identities on the internet before trying them on for size in physical space. "On the telephone line I am anyone / I am anything I wanna be," Hayes sings. It's a naive vision of the web, which has since turned into a hive of trolls and megacorporations, and Hayes's roster of potential alter egos rings a little silly (he lists "Norman Mailer" and "a space invader" as fake identities). But it's not hard to imagine him—or any other young queer person uncertain about their place in the world—typing away on an old gray keyboard, writing himself a more fitting role than the one he felt he had to play in meatspace.

At the end of the '90s, the utopian vision of the web started to fall apart. The dot-com bubble began to pop a few months into the year 2000; as stocks started falling, a jingoistic Republican candidate sneaked his way into the presidency. The Twin Towers came down eight months into George W. Bush's tenure in the White House, and soon enough the United States was embroiled in an endless war in the Middle East. Whatever promise of a better world the internet seemed to hold at the end of the '90s fractured and toppled under the weight of real life.

The cybernetic future envisioned by '90s pop hits "Believe" and "I Want You" (and a handful of album tracks, such as the Britney Spears deep cut "E-mail My Heart") caved. The pop charts of the early aughts were bewilderingly diverse in genre: post-grunge bands like Staind, Creed, and Three Doors Down had throaty, guitar-based number-one hits alongside R&B greats like Aaliyah, Destiny's Child, and Janet Jackson. Pop songs from newcomers Dido and Nelly Furtado mingled with numbers from rappers Nelly, Ludacris, Eve, and Missy Elliott. The techno artist Moby had a hit featuring Gwen Stefani of the ska-rock band No Doubt on vocals; it was a weird time of intense cross-pollination.

In 2001, Apple released the first iteration of the iPod, a stylish and easy-to-use MP3 player that allowed music fans to load thousands of songs onto a single device. The days of toting around a CD wallet and a Discman were over, at least for new adoptees of the technology. At the same time, illegal file-sharing programs such as Napster, Kazaa, and LimeWire made it possible for anyone with an internet connection to download MP3 files directly from other users. The small size of MP3 files made it possible to download songs quickly—if you were meticulous and managed to avoid mislabeled or glitched music, you could pirate whole albums one track at a time.

Both iTunes and Napster made it easy to acquire and listen to music for free. By the end of the aughts, free software such as GarageBand and Audacity allowed aspiring musicians to record, edit, and produce their own songs with little overhead cost. The pioneering social media website MySpace let amateur artists upload their music so other people could stream it, also for free. Growing internet speeds and increasingly accessible technology turned the entire record industry on its head. Before long, this new environment started to change the way new music sounded.

Throughout the 2000s, independent music, newly invigorated by music blogs including Pitchfork and Stereogum, keeled between the gently morose (Interpol, Wilderness, I Love You but I've Chosen Darkness) and the insufferably twee (the Pipettes, I'm from Barcelona, The Boy Least Likely To, Clap Your Hands Say Yeah, etc.). (It also favored bands with entire sentences for names.) Inspired by the general need for escapism under the hellish Bush administration, a new kind of party music emerged from the MP3 generation. Girl Talk, the stage name of American DJ Gregg Gillis, started self-releasing albums made entirely of mashups: recognizable songs split apart into their basic components and stitched back together into a high-energy flow. No longer reliant on vinyl and turntables, DJs could smash together half a dozen tracks into one on their own laptops.

By 2010, digital technology had facilitated a growing network of passionate MP3 bloggers to create a perfect storm for computer music. That year, a group of artists put out records that sounded the way the internet felt. The Los Angeles–based producer Flying Lotus (a.k.a. Stephen Ellison) released his third album *Cosmogramma,* which critic Colin McKean described in a review for the *Quietus* as "a sprawling, post-Web 2.0 cacophony. It's like hurtling through the digital darkness of Spotify with everything blaring at once."[3] Under the name Chuck Person, New York–based electronic artist Daniel Lopatin (who now goes by Oneohtrix Point Never) released a cassette called *Eccojams,* a group of songs made by isolating a few measures of pop songs, slowing them way down, and adding an echo effect to the mix. The syrupy, hypnotic collection would go on to influence the web-native genre vaporwave, whose albums would also be made by artists rummaging through the salvage of existing songs and liquefying them into something new and strange.

In early 2010, a college student at Montreal's McGill University named C. Boucher released her first solo album under the name Grimes. Originally issued as a digital download and limited tape run on the local label Arbutus Records, *Geidi Primes* mixed song titles drawn from Frank Herbert's sci-fi novel *Dune* with layers of distorted synthesizers and woozy, incomprehensible, multitrack vocals. If much of the past decade's indie rock music, like that of Arcade Fire, Wolf Parade, and Fiery Furnaces, was grounded in physical instruments and rousing, Bowie-worthy choruses, then Grimes's debut played like a stray transmission from a distant planet.

Geidi Primes and its follow-up, *Halfaxa,* also first released in 2010, caused a stir among self-publishing online music critics. In a brief interview for the web iteration of the *New York Times* style magazine *T,* Grimes described her music as "post-internet," speaking to the voracious musical omnivorousness that the web enabled.[4] By 2012, Grimes had signed to the storied indie label 4AD, known for putting out albums by British goth bands such as Cocteau Twins and Bauhaus in the '80s.

In January 2012, Grimes released *Visions,* a kaleidoscopic funhouse of electronic pop recorded in GarageBand with a Roland

Juno synthesizer, a handful of vocal pedals, and a sampler. Grimes worked quickly; few of the album's tracks had demos. Instead, they seemed to pour out of her on the spot as she locked herself in her apartment for days on end with all the blinds drawn. A minimal piece of software included for free on Apple laptops, GarageBand was now associated with one of the millennium's most talked-about records.

A crisper, bolder, catchier presentation of the jittery synthpop Grimes had developed on her first two albums, *Visions* furthered the Canadian musician's predilection for atomizing her voice across multiple tracks at once. Like synthpop pioneer Laurie Anderson, she served as her own backup singers, often modulating the pitch or texture of her voice to lend it surreal dimensions. There seemed to be not just one Grimes but a flying army of them whizzing across an unstable sound field from all directions.

Over a fat bassline and tinny drumbeat, Grimes sings high in her head voice on "Oblivion," one of the breakaway singles from *Visions*. Nonverbal vocal gestures—"oohs" and "ah ahs"—drape gauzily over barely discernible lyrics. Only certain phrases emerge from the song's reverb-addled murk. You can make out the refrain "see you on a dark night," if only because it's repeated so many times; the lines "always coming and you'd never have a clue" and "I will wait forever" jump out too. But the song submerges its textual meaning (Boucher wrote it about surviving a sexual assault and subsequently being terrified of men) beneath its musical progression. Tension builds through the verses and then breaks for an indelible coda: a processed voice, or a machine convincingly imitating one, maps out a sequence of low, coarse notes beneath Grimes's floaty glossolalia. The song ends on that sound, a tone that seems like it's coming simultaneously from a human and from a computer, both singing in a middling pitch that's tough to gender.

By obscuring her lyrics and drawing attention instead to her idiosyncratic production, Grimes, a solo artist with a voice high enough to scan as female (she has hesitated to use the word "woman" to describe her gender), flatly refused to write confessional songs.[5] Some male critics floundered when reviewing her music, which did not allow easy entry into her interior emotional state. *Rolling Stone*'s review of *Visions* lamented that "Boucher's voice is all airy top end: she sounds like a cross between a J-pop pipsqueak and Alvin and the Chipmunks. It's an irksome, sometimes shrill sound; often, her lyrics are unintelligible. The result is an emptiness at the center of the record."[6] Without lyrics to cling to, without a pleasingly tempered female voice to hear, certain men heard *Visions* as hollow. They heard Grimes as irritating and childish, lobbing that transparently gendered barb "shrill" at her music.

Dismissed as she might have been by certain reviewers, Grimes attracted a significant following of listeners who heard exciting new space opening up in her weird compositions. She belonged to a new generation of artists who refused to box themselves in to a given genre and shied away from traditional production arrangements. Alongside Grimes, Chuck Person, and Flying Lotus, this wave of internet-savvy auteurs included the omnivorous R&B/pop singer Blood Orange, the electronic provocateur FKA twigs, the unvarnished lo-fi troll Ariel Pink, and the chaotic California hip-hop collective Odd Future Wolf Gang Kill Them All, whose members included the queer and gender-blurring performers Frank Ocean; Syd tha Kid; and Tyler, the Creator. These artists made music in different genres, but they shared an indifference to convention and an aptitude for the tools of the web. All of them were loved and hated by critics at the same time. Depending on who you asked, they were either music's bright new horizon or its explosive end. Within this new online arena, among these artists and others, a wide variety of gender transgressions surged.

As the video-sharing website YouTube gained traction toward the end of the aughts, the relationship between music videos and their viewers fundamentally changed from the MTV model. With free, fast, on-demand streaming videos, anyone could be their own VJ and fire up a clip at will. Few artists have taken advantage of this new landscape as well as Janelle Monáe, the multihyphenate singer, songwriter, producer, and actress born in Kansas City and based in Atlanta, who has filled the second decade of the new millennium with a visual feast of playful and riveting music videos.

Monáe's songs and their videos further a vibrant history of science fiction and Afrofuturism in music, drawing on the legacy of artists such as funk collective Parliament-Funkadelic and jazz visionary Sun Ra and spinning them into her own queer imagining of the future. Her albums, which blend together soul, R&B, pop, and hip-hop, are all concept albums that take place in ambiguous dystopian futures in which androids are systemically oppressed. She plays an android freedom fighter in her visual universe, banding together with other marginalized robots to cast off the tyranny of natural-born humans. In most of her work, she also takes advantage of the radical potential of genderplay and drag.

The music video for Monáe's 2010 song "Tightrope" is set in a psychiatric institution and begins with a caption: "Dancing has long been forbidden for its subversive effects on the residents and its tendency to lead to illegal magical practices." In defiance of the powers that be, Monáe, dressed in a tuxedo and shiny oxford shoes, literally dances her way free of the asylum, a group of fellow dapper androids in tow. The video, as Francesca T. Royster wrote in *Sounding Like a No-No*, "might very well capture what it's like to be black and creative and queer in the twenty-first century, where freedom is still a tightrope walk. If the exuberant group dance scenes are a sign, freedom is clearly the magic of making music."[7] Stillness is captivity, but movement, music, and female dandyism all clear an open space.

In the video for the 2013 single "Q.U.E.E.N.," Monáe finds herself frozen in time and on display in a museum exhibit full of former time-traveling rebels. She's been captured and imprisoned for launching Project Q.U.E.E.N., a "musical weapons program in the twenty-first century." A visitor to the museum sneaks in a forbidden vinyl record and plays it on a turntable that's also on display. A funk guitar line crashes in. Monáe and her bandmates stir to life, once again animated by music's potential for disobedience.

Until 2018, Monáe was fond of saying she preferred dating androids when asked about her sexuality. She finally came out as pansexual in a *Rolling Stone* cover story that ran shortly before the release of her audiovisual album *Dirty Computer*, whose videos dropped the tuxedos in favor of giant pink pants designed to look like vaginas. But she laced references to her queerness throughout her discography years before she was willing to discuss it on record. "Q.U.E.E.N." includes the lines, "Hey brother, can you save my soul from the devil? / Say, is it weird to like the way she wear her tights? . . . Am I a freak because I love watching Mary?" When Monáe sings these lines in the song's video, she's in a group of other black women all wearing black-and-white dresses and short wigs. Their pose and matching costumes call back to the 1960s girl groups the Beatles so voraciously consumed; their hair, though, looks a little more like the Beatles themselves. Monáe poses her questions—*Is it weird to like looking at other women?*—to the girls around her, pointing directly to one of them when she sings the name "Mary." Rather than affirm her fear that she is a freak, Mary sings back to her flirtatiously. It's as if this fictional girl group is reclaiming what the Beatles took from black women fifty years prior—musical communality, sisterhood, and dynamic vocal play—and lacing it with their own homoerotic potential.

No longer aloof about her own queerness, Monáe has proudly stepped into her role as a gay icon. "I want young girls, young boys, nonbinary, gay, straight, queer people who are having a hard time dealing with their sexuality, dealing with feeling ostracized or bullied for just being their unique selves, to know that I see you," she told *Rolling Stone* in her coming-out interview. "Be proud."[8]

Though trans people built networks of social support and medical aid throughout the twentieth century, these structures were necessarily restricted by geography. In the twenty-first century, the proliferation of internet-equipped consumer electronics enabled a new generation of gender nonconformists to communicate across any distance. Trans kids no longer had to move to New York or San Francisco to speak with others like them; they could use Facebook, Twitter, Tumblr, and YouTube to find community. Communication didn't depend on the presence of the physical body, and even the voice was no longer necessary to speak instantaneously to another person in a different town or a different continent, which was useful if you were trans and still literally finding a voice that felt right in your throat.

Against this cultural backdrop, an increasing number of musicians have begun to make work that unstitches the gendered body from its usual schematic of meaning. In 2010, the Seattle songwriter Mike Hadreas released his debut LP under the name Perfume Genius on the New York-based independent label Matador. He wrote *Learning*, a sparse, raw collection of songs written on piano, while living with his parents and in recovery from drug addiction. The album was quietly popular among a certain subset of exquisitely sad gays (among other fans of delicate and earnest music that called to mind the outsider pop songwriter Daniel Johnston), and Hadreas soon had to figure out how to tour his new songs. He enlisted help from Alan Wyffels, a friend who had taken Hadreas to AA meetings in the early days of his recovery. They proved to be an excellent musical match, and while playing Hadreas's songs together, they also fell in love.[9]

In 2014, Perfume Genius released the full-band pop single "Queen," a song that would open Hadreas's music to an increasing number of listeners. Catchy and assertive, "Queen" grapples with the uneasy position of living visibly queer in a world that's not always eager to accept deviations from the heterosexual norm. It's not exactly a pride song; in celebrating himself as a gender non-conforming sexual other, Hadreas explicitly names the straight world's fears. "Don't you know your queen? / Cracked / Peeling / Riddled with disease," he taunts. "No family is safe when I sashay." His voice, an androgynous wisp, floats above a heavy slate of drums and an electric guitar that blares like a fire alarm. The rock instrumentation nods to a vision of normative masculinity, but Hadreas's voice undoes it. He is the nuclear family's worst nightmare, a sick gay artist parading himself through the straight world unashamed. Rather than sanitize himself for a straight audience, Hadreas celebrates the danger he poses to the gendered order.

A month after releasing their third album, *Too Bright*, in October 2014, Perfume Genius appeared on *The Late Show with David Letterman* to perform "Queen." It was the group's network TV debut. Hadreas, backed by a bassist, a drummer, and Wyffels on keys, wore a white power suit over a black leather harness. His lips were painted bright, shiny red, and he bent over the microphone while he sang, as if spitting the words up one by one. He danced, haltingly at first and then incrementally more fluidly.[10] Inside the typically safe and vanilla setting of a late-night show performance slot, Perfume Genius brought an explicitly queer vision into the TV screens and computer monitors of strangers. Watching it at the time felt a little like witnessing a sabotage of all the standards that tended to bound rock music. What traditionally would serve as a vessel for tired straight masculinity, a rock bro with a guitar and some gravel in his voice, had suddenly become vibrant, fluid, and undeniably gay.

It did not seem easy for Hadreas to perform before these cameras, to beam into the homes of people he had never meet, but it did seem necessary. At a time when queer culture's acceptance in the mainstream felt like it depended on queer people's docility, Hadreas refused to comply. He would not make it easy. He would stand out, a vision of complicated gender and open nervousness, daring straight viewers to subsume him into their bland, restrictive vision of what gay people could be. After decades of conciliatory LGBTQ activists trying to convince the straights that their rights posed no threat to their nuclear households, Hadreas went on live TV and sang, "No family is safe when I sashay."

A week after Perfume Genius's TV debut, a twenty-five-year-old electronic producer named Arca released an album called *Xen*. Arca had been in the producer's room during the sessions for rapper Kanye West's abrasive 2013 album *Yeezus*, and she would go on to work with pop chameleon Björk on the albums *Vulnicura* and *Utopia*. In 2014, she was known mostly for the mixes she uploaded to the website SoundCloud, which liquefied hip-hop, dancehall, and reggaeton beats into a gleaming stew.

Xen was Arca's debut LP, and she named it after the feminine alter ego she had cultivated since childhood. "I have this image in my head when I listen to a song of mine that I really love or that I feel happy with. First of all, I feel like I haven't made it, and second of all, I don't bop my head, I move really slowly in a very effeminate way," said Arca in a 2014 interview. "Lastly, I close my eyes and I see this naked being who exists in front of an audience. Everyone is simultaneously attracted to it and repulsed—it looks like it went through suffering but it's beautiful. . . . This being is actually aware of its sex as a weapon and as a threat. Xen is an 'it.' I lean towards calling Xen 'her' in response to the fact that society historically leans towards men having more power. Me calling Xen 'her' is an equalization of that."[11]

Xen appears on the cover of the album bearing her name. Rendered by Arca's frequent collaborator Jesse Kanda, she's a vision of distended femininity, with hips that jut out maybe a foot from her small waist. Her long arms are covered in ripples of loose skin. Her upper body is pale white, but her legs are deep red, as if she's slowly filling up with blood. Kanda's image seems to tease out the subconscious communal shudder prompted by the sight of the naked female form, which is not supposed to be seen under normal circumstances and thus introduces a break into the act of quotidian looking. Even certain streaming services pixelate parts of the album's cover as if it were pornographic.

The music inside *Xen*'s sleeve lives up to the cover's promise of corrupted sensuality, offering alien sound forms that draw upon recognizable genres without replicating them. Rhythms churn, melodies denature, and the occasional voice flickers in and out, filtered to the point of unintelligibility. The fluidity of the music's structures echoes the fluidity of Xen's physicality. Arca explicitly closed the conceptual gap between trans bodies and trans sounds. Using a melting, detuned, chaotic musical vernacular, she articulated the queer embodiment that had run through the synthesizer's history ever since Wendy Carlos first powered up her Moog.

In 2013, an English producer known only as Sophie began putting out a series of idiosyncratic electronic pop singles marked by tactile, plasticized synthesizer sounds and tightly processed, hyperfeminine vocals. Songs such as "Bipp" and "Lemonade" seized on the breathless tone of women gushing about consumer products in advertisements, pairing that overstated artificiality with indelibly catchy melodies. "Hard," the B-side to "Lemonade," embellished Sophie's clanging percussion and rubbery squeaks with lyrics that hinted at a BDSM encounter. "Latex gloves slap so hard," a woman sings. "Hard, hard / I get so hard." At the time, critics assumed that because Sophie was an electronic producer residing in semi-anonymity behind an alias, she must have been a man. It wasn't until 2017, when she released the single "It's Okay to Cry," that she began using she/her pronouns in public.

Sophie's 2018 debut album, *Oil of Every Pearl's Un-Insides*, softens the plastic sheen that coated her early singles. Certain songs, including the pet play wallop "Ponyboy," hit harder than "Hard," webbing a booming, demonic voice over an iron-clad drum beat. But by track four, "Is It Cold in the Water?," Sophie applies her deft grasp of software synths to deep, glistening progressions. The dense knot of her music opens up and starts searching. "Is it cold in the water?" vocalist Cecile Believe asks, stretching out the word "cold" at the top of her range, as if wondering if she should jump into the icy depths below. Tracks bleed into each other, now liquid instead of crystalline. It's not hard to read the album's middle section as a transition narrative: Is it cold in the water? Should I jump? Should I unmake myself, not knowing what I'll be on the other side? Do I give up the cells of what I know for an open plane I've never seen?

Un-Insides congeals again with "Immaterial," a snappy pop anthem seemingly dedicated to legions of "immaterial girls" and "immaterial boys." Sophie nods to pop icon Madonna's 1984 hit "Material Girl" while gently undermining the restraints of material reality, outlining a vision of consciousness unburdened by the body's narrow social connotations. "I can be anything I want," declares Believe. "Without my legs or my hair / Without my genes or my blood / With no name and no type of story / Where do I live? Tell me, where do I exist?" Here, in this indeterminate sphere, matter follows the mind, not the other way around. A body is not a prison; it does not close off possibility. It is not a story completed at birth. A body is a prologue, and its story can be written at will.

Throughout the second decade of the twenty-first century, queer, gender-confounding music has bloomed both in the underground and in the mainstream (and in the blurry, unstable overlap between the two spheres), giving new voice to ancient defections from cis gender categories. Arca's 2017 self-titled follow-up to *Xen* centered the artist's voice and began with a quaking plea: "Quítame la piel de ayer," she sings against a low electronic groan. *Let me shed yesterday's skin*. Brooklyn rapper Young M.A. released the album *Herstory* the same year; it featured her 2016 breakthrough single "OOOUUU," whose video introduced her unapologetic stud presence to the world. Young Thug's 2016 mixtape *Jeffery* featured a photo of the Atlanta rapper posing in a layered blue gown on the cover; inside, his crackling, nasal voice tied together a vibrant mix of genres, from dancehall to synthpop to trap. Big Freedia, the New Orleans bounce pioneer whose voice has appeared on Canadian rapper Drake's "Nice for What" and living legend Beyoncé's "Formation," exploits the joyful potential of colorful drag in music videos for her own rambunctious, playful songs.

In 2018, Björk collaborator and experimental pop artist serpentwithfeet put out his debut LP *soil*, whose songs celebrated gay love and mourned gay heartbreak with a whole chorus of electronically processed, pitch-shifted voices. The same year, enigmatic noise pop musician Yves Tumor released *Safe in the Hands of Love*, a challenging and grotesquely beautiful record that veered between harsh static and crisp, tuneful funk-rock. Tumor, who does not publicly use third-person pronouns, is something of an alt-pop chameleon whose gender presentations vary widely from photo to photo and video to video: a blond wig in one image, a shaved head in the next. *Hands of Love* reflected that malleability in its voraciousness toward genre, all while Tumor's lyrics balanced the deep human need to be loved with the terror that often accompanies pursuing love of any kind as a queer and gender-weird person.

One of the decade's biggest emotional gut-punches arrived in the form of *Blonde*, the 2016 album from pop singer and former Odd Future member Frank Ocean, who came out as queer in a 2012 Tumblr post. The album is something of an ode to former selves, a sequence of memories tied together by Ocean's charismatic and often pitch-shifted voice. He remembers being young and homeless. He remembers awkward first dates with other men. On the album highlight "Nights," his technologically augmented voice rises up the octave as his delivery becomes more tender, more vulnerable, as if breaking away from his masculine-sounding range were a way to soften himself, as if his memories and the way he feels about them could not quite fit within the parameters of acceptable male expression. It's subtle, but "Nights" contains one of the most emotionally disarming instances of pitch-shifting yet recorded. Here, pitch-shifting is not spectacle but intimacy; it provides Ocean with an opportunity to say the things a lower, more historically fraught voice cannot say. "Staying with you when I didn't have an address / Fucking on you when I didn't own a mattress," he sings gently, remembering his own youthful vulnerability and the moments of intimacy it brought.

As Ocean grounds himself in the past, he also situates himself as an emissary of what's to come. "We'll let you guys prophesy / We gon' see the future first," he sings on the album's lead single "Nikes." They're the first lines sung in Ocean's natural pitch; for the first part of the song, his voice is artificially raised, a little cartoonish in its timbre, a little young. When his voice drops, a layer of Auto-Tune clings to it, lending it a sparkle.

In the dreamlike video for "Nikes," which takes place at a party that seems to drift in and out of the real world and a better one, Ocean wears perfectly winged eyeliner, glitter, and a balaclava over his face, a shimmering vision of queer revolution. He stares directly into the camera, and then he goes up in flames—literal flames that shoot up his clothing, later extinguished by crew members on site. He lets the viewer enjoy the illusion of his immolation, and then he reassures us it's just that—an illusion. No harm comes to him. When he starts to sing about prophecy, he appears on an otherwise empty stage in a pearled Balmain jumpsuit, light glancing off his glitter-spangled face as if it were made to touch him. He closes his eyes while he sings and poses a little like David Bowie did in his early videos, holding his arm in front of himself like he's about to bow. In this moment, he is not a target of oppression within the wider, ugly world. In his own world, he is beautiful, bedazzled, and sublime.

On "Wreath," a song from Perfume Genius's fourth album, *No Shape*, Mike Hadreas sings over a quick synthesizer pulse. "Burn off every trace / I wanna hover with no shape," he sings, as if into a strong wind. The song's instrumentation grows denser behind him as its progression unfolds, and it's hard to parse what's machine, what's not. Synthesizers and guitars bleed together, obscuring their origin. "I'm moving just beyond the frame," sings Hadreas, drawing out the last word like he's liquefying his own voice and letting it evaporate into the mist.

"I am not a big fan of my body and would like to leave it," Hadreas said in an NPR interview. "Not die, but retain all my thoughts and be free of my body. I have Crohn's disease, which has caused me to not trust my insides. I feel betrayed by it. I am getting older, and that feels like a betrayal on the outside as well. I do not feel strongly connected to being a man or a woman, which was and still can be confusing. It also doesn't feel attractive. I feel like it would be more attractive or at least easier to comprehend if I picked a side." From this confusion, he wrote "Wreath."[12] The song builds; its instrumentation snowballs, growing louder and prompting Hadreas to sing more boldly. By the end of the song, it sounds as though he is about to sing his way out of his body, as though his voice could lift off and leave the troublesome fact of embodiment behind.

But the voice rises from a person's physical form, just like the desire to leave the body behind originates in the body itself. The difficulty of picking a side, too, weighs on the body, and it was not until recently that I realized the body picks its own side. Trans people, by transitioning, don't force one body into a second shape. They let the only body they have grow into itself until it's whole. Transition isn't a corruption of gender. It's a fulfillment.

In a 2018 interview, the trans Aymara producer Elysia Crampton connected her music—a fluid and spectacular display of shifting beats and surprising melodies—to a history of third-gender expressions in American Indian culture. Her transfeminine ancestors recognized the body as a site of holy becoming, not a hindrance to the expression of the self but the arena where that expression takes place. "The gift the ancestors have given me is this body. The body is also a legitimate document. . . . The body is enough to build agency and confront power—however wounded, however marred, however disabled or prohibited," she said. "That the body is enough is really all I can say at the moment."[13]

In Crampton's compositions, in Perfume Genius's music, in Arca's and Sophie's and Janelle Monáe's and Yves Tumor's songs, I hear a refusal to force the body against its true shape. I hear instead the willingness to let the body choose itself, to let the voice surge up and away from the expectations that would box it in. In their slippery, confounding, and transcendent music, these artists—and the hundreds of others that join them on this path—cast off the claustrophobic molds that would keep them from themselves. Their music twists into new shapes without names, shapes that open a way into a world that lets in the light.

CODA

Whole New World

In October 2017, I went to a Sophie concert in Los Angeles where the pop producer debuted a number of tracks that would later appear on her 2018 album, *Oil of Every Pearl's Un-Insides.* The crowd was mostly young and overflowing with beautiful, chaotic, chimerical genders. All of Sophie's opening acts either were transfeminine or integrated drag into their performances. Sophie's set began with impossibly loud percussion and then the sound of an electronically garbled voice repeating the words "WHOLE NEW WORLD" as the star of the night and her dancers made their way onstage beneath a strobe light. It felt a little like we were all getting away with something, witnessing a performance that felt too pure, too weird, and too ecstatic to belong to this world.

On the T-shirts Sophie sold at the merch stand that night, the evening's date and location were listed as "LA000010302017." The dating convention, all those zeroes in front of the number ten representing the month, is a reference to the concept of deep time: a way of thinking about chronology on a geologic scale rather than an anthropocentric one. The earth is a lot older than the humans destroying it, and it will continue to whir around in space long after we're gone. I'm usually pretty disconsolate when it comes to the geological future, but seeing the day's date represented that way beneath Sophie's name, I shared in her impossible optimism. I could see the zeroes filling up, charting human time far into a future where we as a species not only survive but thrive.

A few years ago I had a trans therapist who believed that trans people were poised to become the catalyst for a radical shift in people's relationship to the earth and to each other. By rewriting the stories of ourselves, by shucking the expectations levied on us at birth and turning ourselves into something new, trans people might show the rest of the world how to unwrite the tragedy of its seemingly inevitable end. I'm not sure a process as personal as transition scales up to the size of an entire planet, especially one populated by millions of people who seem perfectly content to pretend trans people don't exist. And I'm not sure it's fair for us to get slotted into a savior narrative, primed to fix problems most of us didn't create. But again, I'm grateful for the optimism—the belief in transness as transformative both within the body and outside it, as kindling ready to ignite a numbed world.

The music I've written about here doesn't give me hope, exactly, but it does open up space in me to consider the wide possibility of things yet to come. Sophie is a transhumanist, and my former therapist believes in the transcendence of the human spirit; personally, I'm more aligned with the fatalism of Yves Tumor, the noise pop musician who, in a 2017 *Pitchfork* interview, said, "We're doomed. That's it. The world is over. [laughs] Sorry to laugh. But I don't want people to be happy or sad when they listen. I just want them to be hopeful." The interviewer asked what people could possibly have to be hopeful about, given the impending doom. "A happy ending," Tumor said. "And when I say happy ending, I mean that if there is a meteor that's going to destroy the earth, at least there's the most beautiful sunset the world has ever seen right before it crushes us. Maybe my album is that sunset."[1]

Whatever happens, we don't have to walk into it alone. We can find ways to coalesce—to become more ourselves, and in doing so, become better equipped to reach out to each other. There's magic in making yourself, and so often that magic leaks out in the form of music. It disarms you, renders you soft and spontaneous, ready to face the unknown. It binds you to other people, letting you share in sublingual joy. Music dissolves the artificial boundaries we build between each other. In losing yourself, you can better become yourself—one of music's many odd paradoxes that has made it such a fertile home for expressions of gender weirdness. Whether or not you're trans, I hope there's something in this book and the music it points to that helps you feel a little less alone, a little more connected, a little more like whoever you know yourself to be.

ACKNOWLEDGMENTS

This book would not have been written were it not for the support and encouragement of Jessica Hopper and Casey Kittrell at the University of Texas Press. Thank you for your patience and generosity, and for helping me see the thing through every step of the way.

Thank you to my copyeditors, Lynne Ferguson and Sarah Hudgens, for your hard and meticulous work.

Thanks to my editors and far-flung colleagues in the freelance writing world for giving me space to shape my thoughts over the years.

Thank you to Kate Fiello, Misha Bogart-Monteith, and John Vargas for helping me get my head where it needed to be to write. Thanks to Amy and Adam for your love and support, and for letting me ramble about the ideas that would make it into this book. Thanks to Chris, Leslie, and Blair for always welcoming me home.

Thank you to my parents, Paul and Dalia, for instilling in me a lifelong love of music and language.

Thank you to the unpaid and mostly anonymous legions of fan archivists who continually upload vital music history to the web. Your work greatly facilitated my own.

And thank you to Matt, for enduring my lunacy.

NOTES

INTRODUCTION

1. Michael Paramo, "Transphobia Is a White Supremacist Legacy of Colonialism," Medium, July 16, 2018, medium.com/@Michael_Paramo/transphobia-is-a-white-supremacist-legacy-of-colonialism-e50f57240650.
2. Cecily Jones, "Shades of White: Gender, Race, and Slavery in the Carribean," OpenDemocracy, June 25, 2015, www.opendemocracy.net/en/beyond-trafficking-and-slavery/women-and-slavery-in-caribbean-whiteness-and-gilded-cage/.
3. Angela Yvonne Davis, *Blues Legacies and Black Feminism: Gertrude "Ma" Rainey, Bessie Smith and Billie Holiday* (New York: Vintage, 1999), 41.
4. Gayle Wald, *Shout, Sister, Shout! The Untold Story of Rock-and-Roll Trailblazer Sister Rosetta Tharpe* (Boston: Beacon, 2008), x.
5. Molly Miller, "The Badass Riffs of Sister Rosetta Tharpe," Premier Guitar, May 12, 2018, www.premierguitar.com/articles/27313-dr-mollys-guitar-lab-the-badass-riffs-of-sister-rosetta-tharpe.
6. Milo Gooder, "In Conversation with Elysia Crampton," *Tank Magazine* (Spring 2018), tankmagazine.com/tank/2018/tank-talks/elysia-crampton.
7. J. S. Jenkins, "The Voice of the Castrato," *Lancet* 351, no. 9119 (June 20, 1998): 1877–1880.
8. C. De Brosses, *Lettres historiques et critiques sur l'Italie*, 3 vols. (Paris, 1799), 3:246.
9. Wayne Koestenbaum, *The Queen's Throat* (Cambridge: Da Capo Press, 2001), 47.
10. Tyina Steptoe, "Big Mama Thornton, Little Richard, and the Queer Roots of Rock 'n' Roll," *American Quarterly* 70, no. 1 (March 1, 2018): 55–77.
11. Jack Gould, "TV: New Phenomenon," *New York Times*, June 6, 1956, 67.
12. Edward Carpenter, *The Intermediate Sex: A Study of Some Transitional Types of Men and Women* (New York: Mitchell Kennerly, 1921), 111.
13. Koestenbaum, *Queen's Throat*, 190.
14. Ann Powers, *Good Booty: Love and Sex, Black & White, Body and Soul in American Music* (Dey St./William Morrow, 2017).
15. Koestenbaum, *Queen's Throat*, 42.
16. E. Glasberg et al., "The Butch Throat: A Roundtable," *Journal of Popular Music Studies* 30, no. 4 (December 2018): 75–94.
17. Katy Steinmetz, "The Transgender Tipping Point," *Time*, June 9, 2014, time.com/135480/transgender-tipping-point.

1. SCREAMING THE BEATLES

1. *The Ed Sullivan Show*, season 17, episode 19, aired February 9, 1964, on CBS.
2. Ben Cosgrove, "'The Luckiest Generation': LIFE with Teenagers in 1950s America," *Time*, November 29, 2014, time.com/3544391/the-luckiest-generation-life-with-teenagers-in-1950s-america/.
3. Dorian Lynskey, "Beatlemania: 'The Screamers' and Other Tales of Fandom," *Guardian*, September 28, 2013, www.theguardian.com/music/2013/sep/29/beatlemania-screamers-fandom-teenagers-hysteria.
4. Vivek J. Tiwary et al., *The Fifth Beatle: The Brian Epstein Story* (Milwaukie, OR: Dark Horse Books, 2015), 15.
5. Brian Epstein, *A Cellarful of Noise* (London: Souvenir Press, 2011), Kindle.
6. Barbara Ehrenreich, "Screams Heard 'Round the World: The Opening Shot in the Female Sexual Revolution Was Fired by Girls in Bouffants and Bermudas Beatles," *Chicago Tribune*, December 14, 1986, 1–5.
7. Barry Miles, *The Beatles Diary*, vol. 1, *The Beatles Years* (London: Omnibus Press, 2009), Kindle.
8. Wesley Laine, "Beatles Beatles," *Record Mirror*, February 2, 1963, Rock's Backpages Library, accessed June 17, 2019, www.rocksbackpages.com/Library/Article/beatles-beatles.
9. Roger Ebert, review of *A Hard Day's Night*, directed by Richard Lester, October 27, 1996, www.rogerebert.com/reviews/great-movie-a-hard-days-night-1964.
10. Greil Marcus, "Another Version of the Chair," in *The Rolling Stone Illustrated History of Rock & Roll*, ed. James Miller (New York: Random House, 1979), 213.
11. Jonathan Gould, *Can't Buy Me Love: The Beatles, Britain, and America* (New York: Three Rivers Press, 2007), 314.
12. Miles, *Beatles Diary*, vol. 1. Originally published in the *Toronto Telegram*.
13. John Lennon, "Lennon Interview: British Embassy, Washington, DC, 2/11/1964," interview by Jay Spangler, Beatles Interview Database, www.beatlesinterviews.org/db1964.0211be.beatles.html.
14. Richard Harrington, "The Lennon Legend," *Washington Post*, December 14, 1980, www.washingtonpost.com/archive/lifestyle/1980/12/14/the-lennon-legend.

2. OH! YOU PRETTY THINGS

1. "'Pretties for You' Latest Album by Alice Cooper," *Arizona Republic*, May 25, 1969, www.alicecooperechive.com/articles/feature/ariz/690500.
2. John Mendelsohn, "Alice Cooper Is Cruel, Man!," *Entertainment World*, February 20, 1970, 8–13.
3. Marvin H. Hohman Jr., "Purging the Zombatized Void with Alice Cooper," *Creem*, July 1970, quoted in Alice Cooper eChive, alicecooperechive.com/articles/feature/cree/700700.
4. Albert Goldman, "Rock in the Androgynous Zone," *Life*, July 30, 1971, 16.

5. Ben Edmunds and Lenny Kaye, "Alice Cooper: Are You a Boy, or Are You a Girl?" *Crawdaddy*, July 4, 1971, 32–34.
6. Lewis Grossberger, "Alice Cooper of Freaky Rock Fame Is Just an All-American Boy-Girl," *Milwaukee Journal*, June 15, 1971, quoted in Alice Cooper eChive, alicecooperechive.com/articles/feature/mijo/710615.
7. Michael Quigly, "All People Want Is Sex and Violence," *Poppin*, September 1969, 24–34.
8. Philip Auslander, *Performing Glam Rock: Gender and Theatricality in Popular Music* (Ann Arbor: University of Michigan Press, 2006), 78.
9. Robert Christgau, "Consumer Guide," *Village Voice*, March 2, 1972, Robert Christgau: Dean of American Rock Critics, www.robertchristgau.com/xg/cg/cg24.php.
10. Ben Gerson, "Electric Warrior," *Rolling Stone*, January 6, 1972, www.rollingstone.com/music/music-album-reviews/electric-warrior-118646/.
11. Jayne County, "Jayne County, the Trans Rock 'n' Roll Star Who Influenced David Bowie, in Her Own Words," *Interview*, April 19, 2018, www.interviewmagazine.com/culture/jayne-county-trans-rocknroll-star-influenced-david-bowie-words.
12. Legs McNeil and Gillian McCain, *Please Kill Me: The Uncensored Oral History of Punk* (New York: Grove Press, 2016), 105.
13. *Top of the Pops*, season 9, episode 26, aired July 6, 1972, on BBC One.
14. Peter Tatchell, "This Is How LGBT Pride Began in 1972," *Huffington Post*, July 7, 2017, www.huffingtonpost.co.uk/peter-g-tatchell/lgbt-pride_b_17418306.html.
15. Michael Watts, "Oh You Pretty Thing," *Melody Maker*, January 22, 1972, 19.
16. Evelyn McDonnell, "Weird, Wonderful Labelle," *Populism*, February 16, 2009, populismblog.wordpress.com/2009/02/16/weird-wondeful-labelle/. Originally published in the *Miami Herald*.
17. John Rockwell, "Labelle at Met: Sequins, Regions and Acoustics," *New York Times*, October 11, 1974, 25.
18. Martin Weston, "Labelle," *Ebony*, May 1976, 100–108.
19. Wayne Robins, "LaBelle: Phoenix," *Creem*, December 1975, Rock's Backpages Library, accessed June 17, 2019, www.rocksbackpages.com/Library/Article/labelle-iphoenixi.
20. Lynn Van Matre, "Labelle Mines the Silver Lining," *Chicago Tribune*, March 14, 1975, B6.
21. Ken Emerson, "Why Can't America Love New York City's Pop Favorites?," *New York Times*, September 28, 1975, 399.
22. Merrill Reed Weiner, "A Family in Peril: Lou Reed's Sister Sets the Record Straight about His Childhood," *Cuepoint* (blog), Medium, April 13, 2015, medium.com/cuepoint/a-family-in-peril-lou-reed-s-sister-sets-the-record-straight-about-his-childhood-20e8399f84a3.
23. Nick Tosches, review of *Transformer*, recorded by Lou Reed, *Rolling Stone*, January 4, 1973, www.rollingstone.com/music/music-album-reviews/transformer-89126/.
24. *Marc Bolan: The Final Word*, directed by Mark Tinkler (BBC, 2007).

3. WHINING IS GENDER NEUTRAL

1. Legs McNeil and Gillian McCain, *Please Kill Me: The Uncensored Oral History of Punk* (New York: Grove Press, 2016), 34.
2. McNeil and McCain, *Please Kill Me, 14.*
3. Jayne County, "Jayne County, the Trans Rock 'n' Roll Star Who Influenced David Bowie, in Her Own Words," *Interview,* April 19, 2018, www.interview magazine.com/culture/jayne-county-trans-rocknroll-star-influenced-david -bowie-words.
4. McNeil and McCain, *Please Kill Me,* 38.
5. McNeil and McCain, *Please Kill Me,* 52.
6. McNeil and McCain, *Please Kill Me,* 73.
7. McNeil and McCain, *Please Kill Me,* 76.
8. McNeil and McCain, *Please Kill Me,* 102.
9. Patti Smith, "We Can Be Heroes," *Details,* July 1993, www.oceanstar.com /patti/poetry/heroes.htm.
10. Dave Marsh, "Patti Smith: Her Horses Got Wings, They Can Fly," *Rolling Stone,* January 1, 1976, Rock's Backpages Library, accessed June 17, 2019, www.rocksbackpages.com/Library/Article/patti-smith-her-horses-got -wings-they-can-fly.
11. Patti Smith, *Just Kids* (New York: HarperCollins, 2010), 23.
12. Smith, "We Can Be Heroes."
13. Mick Gold, "Patti Smith: Patti in Excelsis Deo," *Street Life,* May 29, 1976, Rock's Back Pages Library, accessed June 17, 2019, www.rocksbackpages .com/Library/Article/patti-smith-patti-in-excelsis-deo.
14. McNeil and McCain, *Please Kill Me,* 103.
15. Smith, *Just Kids,* 140.
16. Victor Bockris and Roberta Bayley, *Patti Smith: An Unauthorized Biography* (New York: Simon & Schuster, 1999), 300–301. Originally published in *Carry-Out* (an LGBT-related chapbook), 1972, 2–17.
17. McNeil and McCain, *Please Kill Me,* 123.
18. McNeil and McCain, *Please Kill Me,* 111.
19. Patti Smith, *Patti Smith Complete* (New York: Harper Perennial, 2006), 27.
20. Simon Reynolds, "'Even as a Child, I Felt like an Alien'," *Observer,* May 22, 2005, www.theguardian.com/music/2005/may/22/popandrock1.
21. Christopher Bollen, "Patti Smith and Robert Mapplethorpe," *Interview,* January 12, 2010, www.interviewmagazine.com/culture/patti-smith-and -robert-mapplethorpe.
22. Smith, *Just Kids,* 251.
23. McNeil and McCain, *Please Kill Me,* 331.
24. McNeil and McCain, *Please Kill Me,* 202.
25. McNeil and McCain, *Please Kill Me,* 196.
26. McNeil and McCain, *Please Kill Me,* 197.
27. Nitsuh Abebe, "Why Poly Styrene's Voice Was Anything but Disposable," Vulture, *New York* magazine, April 26, 2011, www.vulture.com/2011/04/poly -styrene.html.

28. Chas de Whalley, "X-Ray Spex: Oh Bondage! Up Yours!" *Sounds*, October 22, 1977, Rock's Backpages Library, accessed June 17, 2019, www.rocksbackpages.com/Library/Article/x-ray-spex-oh-bondage-up-yours.
29. Nick Kent, "Buzzcocks, The Slits: Thames Polytechnic, Woolwich, London," *New Musical Express*, March 11, 1978, Rock's Backpages Library, accessed June 17, 2019, www.rocksbackpages.com/Library/Article/buzzcocks-the-slits-thames-polytechnicwoolwich-london.
30. Caroline Coon, "Whatever Happened to the Buzzcocks?," *Sounds*, September 17, 1977, Rock's Backpages Library, accessed June 17, 2019, www.rocksbackpages.com/Library/Article/whatever-happened-to-the-buzzcocks.
31. Paul Rambali, "Buzzcocks: The Lust Train Stops Here," *New Musical Express*, October 14, 1978, Rock's Backpages Library, accessed June 17, 2019, www.rocksbackpages.com/Library/Article/buzzcocks-the-lust-train-stops-here.
32. Peter Silverton, "The Buzzcocks: Inside the Hit Factory," *Sounds*, April 7, 1979, Rock's Backpages Library, accessed June 17, 2019, www.rocksbackpages.com/Library/Article/the-buzzcocks-inside-the-hit-factory-.
33. Michael Azerrad, *Our Band Could Be Your Life: Scenes from the American Indie Underground, 1981–1991* (New York: Little, Brown, 2012), Kindle.
34. Josh Eells, "The Secret Life of Transgender Rocker Tom Gabel," *Rolling Stone*, May 31, 2012, www.rollingstone.com/music/music-news/the-secret-life-of-transgender-rocker-tom-gabel-99788/.
35. Laura Jane Grace, "Against Me!'s Transgender Front Woman Laura Jane Grace on Why She Wanted to Play North Carolina," Vulture, *New York* magazine, May 25, 2016, www.vulture.com/2016/05/against-me-laura-jane-grace-playing-north-carolina.html.

4. WRECKERS OF CIVILIZATION

1. Mick Middles, "A History of Joy Division," *Face*, November 1980, Rock's Backpages Library, accessed June 17, 2019, www.rocksbackpages.com/Library/Article/a-history-of-joy-division.
2. John Tobler, "Suicide," *ZigZag*, August 1978, Rock's Backpages Library, accessed June 17, 2019, www.rocksbackpages.com/Library/Article/suicide.
3. "These People Are the Wreckers of Civilisation," *The Daily Mail*, October 19, 1976, 1.
4. Genesis P-Orridge, *Painful but Fabulous: The Lives and Art of Genesis P-Orridge* (New York: Soft Skull, 2002), 21.
5. *The Ballad of Genesis and Lady Jaye*, directed by Marie Losier (New Yorker Films, 2012).
6. Hanna Hanra, "Genesis Breyer P-Orridge: 'Pleasure Is a Weapon,'" *Guardian*, July 30, 2016, www.theguardian.com/lifeandstyle/2016/jul/30/genesis-p-orridge-pleasure-is-a-weapon.
7. Fiona Russell Powell, "Shock and Bore," *New Humanist*, July 17, 2009, newhumanist.org.uk/2095/shock-and-bore.

8. P-Orridge, *Painful but Fabulous*, 54.
9. "Throbbing Gristle—Discipline," YouTube, January 21, 2006, posted by user lelliesandremains, www.youtube.com/watch?v=Y8klW9trVTQ.
10. P-Orridge, *Painful but Fabulous*, 53.
11. P-Orridge, Painful but Fabulous, 77.
12. P-Orridge, Painful but Fabulous, 26.
13. John Stickney, "Four Doors to the Future: Gothic Rock Is Their Thing," *The Williams Record*, October 24, 1967, www.thedoors.com/news/four-doors-to-the-future-gothic-rock-is-their-thing.
14. Cure News, December 1990, picturesofyou.us/fanzines/curenews-10.htm.
15. "Morrissey Says He's 'Humasexual', Not Homosexual," *Guardian*, October 21, 2013, www.theguardian.com/music/2013/oct/21/morrissey-humasexual-not-homosexual-autobiography.
16. Joe Gore, "Guitar Anti-Hero," *Guitar Player*, January 1990, 68.

5. SOFT MACHINES

1. Chris Nelson, liner notes, *Wendy Carlos's Clockwork Orange: Complete Original Score* (Minneapolis: East Side Digital, 2000), Wendy Carlos, accessed July 30, 2019, www.wendycarlos.com/+wcco.html.
2. Robert A. Moog, "Switched-On Brandenburgs," Wendy Carlos, accessed July 30, 2019, www.wendycarlos.com/+sobrand.html.
3. Kurt B. Reighley, "Vocoder Questions," Wendy Carlos, accessed July 30, 2019, www.wendycarlos.com/vocoders.html.
4. "Playboy Interview: Wendy/Walter Carlos," *Playboy*, May 1979, Digital Transgender Archive, www.digitaltransgenderarchive.net/files/nv935298c.
5. Trevor Pinch and Frank Trocco, *Analog Days: The Invention and Impact of the Moog Synthesizer* (Cambridge: Harvard University Press, 2004), 146.
6. "Keith Emerson Biography," Keith Emerson, February 11, 2010, www.keithemerson.com/AboutEmo/emobio.html.
7. Bob Moog, "On Synthesizers," *Keyboard*, January 1980, www.keyboardmag.com/gear/on-synthesizers-wendy-carlos-on-control-devices.
8. Tara Rodgers, *Pink Noises: Women on Electronic Music and Sound* (Durham, NC: Duke University Press, 2010), 9.
9. Jordan Reyes, "The San Francisco Tape Music Center Was an Early Home to the Avant-Garde," Bandcamp Daily, September 18, 2018, daily.bandcamp.com/2018/09/18/san-francisco-tape-music-center-history/.
10. Alan Baker, "An Interview with Pauline Oliveros," American Public Media, January 2003, musicmavericks.publicradio.org/features/interview_oliveros.html.
11. Pauline Oliveros, program notes, The Transparent Tape Music Festival, January 11–12, 2002, Transparent Theater, Berkeley, CA.
12. Baker, "Interview with Pauline Oliveros."
13. Don Shewey, "The Performing Artistry of Laurie Anderson," *New York Times Magazine*, February 6, 1983, 27–46.

14. "Mach 20," YouTube, August 4, 2006, posted by user K8fan, www.youtube.com/watch?v=SirOxIeuNDE. Originally aired on *The New Show*.
15. "Laurie Anderson—Home Studio (Late 80s)—02," YouTube, January 10, 2009, posted by user AouretVolkenVisage, www.youtube.com/watch?v=YajQNIAY78k.
16. *Good Morning Mr. Orwell*, directed by Nam June Paik, aired January 1, 1984, on WNET.
17. Jon Wilde, "Laurie Anderson: Moving Image," *Melody Maker*, May 30, 1987, Rock's Backpages Library, accessed June 17, 2019, www.rocksbackpages.com/Library/Article/laurie-anderson-moving-image.
18. *Home of the Brave*, directed by Laurie Anderson (Cinecom Pictures, 1986).
19. Robert Christgau, "The Knife," Robert Christgau: Dean of American Rock Critics, www.robertchristgau.com/get_artist.php?name=The+Knife.
20. Jess Harvell, review of *Silent Shout Deluxe Edition*, recorded by the Knife, *Pitchfork*, July 19, 2007, pitchfork.com/reviews/albums/10439-silent-shout-deluxe-edition/.
21. The Knife, "Shaking the Habitual Show," Aragon Ballroom, Chicago, April 23, 2014.

6. NOT A WOMAN, NOT A MAN

1. Larry Morgan, "Seeing Prince Open for the Rolling Stones at Los Angeles Memorial Coliseum," K-EARTH 101, February 5, 2018, kearth101.radio.com/blogs/larry-morgan/seeing-prince-open-rolling-stones-los-angeles-memorial-coliseum.
2. Phil Sutcliffe, "Prince: The Entertainment Centre, Sydney, Australia," *Q*, July 1992, Rock's Backpages Library, accessed June 17, 2019, www.rocksbackpages.com/Library/Article/prince-the-entertainment-centre-sydney-australia.
3. Willa Cather, *My Antonia* (Boston: Houghton Mifflin, 1918), 321.
4. *Purple Rain*, directed by Albert Magnoli (Warner Bros. Pictures, 1984).
5. Simon Reynolds, "How Prince's Androgynous Genius Changed the Way We Think about Music and Gender," *Pitchfork*, April 22, 2016, pitchfork.com/features/article/9882-how-princes-androgynous-genius-changed-the-way-we-think-about-music-and-gender/.
6. Joseph Vogel, *This Thing Called Life: Prince and the Crossover Revolution* (New York: Bloomsbury Academic, 2018), 19.
7. Rachel McKibbens, "Minneapolipstick," Poets.org, Academy of American Poets, May 13, 2014, www.poets.org/poetsorg/poem/minneapolipstick.

7. THE FAKE MAKES IT REAL

1. *Orlando*, directed by Sally Potter (Sony Pictures Classics, 1992).
2. Alex Petridis, "'What a Star He Would Be Today': The Extraordinary Musical Legacy of Sylvester," *Guardian*, July 6, 2018, www.theguardian.com/music

/2018/jul/06/what-a-star-he-would-be-today-the-extraordinary-musical-legacy-of-sylvester.

3. *The Nomi Song*, directed by Andrew Horn (Palm, 2005).
4. *The Nomi Song*, directed by Andrew Horn.
5. *Saturday Night Live*, season 5, episode 7, "Martin Sheen/David Bowie," directed by Dave Wilson, aired December 15, 1979, on NBC.
6. "Klaus Nomi—Live In Concert—Full Album," YouTube, August 25, 2018, posted by user dook shalowli, www.youtube.com/watch?v=eTMdFVjwVwU.
7. "Klaus Nomi 1982 Interview," YouTube, May 3, 2008, posted by user trylon perisphere, www.youtube.com/watch?v=dQ4__PGjFQI.
8. *The Nomi Song*, directed by Andrew Horn.
9. *The Nomi Song*, directed by Andrew Horn.
10. Francesca T. Royster, *Sounding Like a No-No: Queer Sounds and Eccentric Acts in the Post-Soul Era* (Ann Arbor: University of Michigan Press, 2012), 119.
11. Parke Puterbaugh, "Anglomania: The Second British Invasion," *Rolling Stone*, November 10, 1983, www.rollingstone.com/music/music-news/anglomania-the-second-british-invasion-52016/.
12. *TopPop*, "Grace Jones—La Vie En Rose," aired December 31, 1977, on AVROTROS.
13. Grace Jones, *I'll Never Write My Memoirs* (New York: Simon & Schuster, 2015), 47.
14. Jones, *I'll Never Write My Memoirs*, 48.
15. Jones, *I'll Never Write My Memoirs*, 73.
16. Jones, *I'll Never Write My Memoirs*, 132.
17. *A One Man Show*, directed by Jean-Paul Goude (Island Records, 1982).
18. Jones, *I'll Never Write My Memoirs*, 105.
19. Kurt Loder, "Eurythmics: Sweet Dreams Come True," *Rolling Stone*, September 29, 1983, www.rollingstone.com/music/music-features/eurythmics-sweet-dreams-come-true-54928/.
20. Laura Mulvey, "Visual Pleasure and Narrative Cinema," *Screen* 16, no. 3 (1975): 6–18.

8. INFINITE UTOPIA

1. Tim Lawrence, *Love Saves the Day: A History of American Dance Music Culture, 1970–1979* (Durham, NC: Duke University Press, 2004), 24.
2. Lawrence, *Love Saves the Day*, 48.
3. Lawrence, *Love Saves the Day*, 25.
4. Lawrence, *Love Saves the Day*, 47.
5. Lawrence, *Love Saves the Day*, 26.
6. Ken Emerson, "Can Rock Ever Learn to Dance Again?," *New York Times*, November 9, 1975, D18.
7. Lawrence, *Love Saves the Day*, 221.
8. Jack Halberstam, *In a Queer Time and Place: Transgender Bodies, Subcultural Lives* (New York: New York University Press, 2005), 2.

9. Lawrence, *Love Saves the Day*, 108.
10. Lawrence, *Love Saves the Day*, 109.
11. Lawrence, *Love Saves the Day*, 220.
12. Lawrence, *Love Saves the Day*, 254.
13. Lawrence, *Love Saves the Day*, 254.
14. Alex Petridis, "'What a Star He Would Be Today': The Extraordinary Musical Legacy of Sylvester," *Guardian*, July 6, 2018, www.theguardian.com/music/2018/jul/06/what-a-star-he-would-be-today-the-extraordinary-musical-legacy-of-sylvester.
15. Petridis, "'What a Star He Would Be Today.'"
16. Jesse Dorris, "Patrick Cowley Is One of Disco's Most Important Producers. These Are His Must-Hear Deep Cuts," *Pitchfork*, January 17, 2018, pitchfork.com/thepitch/patrick-cowley-is-one-of-discos-most-important-producers-these-are-his-must-hear-deep-cuts/.
17. David-Elijah Namod, "A Look Back at Sylvester's Incredible Music—and Incredible Courage," Hoodline, February 22, 2015, hoodline.com/2015/02/sylvester-incredible-music-incredible-courage.
18. Andy Greene, "Flashback: Watch 'Disco Demolition Night' Devolve into Fiery Riot," *Rolling Stone*, July 12, 2017, www.rollingstone.com/music/music-news/flashback-watch-disco-demolition-night-devolve-into-fiery-riot-206237/.
19. *Unsung*, "Frankie Knuckles and the Roots of House Music," aired November 30, 2016, on TV One.
20. Lawrence, *Love Saves the Day*, 221.
21. Simon Reynolds, *Rip It Up and Start Again: Postpunk 1978–1984* (London: Faber & Faber, 2009), 154.
22. Jacob Arnold, "The Warehouse: The Place House Music Got Its Name," Resident Advisor, May 16, 2012, www.residentadvisor.net/features/1597.
23. Frank Broughton, "Frankie Knuckles on the Birth of House Music," *Red Bull Music Academy Daily*, February 21, 2018, daily.redbullmusicacademy.com/2018/02/frankie-knuckles-1995-interview.
24. Broughton, "Frankie Knuckles on the Birth of House Music."
25. Broughton, "Frankie Knuckles on the Birth of House Music."
26. *Unsung*, "Frankie Knuckles and the Roots of House Music."
27. Broughton, "Frankie Knuckles on the Birth of House Music."
28. *Unsung*, "Frankie Knuckles and the Roots of House Music."
29. Alex Frank, "The Story of Jamie Principle and Frankie Knuckles' 'Your Love,' the Sexiest Dance Cut of All Time," Noisey, *Vice*, June 27, 2016, www.vice.com/en_us/article/d7jxzv/jamie-principle-frankie-knuckles-your-love.
30. Terry Church, "Black History Month: Jesse Saunders and House Music," Beatport, February 9, 2010, archive.is/20150424070647/https://news.beatport.com/black-history-jesse-saunders-and-house-music/.
31. Bob Greene, "The Fear of AIDS: A Second Epidemic," *Chicago Tribune*, August 19, 1985, www.chicagotribune.com/news/ct-xpm-1985-08-19-8502240145-story.html.
32. Halberstam, *In a Queer Time and Place*, 2.

9. FUNKY CYBORGS

1. Jeff Chang, *Can't Stop Won't Stop: A History of the Hip-Hop Generation* (New York: Picador, 2005), 79.
2. Frank Broughton, "Interview: DJ Kool Herc," *Red Bull Music Academy Daily*, January 31, 2018, daily.redbullmusicacademy.com/2018/01/kool-herc-interview.
3. Michael A. Gonzales, "The Holy House of Hip-Hop," *New York*, September 22, 2008, nymag.com/anniversary/40th/50665/.
4. Gonzales, "The Holy House of Hip-Hop."
5. Mark Dery, *Flame Wars: The Discourse of Cyberculture* (Durham, NC: Duke University Press, 1994), 193.
6. Chang, *Can't Stop Won't Stop*, 130.
7. Chang, *Can't Stop Won't Stop*, 130.
8. Chang, *Can't Stop Won't Stop*, 131.
9. Dery, *Flame Wars*, 213.
10. Dery, *Flame Wars*, 213–214.
11. bell hooks, *Black Looks: Race and Representation* (New York: Routledge, 2015), 35.
12. Tricia Rose, *Black Noise: Rap Music and Black Culture in Contemporary America* (Middletown, CT: Wesleyan University Press, 1994), Kindle.
13. Frank Owen, "Salt-N-Pepa: Femme Fatales," *Melody Maker*, January 3, 1987, Rock's Backpages Library, accessed June 17, 2019, www.rocksbackpages.com/Library/Article/salt-n-pepa-femme-fatales.
14. Dennis Hunt, "Straight Talk from the Boss," *Los Angeles Times*, August 22, 1993, www.latimes.com/archives/la-xpm-1993-08-22-ca-26294-story.html.
15. Jenna Sauers, "The Making of Mykki Blanco," *Village Voice*, April 10, 2013, www.villagevoice.com/2013/04/10/the-making-of-mykki-blanco/.

10. BUTCH THROATS

1. Darryl Bullock, *David Bowie Made Me Gay: 100 Years of LGBT Music* (New York: Abrams, 2017).
2. Jamie Anderson, "Maxine Feldman: Folk Musician, Lesbian Activist, 1945–2007," Jewish Women's Archive, 2008, jwa.org/weremember/feldman-maxine.
3. Virginia Scharff et al., "Women and the Myth of the American West," Zócalo Public Square, January 12, 2015, www.zocalopublicsquare.org/2015/01/09/women-and-the-myth-of-the-american-west/ideas/up-for-discussion/.
4. B. Ruby Rich, "Standing by Your Girl," *Artforum* 30, no. 10 (Summer 1992), www.artforum.com/print/199206/standing-by-your-girl-33547.
5. Stephen Holden, "Olivia Records Is a Success in 'Women's Music,'" *New York Times*, November 4, 1983, AR16, www.nytimes.com/1983/11/04/arts/pop-jazz-olivia-records-is-a-success-in-women-s-music.html.
6. Holden, "Olivia Records Is a Success."
7. Holden, "Olivia Records Is a Success."

8. Eileen M. Hayes, *Songs in Black and Lavender: Race, Sexual Politics, and Women's Music* (Champaign: University of Illinois Press, 2010), ix.
9. Hayes, *Songs in Black and Lavender*, 6.
10. Cristan Williams, "TERF Hate and Sandy Stone," *Trans Advocate*, August 16, 2014, www.transadvocate.com/terf-violence-and-sandy-stone_n_14360.htm.
11. Williams, "TERF Hate and Sandy Stone."
12. Williams, "TERF Hate and Sandy Stone."
13. Steve Pond, "Tracy Chapman: On Her Own Terms," *Rolling Stone*, September 22, 1988, www.rollingstone.com/music/music-news/tracy-chapman-on-her-own-terms-60993/.
14. Martha Mockus, "Queer Thoughts on Country Music and k.d. lang," in *Queering the Pitch: The New Gay and Lesbian Musicology*, ed. Philip Brett et al. (New York: Routledge, 1994), 261.
15. *The Punk Singer*, directed by Sini Anderson (IFC Films, 2013).
16. Sara Marcus, *Girls to the Front: The True Story of the Riot Grrrl Revolution* (New York: Harper Perennial, 2010), 82–83.
17. Sasha Geffen, "Arca & Jesse Kanda Played with Confusion to Liberate the Pitchfork Crowd." *Chicago Reader*, July 15, 2017, www.chicagoreader.com/Bleader/archives/2017/07/15/arca-and-jesse-kanda-played-with-confusion-to-liberate-the-pitchfork-crowd.
18. Georgia Graham, "Introducing the Multitalented Queer Artist Going on Tour with Radiohead," *Milk*, May 31, 2016, milk.xyz/feature/meet-the-multitalented-queer-artist-going-on-tour-with-radiohead/.

11. GOD IS GAY

1. Kevin Sessums, "Love Child," *Vanity Fair*, June 1995, www.vanityfair.com/news/1995/06/courtney-love-199506.
2. Simon Reynolds, "Belting Out That Most Unfeminine Emotion," *New York Times*, February 9, 1992, www.nytimes.com/1992/02/09/arts/pop-music-belting-out-that-most-unfeminine-emotion.html.
3. James Stafford, "24 Years Ago: Nirvana's 'Nevermind' Becomes the Biggest Album on the Planet," *Diffuser*, January 12, 2016, diffuser.fm/nevermind-reaches-number-one.
4. Juliet Macey, "Men We Love: Remembering Kurt Cobain, a Feminist & LGBTQ Ally Ahead of His Time," *GO Magazine*, February 24, 2017, gomag.com/article/men-love-remembering-kurt-cobain-feminist-lgbtq-ally-ahead-time/.
5. Michael Azerrad, "Nirvana: Inside the Heart and Mind of Kurt Cobain," *Rolling Stone*, April 16, 1992, www.rollingstone.com/music/music-news/nirvana-inside-the-heart-and-mind-of-kurt-cobain-103770/.
6. *Headbangers Ball*, aired October 25, 1991, on MTV.
7. Dennis Cooper, "Love Conquers All," *Spin*, May 1994, www.spin.com/2014/04/courtney-love-spin-1994-hole-cover-story-love-conquers-all/.

8. Lynn Hirschberg, "Strange Love," *Vanity Fair*, September 1992, www.vanityfair.com/hollywood/2016/03/love-story-of-kurt-cobain-courtney-love.
9. Darcey Steinke, "Smashing Their Heads on the Punk Rock," *Spin*, October 1993, www.spin.com/2013/09/nirvana-cover-story-1993-smashing-their-heads-on-the-punk-rock/.
10. Sessums, "Love Child."
11. Sessums, "Love Child."
12. Sessums, "Love Child."
13. David Fricke, review of *Live through This*, recorded by Hole, *Rolling Stone*, April 21, 1994, www.rollingstone.com/music/music-album-reviews/live-through-this-188546/.
14. Sessums, "Love Child."
15. Sessums, "Love Child."
16. Azerrad, "Nirvana."

12. NO SHAPE

1. *The Matrix*, screenplay by Lana Wachowski and Lily Wachowski (Warner Bros. Entertainment, 1997).
2. Patrick Crowley, "Savage Garden's Darren Hayes on Behind-the-Scenes Reactions to His Coming Out, Admiring Michael Jackson and Adam Lambert," *Billboard*, June 19, 2017, www.billboard.com/articles/news/pride/7834056/savage-garden-darren-hayes-coming-out-reactions-interview.
3. Colin McKean, review of *Cosmogramma*, recorded by Flying Lotus, *Quietus*, May 24, 2010, thequietus.com/articles/04312-flying-lotus-cosmogramma-album-review.
4. Abby Aguirre, "Out of This World," *T* magazine, August 18, 2011, tmagazine.blogs.nytimes.com/2011/08/18/out-of-this-world/.
5. Claire Boucher (@Grimezsz), "personally put off by the word 'woman' at least as far as my self id but if u wanna support 'women producers' here's a list of artists who've produced sum of earths best music @abra @kraeji @nbabybell @carolineplz @WondaGurlBeats @KateBushMusic @FKAtwigs," Twitter, March 8, 2018, 4:59 p.m, twitter.com/Grimezsz/status/971913425193394177.
6. Jody Rosen, review of *Visions*, recorded by Grimes, *Rolling Stone*, February 28, 2012, www.rollingstone.com/music/music-album-reviews/visions-205912/.
7. Francesca T. Royster, *Sounding Like a No-No: Queer Sounds and Eccentric Acts in the Post-Soul Era* (Ann Arbor: University of Michigan Press, 2012).
8. Brittany Spanos, "Janelle Monáe Frees Herself," *Rolling Stone*, April 26, 2018, www.rollingstone.com/music/music-features/janelle-Monáe-frees-herself-629204/.
9. Alex Frank, "How Perfume Genius Grew Up and Started Thriving," *The Fader*, 2017, www.thefader.com/2017/02/21/perfume-genius-cover-story-interview-sobriety.
10. *The Late Show with David Letterman*, "Brian Williams/Perfume Genius," season 22, episode 41, aired October 30, 2014, on CBS.

11. Thomas Gorton, "Arca: Xen Master," *Dazed*, December 19, 2014, www.dazed digital.com/music/article/22973/1/arca-xen-master.
12. Robin Hilton, "Perfume Genius Reveals the Doubts and Defiance Behind 'No Shape' Track by Track," All Songs Considered, NPR, May 5, 2017, www .npr.org/sections/allsongs/2017/05/05/527044340/perfume-genius-reveal -the-doubts-and-defiance-behind-no-shape-track-by-track.
13. Theresa Patzschke, "Elysia Crampton on Performance: 'The Gift the Ancestors Have Given Me Is This Body,'" *032c*, June 25, 2018, 032c.com/elysia-cramp ton-on-performance.

CODA

1. Alex Frank, "The Disgusting Beauty of Enigmatic Experimentalist Yves Tumor," *Pitchfork*, January 11, 2017, pitchfork.com/features/rising/10003 -the-disgusting-beauty-of-enigmatic-experimentalist-yves-tumor/.

INDEX

D

E

H

Q

R